Guanxi and Local Green Development in China

This book examines the factors which contribute to local green development in China and employs political ecology to analyze the relationship between power and the environment. Specifically, it looks at which actors control access to resources and are therefore able to promote environmental progress.

Following the reform and opening-up of China in the 1970s, entrepreneurs and local officials profited economically and politically and formed close relationships, known as *guanxi* in China. As a result, they have also been criticized as those responsible for the associated ecological damage. This book does not contest this association, but instead argues that the current literature places too much emphasis on their negative influence and the positive influence of their environmental work has been neglected. Building on three case studies where local green development is being pursued, Shanghai Pudong New Area, Baoding, and Wuning, this book shows how local officials and entrepreneurs can also be the crusaders of a greener environment at the local level in China.

This book will be of great interest to students and scholars of Chinese studies, with a particular interest in environmental policy and politics, business and society, as well as those interested in sustainable development more broadly.

Chunhong Sheng is a postdoctoral fellow at the China Center for Special Economic Zone Research, Shenzhen University, China.

Routledge Studies in Energy Policy

Making Electricity Resilient
Risk and Security in a Liberalized Infrastructure
Antti Silvast

Energy Policy in China
Chi-Jen Yang

Fossil Fuel Subsidy Reforms
A Guide to Economic and Political Complexity
Jun Rentschler

Low Carbon Politics
A Cultural Approach Focusing on Low Carbon Electricity
David Toke

Governing Shale Gas
Development, Citizen Participation and Decision Making in the US, Canada, Australia and Europe
John Whitton, Matthew Cotton, Ioan M. Charnley-Parry and Kathy Brasier

Business Battles in the US Energy Sector
Lessons for a Clean Energy Transition
Christian Downie

***Guanxi* and Local Green Development in China**
The Role of Entrepreneurs and Local Leaders
Chunhong Sheng

Energy Policies and Climate Change in China
Actors, Implementation and Future Prospects
Han Lin

For further details please visit the series page on the Routledge website: www.routledge.com/books/series/RSIEP/

Guanxi and Local Green Development in China

The Role of Entrepreneurs and Local Leaders

Chunhong Sheng

First published 2020
by Routledge
2 Park Square, Milton Park, Abingdon, Oxon OX14 4RN

and by Routledge
605 Third Avenue, New York, NY 10017

First issued in paperback 2020

Routledge is an imprint of the Taylor & Francis Group, an informa business

© 2020 Chunhong Sheng

The right of Chunhong Sheng to be identified as author of this work has been asserted by her in accordance with sections 77 and 78 of the Copyright, Designs and Patents Act 1988.

All rights reserved. No part of this book may be reprinted or reproduced or utilized in any form or by any electronic, mechanical, or other means, now known or hereafter invented, including photocopying and recording, or in any information storage or retrieval system, without permission in writing from the publishers.

Trademark notice: Product or corporate names may be trademarks or registered trademarks, and are used only for identification and explanation without intent to infringe.

British Library Cataloguing-in-Publication Data
A catalogue record for this book is available from the British Library

Library of Congress Cataloging-in-Publication Data
A catalog record has been requested for this book

ISBN 13: 978-0-367-72750-5 (pbk)
ISBN 13: 978-0-367-00197-1 (hbk)

Typeset in Times New Roman
by Wearset Ltd, Boldon, Tyne and Wear

Contents

List of illustrations vi
Preface vii
Acknowledgments viii
List of abbreviations x

1 The boom of local green development in China 1

2 China's local green development background 24

3 A run-down city regains competence: Shanghai 49

4 A polluted city's path towards low-carbon pioneering: Baoding 76

5 A poor county's green leap forward: "Green Rising-Up" in Wuning 105

6 A comparative analysis of green development 133

7 A political ecology of local green development 159

Appendix: interview and fieldwork information 184
Index 193

Illustrations

Figures

2.1	Power investment in China from 2009 to 2017 (in billion RMB)	28
2.2	Fragmented local authoritarianism in China	29
2.3	Environmental petition data in China from 1994 to 2013	32
3.1	1995 Pudong land use structure	64

Tables

1.1	Local demonstration projects for green development	2
1.2	General information about Shanghai, Baoding, and Wuning 2016	13

Preface

I first became interested in environmental pollution, climate change, and other common public problems while studying international relations at Tongji University in Shanghai. The idea of the growing number of people sharing the planet and the reality of a "nation state" led me to think about how common problems are being addressed by supranational organizations. At that time, I was eager to work with an international NGO. Therefore, I applied to a PhD program abroad in order to sharpen my language skills and gain international experience.

I was accepted to study in the Environmental Policy Research Center (FFU) at the Free University of Berlin. During my studies there, I learned more about the serious environmental challenges facing China and the rest of the world, especially from my international colleagues. Together, we searched for best practices or solutions to some of these pressing environmental problems. In many classes I attended at the Free University of Berlin, China was criticized for its levels of environmental pollution and its need for urgent changes to its economic development model. Are there best practices that could change China's development path? Considering this question of how (or even whether) China can resolve its serious environmental degradation shifted my focus from international issues to Chinese issues in my dissertation—which ultimately evolved into this book.

During my fieldwork in China, I first examined the role of international organizations' influence in the country. Later, I started to look at the role of the central government as well. However, after completing my fieldwork, I came to realize that essential change is based on the local context, and particularly the local power structure. The push for environmental change comes mainly from within Chinese localities, not from external forces. I have found that the "love for one's hometown and people" is essential for local environmental progress. If local residents, businesses, and governments can change their behavior, it will lead to better practices on a national or even global scale. Yet, there are some problems related to China's local power structure and environmental change that complicate this approach, which have encouraged me to consider environmental justice issues in China as a future research topic.

Acknowledgments

First and foremost, I would like to thank my parents, Guangwen and Jiju. As farmers they gave me the freedom and courage to pursue my studies and even go abroad, instead of giving up. In addition, I received help from many people during my years of study. My sincere thanks go to the people who supported education in poor areas in China. My studies and research were made possible by the generous financial support from the China Scholarship Council Program. I also offer thanks to Hui Zhang at the education office of the Chinese embassy in Berlin.

I am most thankful to my supervisor, Professor Dr. Miranda Schreurs, for her mentoring and encouragement. She patiently read my manuscript word by word, giving me suggestions, not only about academic writing, but also about language improvement. She has the incredible power to inspire students to discover research topics that speak to their passions. I have benefited from the diverse research topics presented by our colleagues in the Environmental Policy Research Center of the Free University of Berlin and Miranda's insightful comments in PhD colloquium every Wednesday evening.

I also want to thank Professor Dr. Bettina Gransow, Dr. Klaus Jacob, Dr. Eva Sternfeld and Professor Carina Sprungk, my committee members, as well as Professor Martin Jänicke and Professor Yawei Chen, who did not hesitate to share their precious time to read parts of my dissertation. The Free University of Berlin gave me the opportunity to learn from Professor Haifeng Huang, Professor Xiangshu Zhang, Professor Xiaoyi Wang, and Professor Fengting Li. They provided their comments on my work from a Chinese perspective.

It was valuable to have a writing group to read and critique one another's chapters and communicate about common issues in our PhD studies. I would like to thank Karoline Steinbacher, Sascha Hahn, Weila Gong, Hamed Beheshti, Jens Marquardt, Eva Öller, Yun Cao, und Nhlanhla Sibisi for their support.

During my fieldwork, many people helped me to carry out my research in Shanghai, Baoding, and Wuning. I am grateful to my friends, Haibin Han, Yaning Liu, and Mayinu Shanatibieke who used their personal connections to help me build relationships with interviewees. I also appreciate the trust of interviewees who did not know me before this research.

As a non-native English speaker, I am grateful to have found two wonderful proofreaders, Jessica Wallach and Catie Phares, who improved my manuscript effectively and patiently. I also would like to thank Richard Forrest, Almas Haider, and Rainer Quitzow for their comments.

Finally, I thank my husband, Julian Barg, for his support, encouragement, and companionship over the years of PhD study with all its ups and downs. And my lovely daughter, Freya Barg, who brings me great happiness and is an inspiration for my work.

Abbreviations

ACCA	Administration Center for China Agenda 21
ADB	Asian Development Bank
BIPV	Building Integrated Photovoltaics
CCP	Chinese Communist Party
CEO	Chief Executive Officer
CLAPV	Center for Legal Assistance to Pollution Victims
CPIA	China Photovoltaic Industry Association
CSIGC	China South Industries Group Corporation
CSUS	Chinese Society for Urban Studies
CWPC	China Wind Power Center
ENGOs	Environmental Non-Governmental Organizations
EPBs	Environmental Protection Bureaus
EVC	Electric Valley of China
FDI	Foreign Direct Investment
FON	Friends of Nature
GDP	Gross Domestic Product
GWth	Gig watts-thermal
HTZ	High-tech Zone
ICLEI	Local Governments for Sustainability
IFC	International Finance Corporation
IMF	International Monetary Fund
kW	kilowatt
LEDs	light emitting diodes
MEE	Ministry of Ecology and Environment
MEP	Ministry of Environmental Protection
MHURD	Ministry of Housing and Urban-rural Development
MNCs	Multinational Corporations
MoST	Ministry of Science and Technology
mu	Chinese unit of area = 0.0667 hectares
NCEPU	North China Electric Power University
NDRC	National Development and Reform Commission
NEA	National Energy Administration
NIMBY	not in my backyard

NPC	National People's Congress
PX	Para xylene
R&D	Research and Development
RMB	Renminbi
SCNPC	Standing Committee of the National People's Congress
SOEs	State-owned Enterprises
Solar PV	solar photovoltaic
TVEs	Township and Village Enterprises
UN	United Nations
UNEP	United Nations Environment Program
UNESCO	United Nations Educational, Scientific and Cultural Organization
WWF	World Wide Fund for Nature
Yingli	Yingli Solar

1 The boom of local green development in China

Introduction

Local governments in China have long embraced the traditional model of development, which emphasizes economic growth without serious consideration for environmental protection. Recently, however, many local governments—and especially municipal governments—have started to advocate for environmentally sustainable development as a means to a better quality of life, including in areas that are both affluent and poor, industrialized and agricultural, large and small. China's development has had, and continues to have, a profound impact on the country's own environment, as well as the world in general. As China transitions towards greater environmental awareness and sustainability, local support of these "greener" aims will be of paramount importance. Thus, this research investigates several local governments that have supported green development strategies, along with the motivations and powers driving these decisions.

"Eco," "low-carbon," "green," and "circular" have become buzzwords for describing environmentally sound development (H. Li, 2015). The Chinese government began to encourage local governments to pursue "clean and green" objectives using demonstration programs in the early 1990s. The "Pilot Hygiene City/County" was launched in 1990. Since 1996, pilot ecological demonstrations became popular across several cities and counties. In 2004, the national government's focus was on forest cities and counties. In 2011, energy-saving and emission-reduction pilot programs were launched by the State Council. In 2012, the National Development and Reform Commission (NDRC) chose low-carbon pilot provinces and cities; in 2013, the NDRC launched a circular economy pilot, and in 2017, the first round of its "Ecological Civilization" pilot began.

For years, China's central government continued to launch these demonstration projects aimed at incentivizing local governments to be greener. Yet, in spite of the programs, the country's environment continued to degrade. This study questions the real motivations behind the green development of local governments—particularly those of governments that declared they would be pursuing green development even without the recognition of the central government.

Table 1.1 Local demonstration projects for green development

National program	Governmental departments	Year	Numbers of local governments
Hygiene city	National Health Commission	1990	266 cities and 47 districts of the municipal area
Ecological demonstration zone	Ministry of Ecology and Environment (MEE)	1996	533 (cities, districts, and counties)
Forest city	National Forest and Grassland Administration/Ministry of Natural Resources	2004	165 cities
Energy saving and emission reduction city	State council	2011	30 cities
Low-carbon city	NDRC	2012	6 provinces, 4 provincial-level cities, and 32 municipalities
Circular economy city	NDRC	2013	66 cities and 36 counties
Ecological civilization city	MEE	2017	95 cities and 36 counties

Sources: National Health Commission of the People's Republic of China (PRC), Ministry of Ecology and Environment of PRC, National Development and Reform Commission (NDRC), the State Council of PRC; NDRC (2010, 2012).

In contrast to the number of green titles and recognitions that local governments seem eager to obtain, many environmental scholars argue that these governments have few real incentives to protect the environment (Economy, 2007; Lieberthal, 2007, pp. 88–96; Shapiro, 2012; Shirk, 2010). The central government has observed that some local governments pursue economic growth at the cost of environmental protection (Xi, 2014), leading to public protest against these governments (Martens, 2006). In general, local governments have indeed failed to protect the environment and it has resulted in serious pollution concerns.

Yet, if local governments largely lack incentives for environmental protection, then why do some advocate green development? What factors lead them towards (or away from) considering the environment in their development plans?

Arguments for whether (and how) local green efforts work

Scholars have explored the "black box" of local environmental politics from many different perspectives, using theories supported by empirical evidence. Two major schools of thought have emerged in this regard, one originated from the perspective of the role of civil society and the other from the role of central government in local environmental development strategies.

The role of civil society

The first of these groups supports an emerging and dynamic theoretical area that focuses on civil society's role in environmental governance (Cooper, 2006; Economy, 2005; Ho, 2001; Knup, 1997; Lo & Tang, 2006; Mol & Carter, 2006; Wu, 2009; G. Yang, 2005). This theoretical explanation is based on the experiences of many industrialized countries in which civil society has played an important role in improving environmental protection (Dryzek, Hunold, Schlosberg, Downes, & Hernes, 2002; Wu, 2009). China's central government has given more freedom and responsibilities to civil society so that it can supervise local governments in terms of environmental protection (Ho, 2001; Lo & Tang, 2006; Mol & Carter, 2006; NPC, 2014; Sun & Zhao, 2008). For example, the revised Environmental Protection Law of 2015 (Friends of Nature, 2019) empowered environmental non-governmental organizations (ENGOs) to initiate public litigation against environmental polluters. Similarly, many empirical studies have found that civil society is able to instigate positive environmental changes at the local level, particularly through demonstrations, petitions, and the employment of new media (Cooper, 2006; Deng & Yang, 2013; Lang & Xu, 2013; Lee & Ho, 2014; Shao, Lu, & Wu, 2012). For instance, the "rise of a green public sphere" challenged the Yunnan government's decision to dam the Nu River, and with the help of the new media, opponents mobilized resources for public environmental protests (G. Yang & Calhoun, 2007). Likewise, in the 2000s, citizens succeeded in stopping waste incinerator projects in several cities through protests (Lang & Xu, 2013; Lee & Ho, 2014).

Despite this progress, many scholars emphasize the limited or constrained role of civil society in China's environmental politics, especially regarding the ability to effect lasting, fundamental change in local government policies and behaviors (Economy, 2005; Ho, 2001; Lo & Leung, 2000; Schwartz, 2004; Stally & Yang, 2006). This second group argues that environmentalists in China rarely challenge the government openly (Ho, 2001). Chinese civil society and ENGOs are under tight political control, which limits their participation in environmental policymaking processes (Lo & Leung, 2000). Schwartz (2004) concludes that civil society does not challenge the state, but rather, that it is state led, and therefore has a limited impact. While ENGOs can play a role in promoting environmental policy implementation at the local level, they are unable to impose their influence on policy design (Fuerst & Holdaway, 2015), change government policies, and/or affect officials' behaviors (Tang & Zhang, 2008). Their protests or petitions may force local governments to stop or relocate certain projects with negative environmental impacts; however, they cannot change local development strategies. Hence, the civil society approach is an important one, but it is not sufficient to explain the changing attitudes of local governments towards green development.

The role of the central government

Another noticeable and influential group of scholars notes the Chinese political character, as an authoritarian, hierarchical party-state, and its influence on local environmental governance (Jahiel, 1997, 1998; Lieberthal, 1997, 2007; Ma & Ortolano, 2000, pp. 43–54; Ross, 1992). In recent years, the central government has tried to strengthen its authority through administrative regulations to prompt local leaders to act on environmental protection (Lo & Tang, 2006; Mol, 2006; A. Wang, 2013). Van Rooij (2006) finds that national environmental "political campaigns" pressured local governments to enhance environmental law enforcement at the local level as a short-term political tool. At the same time, the central government attempted to add more weight to environmental protection in local leaders' performance evaluations (Lo & Tang, 2006; A. Wang, 2013). Nevertheless, the reality is that the central government still does not prioritize environmental protection over economic growth. Environmental protection remains merely a supplementary or supporting element of this economic growth, which is the key source of the Chinese Communist Party's (CCP's) legitimacy (A. Wang, 2013).

Another branch of scholars examines local governments' implementation of the central government's environmental policies. These scholars have identified several reasons for the poor and ineffective implementation of environmental policies at the local level: the lack of incentives for local officials to realize sustainability, low public participation, and the dominance of business interests (Kostka, 2014; Kostka & Mol, 2013; Skinner, Kuhn, & Joseph, 2001). The rotation of local leaders may also prohibit consistent implementation of the central government's environmental initiatives at the local level (Eaton & Kostka, 2014). This scholarship mainly addresses the failure of local governments to implement the central government's environmental policies and is unable to provide satisfying answers regarding the changing behaviors of some local governments in promoting green development strategies.

One leading argument from this scholarship is that the Chinese political system has created a strong incentive system for local officials to pursue economic growth in cooperation with business owners, while these officials have few incentives to protect the environment (Jahiel, 1997; Lieberthal, 1997, 2007; Ross, 1992; Shapiro, 2012, p. 10). Within the environmental administration system, local Environmental Protection Bureaus (EPBs) have failed to enforce environmental laws and regulations as they are under the leadership of local governments, which limits their ability to check the pro-growth strategies pursued by local government leaders (Jahiel, 1997, 1998; Lieberthal, 1997; McElwee; 2011, pp. 3–15). The central government's rule of law in environmental protection is weak and restricted at the local level, despite the well-structured environmental laws and regulations designed by the central government (Beyer, 2006; Gang, 2009, pp. 33–40; McElwee; 2011, pp. 3–15; Shapiro, 2012, p. 57).

Why, then, do local governments matter in ecological protection? The central government has transferred many political and economic duties and rights to local governments (Shapiro, 2012), including the responsibility for local environmental protection, and granted autonomy and power to local governments by initiating fiscal and administrative reforms (Guthrie, 2012, pp. 121–123; Morton, 2006; Oi, 1992; Zhang & Zou, 1998). Thanks to this strong decentralization, local governments have more autonomy than ever before, making China one of the most decentralized countries in East Asia (Oi, Rozelle, Zhou, & Walter, 2010).

Moreover, in the context of China's environmental challenges, Jonathan Watts asserts that "power lies neither at the top nor the bottom, but within a middle class of developers, polluters, and local officials who are difficult to regulate, monitor, and challenge" (Shapiro, 2012, p. 10). The autonomy of local governments enables local officials to directly manage local resources and affairs. These governments can employ preferential policies towards industries related to green or polluted industries, and either protect the local ecology or allow it to be irreversibly damaged.

This book questions the motivations of local green development efforts in China, which may respond either to the orders of the central government or to pressure from the public. Some local governments may prioritize national titles and funds, while others prioritize local public approval. This work seeks to clarify how and why some local officials and business owners voluntarily advance local environmental initiatives. The indicator for whether an initiative can be termed "local" depends on whether it was advocated *before* the central government's green development requirements. Among all of the targets and requirements set by the central government, some of local governments have stressed environmental protection. Furthermore, some local governments supported environmentally friendly industries or industries with less adverse environmental impact. The book's findings reveal the complex role of local officials and business owners in advocating for environmental protection.

The political ecology logic of local green development

The developing area of political ecology theory stresses that environmental changes can be best explained through the study of actors' power to access and control resources (Peet, 2004). Accordingly, in contrast to a study of weak or ineffectual actors in local environmental politics, the analysis of powerful actors (usually local officials and business owners) can better advance our understanding of the distribution of resources and how the environment can be changed at the local level. In the Chinese local context, municipal governments and businesses are the most prominent decision-makers in local affairs, including local development strategy. Therefore, political ecology leads this study to focus on these powerful actors and their impact on the environment.

This research integrates theories and literatures on entrepreneurs, political economy, and social capital to help explain the growing interest of some Chinese communities in local green development. The first theory examined addresses the power of entrepreneurs. It emphasizes the innovative role of entrepreneurs as they mobilize resources for a new business. The second theory deals with industrial development in political economy, and how political actors gather resources to promote economic development (mainly through industrial policies). The third theory relates to social capital and the unique Chinese concept of *guanxi*—that is, individuals' use of trust networks and sociocultural power to gain resources for certain purposes.

The rise of Chinese entrepreneurs and their "green" businesses

According to Schumpeter, an entrepreneur aims

> to reform or revolutionize the pattern of production by exploiting an invention or, more generally, an untried technological possibility for producing a new commodity or producing an old one in a new way, or by opening up a new source of supply of materials or a new outlet for products, or by reorganizing an industry.
>
> (Hamilton & Harper, 1994, p. 4)

In other words, "it is his (an entrepreneur's) job to locate new ideas and put them into effect" (Baumol, 1968, p. 65). In this study, entrepreneurs with "green" businesses are defined as those who first developed firms that offer environmentally friendly products or services.

Scholars note that entrepreneurs have contributed enormously to China's rapid economic development (Chen & Dickson, 2010, pp. 18–37; Djankov, Qian, Roland, & Zhuravskaya, 2006; Huang, 2008; Liao & Sohmen, 2001; Malik, 1997; Nee & Young, 1991; Tsai, 2007; K. Yang, 2012). The household responsibility system reform has loosened the control of farmers by the governments and, combined with the motivation to pursue economic benefits, gave birth to entrepreneurship in China and represented the moment when the Chinese economy took off. As Rostow observes, "A requirement for take-off is, therefore, a class of farmers willing and able to respond to the possibilities opened up for them by new techniques, land-holding arrangements, transport facilities, and forms of market and credit organization" (Rostow, 1967, pp. 51–52). Since farmer-entrepreneurs have limited resources to start businesses, they usually make use of the collective resources and assets of their communes (collectively managed farms) to set up township and village enterprises (TVEs) (Che & Qian, 1998; Harvey, 2005, pp. 125–126; Jin & Qian, 1998). Huang (2008) argues that the Chinese economic miracle was created by such bottom-up private entrepreneurship. In this way, the liberation of farmers was the basis of China's market reform that replaced the central planning system in many sectors (Oi, 1999).

Another important group of entrepreneurs consists of cadre-entrepreneurs, who either make use of public property to develop public enterprises or have formerly worked in government/government-affiliated organizations before starting their own enterprises. The wave of market forces broke down "the iron rice bowl" (*tie fanwan*) system since the 1980s, in which jobs were planned by the government and were lifelong positions (Ding, Goodall, & Warner, 2000; Ding

& Warner, 2001). When cadre-entrepreneurs leave their jobs and enter the market instead, this is now called "jumping into the sea" (*xiahai*) (Dickson, 2003; D. Li, 1998; Liu, 2001). Many ambitious government officials have left the political system in order to use their knowledge and social relationships in the wider market. The common trait among all cadre-entrepreneurs is that they have strong personal and political ties with the government (Dickson, 2003), making it hard, at times, to separate their dual roles as cadres and entrepreneurs.

Aside from acknowledging the role of entrepreneurs in economic development, most of the literature on environmental studies focuses on the destructive role of business owners in local environmental governance; they are described as actors who chase profits and impede the implementation of environmental laws and regulations under the protection of the local governments (Economy, 2007; Ip, 2009; Shapiro, 2012; Shirk, 2010). This study deconstructs this monolithic image of business owners by studying the rise of entrepreneurs with businesses related to green or environmentally friendly products and services, and further examining these individuals' roles in local green development. The book studies the emergence of businesses that offer products or services to meet the demands of green consumerism in the market and uses the term "green entrepreneurs" to categorize those at the helm of such businesses or those proposing green development ideas.

The nature of these green businesses can vary across many sectors. Dynamic private entrepreneurs and their companies are fast entering the state-dominated energy sector in China, and particularly the prominent renewable energy sector (Martinot, Li, & Mastny, 2007; REN21, 2015; Q. Wang, 2010). The global solar and wind energy sector is crowded with Chinese entrepreneurs, and Chinese companies are world leaders in this regard; Yingli Green Energy (Yingli) is ranked among the top 10 competitors in the global 2018 solar module market, and Xinjiang Goldwind is among the top 10 wind turbine companies in the international market (Bloomberg New Energy Finance, n.d; Efstathiou, 2018). Entrepreneurs are also the main contributors to China's leadership in solar water thermal capacity (Mauthner, Weiss, & Spoerk-Duer, 2014). Ming Huang's Himin and Xinjian Xu's Sunrain are the world leaders in solar thermal production. In Wuning County of Jiangxi Province, more than 90% of all small hydropower stations are deployed by entrepreneurs. The rapid development of electric bicycle and electric vehicle businesses further adds to the market power of Chinese green businesses (Weinert, Ma, Yang, & Cherry, 2007; Weinert, Ogden, Sperling, & Burke, 2008). In addition to exploring renewable energy, many entrepreneurs have pursued offerings in the energy-saving and energy-efficiency fields (e.g., the energy-saving lamp industry). As these examples (and many others) demonstrate, private entrepreneurs have played a crucial role in China's rapid development of green industries.

The growth of green tertiary industries—including finance, trade, services, and real estate—also requires careful examination. One of the most influential tertiary industries is real estate, which, along with the finance industry, has a particularly close relationship with local government. Local governments sell land use rights to real estate developers as a major source of local revenue and use land as a guarantee to gain capital loans from banks for local development (Cartier, 2001; G. Lin & Yi, 2011; Lu & Sun, 2013). In light of this relationship, real estate developers can have a strong influence on local governments' policymaking. For instance, Wuning's real estate companies advertise the ecological benefits of their properties in order to sell their products (Y. Wang & Tong, 2013). The studies in this book focus on economic or financial issues related to the real estate industry and local government (Cartier, 2001; G. Lin & Yi, 2011; Lu & Sun, 2013). Through these studies, the book examines the relationship between the rise of China's real estate industry, its relationship to local government, and its impact on local environmental protection, thereby addressing a significant gap in the literature regarding the influence of green businesses and entrepreneurs on local green development strategies.

Local leaders and a greener future for governing regions

Local government officials in China have extensive control in terms of establishing industrial subsidies and policies to decide how to use the local resources in their ruling areas for economic development (Qian, 2002). After decentralization in the 1980s, local governments enjoyed considerable autonomy and authority in handling their own local resources and affairs, with some even referring to the resulting situation as "Chinese style federalism" (Montinola, Qian, & Weingast, 1995; Qian & Weingast, 1997; Shirk, 1993, pp. 335–336). "The government has gradually pushed ownership-like control down the government administrative hierarchy to the localities" (Guthrie, 2009, p. 39), so that local governments control local resources and are responsible for decision-making with respect to local development strategies. Local leaders also won the right to appoint local officials, which made it possible to select people with rich local knowledge and experience and create a high-quality and efficient local personnel system (Burns, 1989). The ability of local leaders and officials to implement industrial policies that are best suited to the local conditions is one important factor of local economic success (Rodrik, 2008, pp. 154–164). Hence, this study focuses on local officials who can influence local industrial policymaking by providing advice and suggestions to local leaders about which industries should be supported through preferential industrial policies.

With central political stability, the Chinese economic reform policies were deeply rooted in the local conditions, and many innovative local experiments gradually became national policies (Chen & Dickson, 2010, p. 10; Guthrie, 2012, p. 13; Naughton, 2007, p. 107), such as the rural household responsibility reform and the TVEs (Hong, 1995; Hsueh, 2011, pp. 1–10; J. Lin, 1992; Peng, 2001).

In the literature on China's economic development, many political economists emphasize the importance of local governments' political power to make use of their respective resources in order to develop their area's economy (Chen & Dickson, 2010, p. 8; N. Lin, 1995; Lin & Liu, 2000; Montinola et al., 1995;

Oi, 1992, 1995; Tsui & Wang, 2004; Wong, 1991; Zhang & Zou, 1998). China's economic achievement shares many similarities with the paradigm of East Asian countries and regions in which government investment is concentrated in certain industries. The government supports certain industries in order to turn new technologies into production, and then exposes them to international competition (Wade, 1990, p. 26). Rodrik (2006, pp. 9–42) finds that successful industrial policies are context specific and require "considerable local knowledge," which means the national government should leave sufficient space for innovations at the local level. Thus, China's central government grants local officials the freedom to pursue different development strategies (Guthrie, 2012, p. 43).

The literature on industrial policies focuses on explaining local governments' contributions to economic growth (Oi, 1992; Walder, 1995). However, it does not address whether local officials consider environmental elements in the process of selecting strategic industries, nor does it explore the environmental impact of these industrial policies. Nevertheless, some local governments and officials choose to prioritize green businesses, which suggests that they do, in fact, consider environmental elements and impacts. This research reconstructs the process by which certain green business sectors became key industries supported by local holders of political power. The dedicated efforts of some local officials who envision a better future for their governing regions have pushed green ideas and policies onto the agenda of local governments (Morton, 2006, pp. 181–182). These local officials choose industries that are not only high-tech and strategic, but also have less negative environmental impacts on their areas.

It is common for local governments to regard green businesses as key industries to be supported in industrial parks, as reflected by the environmentally friendly nature of the industries within such parks and the priority given to them by the national government. Despite these conditions, few local governments have moved from these green industrial policies to a broader local green development strategy. This study narrowly focuses on those locals which made green businesses their top priority among various industries, and an area with full support from local leaders. Local leaders play a decisive role in green development strategy. If local leaders do not agree with the local officials who propose to support green industrial policies, then environmentally sustainable development is impossible. For this study's purposes, "local leader" means the secretary of the local CCP, or leaders of local governments who are top officials in the local CCP party and/or other local governments. These local leaders (especially the secretary of the CCP) have considerable power to command public property (e.g., land and capital) and personnel working in local government administrations to implement their development strategies (Chen & Dickson, 2010, p. 30; Guthrie, 2012, p. 38; Hsueh, 2011, p. 196; Morton, 2006, p. 170; Naughton, 2007, p. 118).

In the extant literature on local governments and environmental protection, local officials and leaders are assumed to pursue economic growth at the cost of environmental protection (Economy, 2010; Heilmann, 2008; Jahiel, 1997; Lieberthal, 1997, 2007; Morton, 2006; Ross, 1992; Shapiro, 2012, p. 10). This perception simplifies the complicated circumstances and decisions that arise when local officials and leaders choose which industries to support and which development strategy is best for their region. Like the rational man assumption, this assumption may also be misleading when it comes to pinpointing the factors that contribute to local green development. It is possible that local officials and leaders may purposely choose industries that are both environmentally friendly and economically promising. Examples of such choices can be seen in the provincial-level cities of Beijing, Shanghai, Tianjin, and Chongqing, all of which embraced campaigns to upgrade their industries and pursue environmentally friendly tertiary industries. This research fills a gap in the literature on the role of local officials/leaders in environmental governance via an in-depth study of how local leaders decide to pursue green development strategies.

Interactions between powerful actors: social capital or "guanxi"

The sociocultural power of entrepreneurs and local officials lies mainly in their personal connections—their social capital, or *guanxi*, described by Putnam:

> By analogy with notions of physical capital and human capital—tools and training that enhance individual productivity—the core idea of social capital theory is that social networks have value. Social capital refers to connections among individuals—social networks and the norms of reciprocity and trustworthiness that arise from them.
>
> (Putnam, 2000, p. 16)

Entrepreneurs and local officials and leaders use their social capital or *guanxi* to realize their aims and advance their respective businesses and development strategies, including green development strategies. Guthrie observes that "the Chinese culture creates a deep psychological tendency for individuals to actively cultivate and manipulate social relations for instrumental ends" (2012, p. 86). Although *guanxi* is a cultural phenomenon, it can determine whether actors are able to control or access resources to reach their goal or not, an important form of power in political ecology. For entrepreneurs, *guanxi* or social capital is a particularly crucial form of personal power that can be used to gain support for their ideas (Fan, 2002a, 2002b). The importance of *guanxi* as a cultural phenomenon is emphasized by several experts on business relationships within China (Ledeneva, 2008; Tsai, 2004, 2007; H. Wang, 2000). These scholars argue that *guanxi* is an informal power that strongly influences the distribution of resources and the usage of local resources.

The *guanxi* between entrepreneurs and local officials is one of the main subjects of this book. Many scholars have highlighted that entrepreneurs need the support of political power (Batjargal & Liu, 2004; Dickson, 2003; J. Li, Chen, Li, & Matlay, 2006; McMillan & Woodruff, 2003; Peng, 2001; Tan, 1996; K. Yang, 2012). There are myriad challenges involved in conducting business at the local level: local governments hold many necessary resources (e.g., land, capital, and infrastructure); these governments may seek rent from entrepreneurs; and the local arena can involve weak private property rights and rule of law (Hsueh, 2011, p. 196; Leng, 2009; Naughton, 2007; Szamosszegi & Kyle, 2011). Accordingly, entrepreneurs actively seek to build connections with local officials and leaders to overcome these challenges (Ledeneva, 2008; Park & Luo, 2001; H. Wang, 2000; Xin & Pearce, 1996). A local social relationship can legitimize the property rights of a firm, as it is built on political connections with local government officials (Ahlstrom & Bruton, 2001; Carlisle & Flynn, 2005; Heberer, 2003; Tsai, 2004). Entrepreneurs who have good *guanxi* with government officials are likely to be more successful in their businesses (Ai, 2006; Park & Luo, 2001). To this end, some entrepreneurs even enter local politics as members of the local people's congress (K. Yang, 2012). Dickson (2003) uses the term "red capitalists" to describe Chinese private entrepreneurs' close relationship with political power.

Local officials also rely on their own *guanxi* to connect with entrepreneurs to determine the right businesses for their regions. Government officials' reliance on entrepreneurs in this way has been underexplored in the literature, which mostly focuses instead on entrepreneurs' *guanxi* in the direction of local officials. The cooperation between local government officials and entrepreneurs is at the core of China's explosive economic growth; this was especially true for rural industry at the beginning of the reform and opening-up (Oi, 1995, 1999). Local officials need to gain business information from entrepreneurs to create suitable industrial policies and achieve local economic growth (Rodrik, 2008, p. 100). They also compete with other regional governments for entrepreneurs (especially in areas prime for industrial upgrading, e.g., high-tech and eco-friendly industries), as reflected in many preferential industrial policies. It is common for local governments to organize visits to more economically advanced regions in order to attract entrepreneurs to set up businesses and invest in their industrial parks. During this process, local officials customarily employ their *guanxi* to connect with entrepreneurs, particularly those who have relationships with their governing regions.

While many studies focus extensively on the impact of *guanxi* between local officials and business owners in terms of economic development, this book considers the role of *guanxi* in environmental development. The social capital between local officials and entrepreneurs depends on what their *guanxi* is rooted in: if it is based on the common aim to develop the local economy, then local officials will protect entrepreneurs from environmental audits made by local EPBs and from central government supervision, as noted by Shirk:

> Local officials benefit more by colluding with local business to promote economic growth by spending on big development projects than by providing such social goods as environmental protection, health care, education, and quality food and medicine that are mandated but not fully funded by the central government.
>
> (Shirk, 2010, p. 19)

However, *guanxi* can be used for ecological protection as well as economic benefit (Kostka, 2013; Ma and Ortolano, 2000, pp. 82–95). Local officials' and leaders' social capital or *guanxi* can support green entrepreneurs and help them overcome problems they confront. Those actors who have such connections are in a better position to reach their aim of green development strategy, particularly when a green business or idea is threatened by factors like shortage of capital or political disagreement from upper-level government. When *guanxi* is available to green entrepreneurs, local officials, and local leaders, they all have a greater chance of overcoming these barriers. The context and nature of the *guanxi* deployed depends on the actors' aims and wishes. This study emphasizes *guanxi* as a means to support actors in realizing green development.

Local green experiments and experiences

As Schreurs concludes, there are many front runners in local governments who represent the people's will to protect the environment, and who take initiatives in policymaking and action to show their influence and to make some difference (Schreurs, 2008). Local governments experiment with different kinds of green development strategies based on their local conditions. Some put effort into upgrading their local economy from secondary to tertiary industries. Other governments focus on the development of renewable energy and applications of renewable energy products in their jurisdictions. Yet another group of local governments use their regional ecological conditions to develop ecotourism industries. These distinct green development experiments can provide lessons and experiences to other local governments, not only in China, but worldwide.

As noted, the Chinese economic development model has relied on initial experiments introduced by a few local governments (White, 1998). Those that are successful are later applied to other regions or imitated by others (Heilmann, 2008). The Fengyang household responsibility system, which terminated the people's commune system and turned farmland into local farmers' hands, was initially secretly tested by farmers at the local level (Qian, 2000; Zhou, 1996). Further, the Shenzhen economic policies were invented by local individuals who had connections with businesses abroad; they rented urban land to business owners in order to develop the local economy (Zhu, 1994). At the beginning of the era of reform and opening-up, Shenzhen's experiences and policies were adopted by the central government (Yuan et al., 2010; Zhu, 1994). They were then allowed to spread to other areas in China.

The innovative policies of local governments have become solutions to many larger economic problems. The experiments and experiences that some local governments have undergone during the process of green development may similarly provide solutions for China's environmental problems.

Research design

In this book, local governments include those of provinces, cities, counties, and townships, according to the Chinese administrative system. Green development is

Table 1.2 General information about Shanghai, Baoding, and Wuning 2016

	Shanghai	Baoding	Wuning
Population/million	24.25	10.42	0.37
Area/km²	6,340.5	22,109	3,507
Gross Domestic Product (GDP)/ billion RMB	2,746	311	10.7
Urban household income (RMB)	57,692	25,680	27,859
Rural household income (RMB)	25,520	11,612	12,897
Green development strategy	Develop Pudong	Pioneer low-carbon city	Green rising-up

Sources: various sources, including 2016 nian Shanghaishi guomin jingji yu shehui fazhan gongbao [Statistical Communique of Shanghai on the 2016 Economic and Social Development]; 2016 nian Baodingshi guomin jingji yu shehui fazhan gongbao [Statistical Communiqué of Baoding on the 2016 Economic and Social Development]; and 2016 nian Wuningxian guomin jingji yu shehui fazhan gongbao [Statistical Communiqué of Wuning on the 2016 Economic and Social Development].

an umbrella concept, which includes all kinds of development strategies addressing not only economic development but also ecological protection. Related ideas of green development can include sustainable development, ecological development, low-carbon development, and the formation of a circular economy.

This work uses a comparative case design with three different case studies, conducted during three fieldwork trips, to research the green development phenomenon at the local government level. The three exemplary case studies range from a metropolis, the Pudong district of Shanghai, to a small county, Wuning. The third study location, Baoding, was chosen because it is a pioneer low-carbon city. Baoding is also an excellent example of why a relatively poor and less-developed city may choose a green development strategy. Shanghai was selected because it represents a megacity's efforts towards green development, while Wuning exemplifies a peripheral, agricultural, and poor town endeavoring to advance using green development strategies.

The book follows the most different systems design, with the same results and aims to examine the same independent variables for all three cases. This study aims to identify the motivations and powers behind why local governments with different political statuses, levels of economic development, and social contexts may decide to pursue green development.

Various sources were gathered to illustrate and support the three cases, including government documents, media reports, observations, archival materials, and interviews. There was also an abundance of resources available from government websites.

Questioning local green development

As Adams notes, "Development is not necessarily good" (2009, p. 377). But local green development can involve different aims, and sometimes achieve a win-win situation alongside economic development. This book focuses on the transition point of the three case studies to explain why and how local green development can offer economic benefits. The study stresses the need for the support of local powerful actors and the efforts of local people in this regard and finds that some places' ecological benefits do not follow the environmental Kuznets curve regardless of the economic development levels.

This book also emphasizes the efforts of poor regions to pursue relatively greener development plans or industries, even though many are not "green cities" according to common criteria. For instance, the case of Baoding is somewhat controversial because of the serious air pollution in the region. The case answers the questions of why a poor city may be attracted by low-carbon development, and what important factors may contribute to the decision to pursue this development.

Beyond asking why some local governments choose to pursue green development, the book also raises questions regarding the environmental and social justice issues involved with green development. Green development is generally considered to be a positive change that will contribute to China's environmental governance transition. Yet, during the process of local green development, environmental benefits and costs may be distributed in an unbalanced manner, with the benefits tending to go to the most powerful actors (e.g., local officials and industries), who have the power of allocation; conversely, weak political actors (e.g., low-income local residents) tend to carry the costs (Heynen, Perkins, & Roy, 2006; Njeru, 2006; Pelling, 1999; Swyngedouw & Heynen, 2003). Political ecology emphasizes that powerful actors typically have a significant influence on the ecology while the interests of weak actors are often neglected or improperly protected (Adams, 2009).

Entrepreneurs and local officials have the most power to define what green development will look like for the area. Through various environmental projects, they allocate local resources like land and capital, which may have a negative effect on local environment and people. The growing popularity of renewable energy industrial parks, low-carbon cities or eco-cities, and ecotourism demands large amounts of land confiscation, change of land use patterns, relocation of local people, and commercialization of natural resources, which may carry negative social and environmental impacts (Shiuh-Shen, 2013; G. Wang et al., 2012).

Moreover, there are few channels for public participation in local decision-making processes, as these are mainly controlled by local governments and industries. The task of this study is to identify the persons who support green development, their means of carrying out green development, and the implications of this process for the local people and ecology. After identifying the most powerful actors, this study will analyze their interests and incentives to elucidate local green development.

One of the most profound consequences of local green development strategies is the rapid urbanization led by local governments. Local development strategies have provided good reasons for local governments to take more resources, like land and labor, from rural areas in order to support industrialization and urbanization, including green development strategies. According to the United Nations China National Human Development Report 2013, as of 2018, nearly 60% of the population lives in cities, and by 2030, 70% of the population will be living in cities (United Nations, 2013). Even county-level governments are actively promoting urbanization. Wuning, as a small county, has an ambitious city planning program which covers 124 kilometers (Xiu & Zou, 2015). This book examines the land and capital transfers between entrepreneurs, industrial parks, banks, and local governments that occurred during urbanization under green development strategies, with the intention of offering insight on the social and environmental problems related to land issues.

The structure of the book

The book comprises seven chapters, including this introduction. The second chapter explains the context of local green development and focuses on three primary influences on local green development: global green development trends which have an influence on entrepreneurs; the national requirement for ecological protection which has influenced local officials and entrepreneurs; and local demands for environmental protection through petitions and protests which challenge the close relationships among local officials and entrepreneurs.

The third chapter describes the case of Shanghai Pudong, which has been referred to as "the window of China"—a symbol of modernization and development (Xinhua, 2009). Through the "Develop Pudong" strategy, the whole county was turned into an urban area; within a decade, it came to define the skyline of Shanghai. This chapter focuses on Pudong as a model of green development. Shanghai was behind other regions economically at the beginning of the reform and opening-up period, but with the launch of the Pudong strategy, it became a pioneer. Pudong is now a leading experimental zone in China.

The book's fourth chapter is a case study of Baoding, one of the first low-carbon cities in China. It has strong renewable energy industries and is a national renewable energy equipment base. The city's efforts in low-carbon development have been recognized not only by the national government but also by the international community, with the World Wide Fund for Nature (WWF) calling Baoding a "carbon positive" city (WWF, 2008). This chapter explores how a poor and polluted city became a pioneer in green development.

The fifth chapter presents the case of Wuning, a small agricultural county struggling to achieve green development. Wuning has long been a sparsely industrialized forest county but has developed quickly under the "Green Rising-Up" strategy. The face of the city has changed due to the modern city planning, and Wuning now aims to be one of the most beautiful counties with green industries in China.

The sixth chapter is a comparative analysis of the three case studies, which seeks to find shared key factors in green development across the three Chinese locations, thereby charting a pattern of local green development. Additionally, this chapter comments on the influence of green development on the local people and ecology.

The last chapter contains the conclusions of this study and addresses the two research questions, explaining why and how local green development may be achieved.

References

Adams, W. (2009). *Green development: Environment and sustainability in a developing world (3rd edition)*. London: Routledge.

Ahlstrom, D., & Bruton, G. D. (2001). Learning from successful local private firms in China: Establishing legitimacy. *The Academy of Management Executive, 15*(4), 72–83.

Ai, J. (2006). Guanxi networks in China: Its importance and future trends. *China & World Economy, 14*(5), 105–118.

Batjargal, B., & Liu, M. (2004). Entrepreneurs' access to private equity in China: The role of social capital. *Organization Science, 15*(2), 159–172.

Baumol, W. J. (1968). Entrepreneurship in economic theory. *The American Economic Review, 58*(2), 64–71.

Beyer, S. (2006). Environmental law and policy in the People's Republic of China. *Chinese Journal of International Law, 5*(1), 185–211.

Bloomberg New Energy Finance. (n.d.). Global market share of solar module manufacturers in 2013. In Statista—The Statistics Portal. Retrieved from www.statista.com/statistics/269812/global-market-share-of-solar-pv-module-manufacturers/.

Burns, J. P. (Ed.). (1989). *The Chinese Communist Party's nomenklatura system: A documentary study of party control of leadership selection, 1979–1984*. New York: ME Sharpe Inc.

Carlisle, E., & Flynn, D. (2005). Small business survival in China: Guanxi, legitimacy, and social capital. *Journal of Developmental Entrepreneurship, 10*(01), 79–96.

Cartier, C. (2001). "Zone fever," the arable land debate, and real estate speculation: China's evolving land use regime and its geographical contradictions. *Journal of Contemporary China, 10*(28), 445–469.

Che, J., & Qian, Y. (1998). Institutional environment, community government, and corporate governance: Understanding China's township village enterprises. *Journal of Law, Economics, and Organization, 14*(1), 1–23.

Chen, J., & Dickson, B. J. (2010). *Allies of the state: China's private entrepreneurs and democratic change*. USA: Harvard University Press.

Cooper, C. M. (2006). "This is our say in": The civil society of environmental NGOs in South-West China. *Government and Opposition, 41*(1), 109–136.

Deng, Y., & Yang, G. (2013). Pollution and protest in China: Environmental mobilization in context. *The China Quarterly, 214*, 321–336.

Dickson, B. J. (2003). *Red capitalists in China: The party, private entrepreneurs, and prospects for political change*. Cambridge: Cambridge University Press.

Ding, D. Z., Goodall, K., & Warner, M. (2000). The end of the "iron rice-bowl": Whither Chinese human resource management? *International Journal of Human Resource Management, 11*(2), 217–236.

Ding, D. Z., & Warner, M. (2001). China's labor-management system reforms: Breaking the 'Three Old Irons' (1978–1999). *Asia Pacific Journal of Management, 18*(3), 315–334.

Djankov, S., Qian, Y., Roland, G., & Zhuravskaya, E. (2006). Entrepreneurship in China and Russia compared. *Journal of the European Economic Association, 4*(2–3), 352–365.

Dryzek, J. S., Hunold, C., Schlosberg, D., Downes, D., & Hernes, H. K. (2002). Environmental transformation of the state: the USA, Norway, Germany and the UK. *Political studies, 50*(4), 659–682.

Eaton, S., & Kostka, G. (2013). Authoritarian environmentalism undermined? Local leaders' time horizons and environmental policy implementation. *The China Quarterly, 218*, 359–380.

Economy, E. (2005, May 07). China's environmental movement. Testimony before the Congressional Executive Commission on China Roundtable on Environmental NGOs in China: Encouraging Action and Addressing Public Grievances, 7. Retrieved from www.cfr.org/publication/7770/.

Economy, E. (2007). The great leap backward? The costs of China's environmental crisis. *Foreign Affairs, 86*, 38–59.

Efstathiou Jr. J. (2018). These four power giants rule the world's growing wind market. Bloomberg. Retrieved from www.bloomberg.com/news/articles/2018-02-26/these-four-power-giants-rule-the-world-s-growing-wind-market.

Fan, Y. (2002a). Ganxi's consequences: Personal gains at social cost. *Journal of Business Ethics, 38*(4), 371–380.

Fan, Y. (2002b). Questioning guanxi: Definition, classification and implications. *International Business Review, 11*(5), 543–561.

Friends of Nature [FON] (2019). Huanjing Gongyi Susong Jianbao [A brief report on public environmental litigation]. Retrieved from www.fon.org.cn/index.php?option=com_k2&view=itemlist&layout=category&Itemid=178.

Fuerst, K., & Holdaway, J. (2015). Environment and health in China: The role of environmental NGOs in policy innovation. In A. Fulda (Ed.), *Civil society contributions to policy innovation in the PR China: Environment, social development and international cooperation* (pp. 33–76). Hampshire: Palgrave Macmillan.

Gang, C. (2009). *Politics of China's environmental protection: Problems and progress (Vol. 17)*. Singapore: World Scientific.

Guthrie, D. (2009). *China and globalization: The social, economic and political transformation of Chinese society*. New York: Routledge.

Guthrie, D. (2012). China and globalization: The social, economic and political transformation of Chinese society. New York: Routledge.

Hamilton, R. T., & Harper, D. A. (1994). The entrepreneur in theory and practice. *Journal of Economic Studies, 21*(6), 3–18.

Harvey, D. (2005). *A brief history of neoliberalism*. Oxford: Oxford University Press.

Heberer, T. (2003). *Private entrepreneurs in China and Vietnam: Social and political functioning of strategic groups (Vol. 4)*. Leiden: Brill.

Heilmann, S. (2008). Policy experimentation in China's economic rise. *Studies in Comparative International Development, 43*(1), 1–26.

Heynen, N., Perkins, H. A., & Roy, P. (2006). The political ecology of uneven urban green space the impact of political economy on race and ethnicity in producing environmental inequality in Milwaukee. *Urban Affairs Review, 42*(1), 3–25.

Ho, P. (2001). Greening without conflict? Environmentalism, NGOs and civil society in China. *Development and Change, 32*(5), 893–921.

Hong, C. (1995). Zhongguo xiangzhen qiye chanquan gaige yu zhongyang-difang quanli de hudong [The property right reform of TVEs and its interaction with the central-local relationship]. *Modern China Studies*, No. 1. Retrieved from www.modernchinastudies. org/us/issues/past-issues/45-mcs-1995-issue-1/254-2011-12-29-11-30-06.html.

Hsueh, R. (2011). *China's regulatory state: A new strategy for globalization*. New York: Cornell University Press.

Huang, Y. (2008). *Capitalism with Chinese characteristics: Entrepreneurship and the state (Vol. 1)*. Cambridge: Cambridge University Press.

Ip, P. K. (2009). The challenge of developing a business ethics in China. *Journal of Business Ethics*, 88, 211–224.

Jahiel, A. R. (1997). Research note. The contradictory impact of reform on environmental protection in China. *The China Quarterly, 149*, 81–103.

Jahiel, A. R. (1998). The organization of environmental protection in China. *The China Quarterly, 156*, 757–787.

Jin, H., & Qian, Y. (1998). Public versus private ownership of firms: Evidence from rural China. *Quarterly Journal of Economics*, 773–808.

Knup, E. (1997). Environmental NGOs in China: An overview. *China Environment Series, 1*(3), 9–15.

Kostka, G. (2013). Environmental protection bureau leadership at the provincial level in China: examining diverging career backgrounds and appointment patterns. *Journal of Environmental Policy & Planning, 15*(1), 41–63.

Kostka, G. (2014). Barriers to the implementation of environmental policies at the local level in China. *World Bank Policy Research Working Paper* (7016).

Kostka, G., & Mol, A. P. (2013). Implementation and participation in China's local environmental politics: Challenges and innovations. *Journal of Environmental Policy & Planning, 15*(1), 3–16.

Lang, G., & Xu, Y. (2013). Anti-incinerator campaigns and the evolution of protest politics in China. *Environmental Politics, 22*(5), 832–848.

Ledeneva, A. (2008). Blat and guanxi: Informal practices in Russia and China. *Comparative Studies in Society and History, 50*(01), 118–144.

Lee, K., & Ho, M.-s. (2014). The Maoming anti-PX protest of 2014. *China Perspectives*, 2014(3).

Leng, J. (2009). *Corporate governance and financial reform in China's transition economy (Vol. 1)*. Hong Kong: Hong Kong University Press.

Li, D. D. (1998). Changing incentives of the Chinese bureaucracy. *The American Economic Review, 88*(2), 393–397.

Li, H. L. (2015, September 04). Current situation and trend of Chinese eco-city development. Presentation at the ICLEI World Congress, Seoul, Republic of Korea, April 8–12, 2015. Retrieved from http://worldcongress2015.iclei.org/wp-content/uploads/2015/04/SP1_04_-Hailong-Li.pdf.

Li, J., Chen, G., Li, J., & Matlay, H. (2006). Who are the Chinese private entrepreneurs? A study of entrepreneurial attributes and business governance. *Journal of Small Business and Enterprise Development, 13*(2), 148–160.

Liao, D., & Sohmen, P. (2001). The development of modern entrepreneurship in China. *Stanford Journal of East Asian Affairs, 1*(1), 27–33.

Lieberthal, K. (1997). China's governing system and its impact on environmental policy implementation. *China Environment Series, 1*(1997), 3–8.

Lieberthal, K. (2007). Scorched earth: Will environmental risks in China overwhelm its opportunities? In E. Economy & K. Lieberthal (Eds.), *Harvard Business Review, 85*, 88–96.

Lin, G. C., & Yi, F. (2011). Urbanization of capital or capitalization on urban land? Land development and local public finance in urbanizing China. *Urban Geography, 32*(1), 50–79.

Lin, J. Y. (1992). Rural reforms and agricultural growth in China. *The American Economic Review*, 34–51.
Lin, N. (1995). Local market socialism: Local corporatism in action in rural China. *Theory and Society*, 24(3), 301–354.
Lin, J. Y., & Liu, Z. (2000). Fiscal decentralization and economic growth in China. *Economic Development and Cultural Change*, 49(1), 1–21.
Liu, X. R. (2001). *Jumping into the sea: From academics to entrepreneurs in South China*. Maryland: Rowman & Littlefield.
Lo, W.-H., & Tang, S.-Y. (2006). Institutional reform, economic changes, and local environmental management in China: The case of Guangdong Province. *Environmental Politics*, 15(02), 190–210.
Lo, C. W. H., & Leung, S. W. (2000). Environmental agency and public opinion in Guangzhou: The limits of a popular approach to environmental governance. *The China Quarterly*, 163, 677–704.
Lu, Y., & Sun, T. (2013). Local government financing platforms in China: A fortune or misfortune? *International Monetary Fund Working Paper 13*(243), 1–30. Retrieved from www.imf.org/external/pubs/ft/wp/2013/wp13243.pdf.
Ma, X., & Ortolano, L. (2000). *Environmental regulation in China: Institutions, enforcement, and compliance*. Maryland: Rowman & Littlefield Publishers.
Malik, R. (1997). *Chinese entrepreneurs in the economic development of China*. Westport: Greenwood Publishing Group.
Martinot, E., Li, J., & Mastny, L. (2007). *Powering China's development: The role of renewable energy*. Washington, DC: Worldwatch Institute.
Martens 1, S. (2006). Public participation with Chinese characteristics: Citizen consumers in China's environmental management. *Environmental Politics*, 15(02), 211–230.
Mauthner, F., Weiss, W., & Spoerk-Duer (2015). Solar heat worldwide markets and contribution to energy supply 2013 Solar heat worldwide edition 2015 (p. 4). Solar Heating & Cooling Programme International Energy Agency. Retrieved from www.iea-shc.org/data/sites/1/publications/Solar-Heat-Worldwide-2015.pdf.
McElwee, C. R. (2011). *Environmental Law in China: Managing Risk and Ensuring Compliance*. Oxford New York: Oxford University Press.
McMillan, J., & Woodruff, C. (2003). The central role of entrepreneurs in transition economies. In G. Fields & G. Pfeffermann (Eds.), *Pathways out of poverty: Private firms and economic mobility in developing countries* (pp. 105–121). Boston: Kluwer Academic Publishers.
Mol, A. P., & Carter, N. T. (2006). China's environmental governance in transition. *Environmental Politics*, 15(02), 149–170.
Montinola, G., Qian, Y., & Weingast, B. R. (1995). Federalism, Chinese style: the political basis for economic success in China. *World Politics*, 48(01), 50–81.
Morton, K. (2006). *International aid and China's environment: Taming the Yellow Dragon (Vol. 25)*. London: Routledge.
National Development and Reform Commission [NDRC]. (2010). Guojia Fagaiwei guanyu kaizhan ditan shengqu he ditan chengshi shidian gongzuo de tongzhi (fagai qihou 1587(2010))[NDRC: The notice of launching low-carbon pilot provinces and cities (climate changeNDRC No. 1587(2010))]. Retrieved from http://bgt.ndrc.gov.cn/zcfb/201008/t20100810_498787.html.
National Development and Reform Commission [NDRC]. (2012). Guojia Fagaiwei guanyu kaizhan di er pi guojia ditan shengqu he ditan chengshi shidian gongzuo de tongzhi [NDRC: The notice of launching a second round of low-carbon pilot provinces and cities]. Retrieved from www.ndrc.gov.cn/gzdt/201212/t20121205_517506.html.

National People's Congress (NPC) (2014). Zhonghua renmin gongheguo huanjing baohufa [Environmental protection law of the People's Republic of China]. Retrieved from www.npc.gov.cn/npc/xinwen/2014-04/25/content_1861279.htm.
Naughton, B. (2007). *The Chinese economy: Transitions and growth (Vol. 1)*. Cambridge: MIT Press Books.
Nee, V., & Young, F. W. (1991). Peasant entrepreneurs in China's "second economy": An institutional analysis. *Economic Development and Cultural Change, 293*–310.
Njeru, J. (2006). The urban political ecology of plastic bag waste problem in Nairobi, Kenya. *Geoforum, 37*(6), 1046–1058.
Oi, J. C. (1992). Fiscal reform and the economic foundations of local state corporatism in China. *World Politics, 45*(1), 99–126.
Oi, J. C. (1995). The role of the local state in China's transitional economy. *The China Quarterly, 144*(1), 1132–1149.
Oi, J. C. (1999). *Rural China takes off: Institutional foundations of economic reform.* California: University of California Press.
Oi, J. C., Rozelle, S., Zhou, X., & Walter, H. (2010). *Growing pains: Tensions and opportunity in China's transformation.* Stanford: Walter H. Shorenstein Asia-Pacific Research Center.
Park, S. H., & Luo, Y. (2001). Guanxi and organizational dynamics: Organizational networking in Chinese firms. *Strategic Management Journal, 22*(5), 455–477.
Peet, R. (2004). Liberation ecologies: Environment, development and social movements. In R. P. M. Watts (Ed.), *Liberation Ecologies* (pp. 1–45). London: Routledge.
Pelling, M. (1999). The political ecology of flood hazard in urban Guyana. *Geoforum, 30*(3), 249–261.
Peng, M. W. (2001). How entrepreneurs create wealth in transition economies. *The Academy of Management Executive, 15*(1), 95–108.
Putnam, R. D. (2000). *Bowling alone: The collapse and revival of American community.* New York: Simon & Schuster.
Qian, Y. (2000). The process of China's market transition (1978–1998): The evolutionary, historical, and comparative perspectives. *Journal of Institutional and Theoretical Economics (JITE)/Zeitschrift für die gesamte Staatswissenschaft*, 151–171.
Qian, Y. (2002, July 21). How reform worked in China. *William Davidson Institute Working Paper Number 473.* Advance online publication. doi: http://libguides.scu.edu.au/content.php?pid=161580&sid=2263819.
Qian, Y., & Weingast, B. R. (1997). Federalism as a commitment to preserving market incentives. *Journal of Economic Perspectives, 11*(4), 83–92.
REN21. (2015). Renewables 2015 global status report. Retrieved from www.ren21.net/status-of-renewables/global-status-report/.
Rodrik, D. (2006). What's so special about China's exports? *China & World Economy, 14*(5), 1–19. Princeton: Princeton University Press.
Rodrik, D. (2008). *One economics, many recipes: Globalization, institutions, and economic growth.* Princeton: Princeton University Press.
Ross, L. (1992). The politics of environmental policy in the People's Republic of China. *Policy Studies Journal, 20*(4), 628–642.
Rostow, W. W. (1967). *The stages of economic growth: A non-communist manifesto.* Cambridge: Cambridge University Press.
Schreurs, M. A. (2008). From the bottom up local and subnational climate change politics. *Journal of Environment & Development, 17*(4), 343–355.
Schwartz, J. (2004). Environmental NGOs in China: Roles and limits. *Pacific Affairs*, 28–49.

Shao, G., Lu, J., & Wu, J. (2012). New media and civic engagement in China: The case of the Xiamen PX Event. *China Media Research, 8*(2), 76–82.
Shapiro, J. (2012). *China's environmental challenges.* Cambridge: Polity.
Shirk, S. L. (1993). *The political logic of economic reform in China.* California: University of California Press.
Shirk, S. L. (2010). Changing media, changing China. In S. L. Shirk (Ed.), *Changing media, changing China* (pp. 1–37). Oxford: Oxford University Press.
Shiuh-Shen, C. (2013). Chinese eco-cities: A perspective of land-speculation-oriented local entrepreneurialism. *China Information, 27*(2), 173–196.
Skinner, M. W., Kuhn, R. G., & Joseph, A. E. (2001). Agricultural land protection in China: a case study of local governance in Zhejiang Province. *Land Use Policy, 18*(4), 329–340.
Stalley, P., & Yang, D. (2006). An emerging environmental movement in China? *The China Quarterly, 186*, 333–356.
Sun, Y., & Zhao, D. (2008). Environmental campaigns. In K. J. O'Brien (Ed.), *Popular protest in China* (pp. 144–162). USA: Harvard University Press.
Swyngedouw, E., & Heynen, N. C. (2003). Urban political ecology, justice and the politics of scale. *Antipode, 35*(5), 898–918.
Szamosszegi, A., & Kyle, C. (2011, October 26). An analysis of state-owned enterprises and state capitalism in China: Capital Trade, Incorporated for US-China Economic and Security Review Commission. Retrieved from www.uscc.gov/sites/default/files/Research/10_26_11_CapitalTradeSOEStudy.pdf.
Tan, J. (1996). Regulatory environment and strategic orientations in a transitional economy: A study of Chinese private enterprise. *Entrepreneurship: Theory and Practice*, 31–44.
Tang, S.-Y., & Zhan, X. (2008). Civic environmental NGOs, civil society, and democratization in China. *Journal of Development Studies, 44*(3), 425–448.
Tsai, K. S. (2004). *Back-alley banking: Private entrepreneurs in China.* New York: Cornell University Press.
Tsai, K. S. (2007). *Capitalism without democracy: The private sector in contemporary China.* New York: Cornell University Press.
Tsui, K.-y., & Wang, Y. (2004). Between separate stoves and a single menu: Fiscal decentralization in China. *The China Quarterly, 177*, 71–90.
United Nations. (2013). China National Human Development Report 2013. Sustainable and livable cities: Towards ecological civilization. Retrieved from www.cn.undp.org/content/china/zh/home/library/human_development/china-human-development-report-2013.html.
Van Rooij, B. (2006). Implementation of Chinese environmental law: Regular enforcement and political campaigns. *Development and Change, 37*(1), 57–74.
Wade, R. (1990). *Governing the market: Economic theory and the role of government in East Asian industrialization.* New Jersey: Princeton University Press.
Walder, A. G. (1995). Local governments as industrial firms: An organizational analysis of China's transitional economy. *American Journal of Sociology, 101*(2), 263–301.
Wang, A. (2013). The search for sustainable legitimacy: Environmental law and bureaucracy in China. *37 Harvard Environmental Law Review 365; UCLA School of Law Research Paper No. 13–31.* Retrieved from http://papers.ssrn.com/sol3/papers.cfm?abstract_id=2128167.
Wang, G., Innes, J. L., Wu, S. W., Krzyzanowski, J., Yin, Y., Dai, S., … Liu, S. (2012). National park development in China: conservation or commercialization? *Ambio, 41*(3), 247–261.

Wang, H. (2000). Informal institutions and foreign investment in China. *The Pacific Review, 13*(4), 525–556.

Wang, Q. (2010). Effective policies for renewable energy—the example of China's wind power—lessons for China's photovoltaic power. *Renewable and Sustainable Energy Reviews, 14*(2), 702–712.

Wang, Y., & Tong, S. (2013, January 30). Yizuo Quanguo zuimei xiancheng zhengzai jueqi [The rise of one of the most beautiful counties]. *Wuning Xinwen*. Retrieved from www.jjwn.com/news/bencandy.php?fid=48&id=1483.

Weinert, J. X., Ma, C., Yang, X., & Cherry, C. R. (2007). Electric two-wheelers in China: effect on travel behavior, mode shift, and user safety perceptions in a medium-sized city. *Transportation Research Record: Journal of the Transportation Research Board, 2038*(1), 62–68.

Weinert, J., Ogden, J., Sperling, D., & Burke, A. (2008). The future of electric two-wheelers and electric vehicles in China. *Energy Policy, 36*(7), 2544–2555.

White, L. T. (1998). *Unstately Power: Volume 1, Local Causes of China's Economic Reforms*. New York: ME Sharpe.

Wong, C. P. W. (1991). Central–local relations in an era of fiscal decline: The paradox of fiscal decentralization in post-Mao China. *The China Quarterly, 128*, 691–715.

Wu, F. S. (2009). Environmental politics in China: An issue area in review. *Journal of Chinese Political Science, 14*(4), 383–406.

WWF. (2008). Low carbon initiative in China. Retrieved from http://en.wwfchina.org/en/what_we_do/climate___energy/mitigation/lcci/.

Xi, J. (2014). Ba, lushui qingshan jiushi jinshan yinshang, guanyu dali tuijin shengtai wenming jianshe [chapter 8, clean water and green mountains are gold and silver mountains, strengthening the promotion of ecological civilization] in Zhonggong Zhongyang Xuanchuanbu [Publicity Department of the Communist Party of China] (Ed.), *Xi Jinping Zongshuji xilie zhongyao jianghua duben [Speech collection of General Secretary of Xi Jinping]*. Retrieved from http://theory.people.com.cn/n/2014/0711/c40531-25267092.html.

Xin, K. K., & Pearce, J. L. (1996). Guanxi: Connections as substitutes for formal institutional support. *Academy of Management Journal, 39*(6), 1641–1658.

Xinhua. (2009). Shanghai Pudong: Zhongguo gaige kaifang de chuangkou (Shanghai Puodng: The window of reform of China's reform and opening-up). Retrieved from http://city.finance.sina.com.cn/city/2009-09-22/115971.html.

Xiu, J., & Zou, Y. (2015, August 18, 2015). Chengqu jianshe jingquhua, shanshui Wuning yao dang quanguo zuimei xiancheng [Construct urban area into a tourist resort, Wuning strive to become of the most beautiful counties in China]. Retrieved from www.jxnews.com.cn/xxrb/system/2015/08/18/014163616.shtml.

Yang, G. (2005). Environmental NGOs and institutional dynamics in China. *The China Quarterly, 181*(1), 46–66.

Yang, G., & Calhoun, C. (2007). Media, civil society, and the rise of a green public sphere in China. *China Information, 21*(2), 211–236.

Yang, K. (2012). *Entrepreneurship in China*. Surrey: Ashgate Publishing.

Yuan, Y., Guo, H., Xu, H., Li, W., Luo, S., Lin, H., & Yuan, Y. (2010). China's first special economic zone: The case of Shenzhen. In D. Z. Zeng (Ed.), *Building engines for growth and competitiveness in China: Experience with special economic zones and industrial clusters* (pp. 55–86). Washington DC: The World Bank.

Zhang, T., & Zou, H. F. (1998). Fiscal decentralization, public spending, and economic growth in China. *Journal of Public Economics, 67*(2), 221–240.

Zhou, K. X. (1996). *How the farmers changed China: Power of the people*. Boulder: Westview.
Zhu, J. (1994). Changing land policy and its impact on local growth: the experience of the Shenzhen Special Economic Zone, China, in the 1980s. *Urban Studies, 31*(10), 1611–1623.

2 China's local green development background

Introduction

China's local green development has occurred against a background of severe environmental pollution and been influenced by international, national, and bottom-up powers. The country's pollution has reached unparalleled levels, particularly in urban areas, posing not only serious health problems to the public, but also enormous economic damage (Chan & Yao, 2008; X. Wang & Mauzerall, 2006). Domestically, the Ministry of Ecology and Environment (MEE) (formerly known as the Ministry of Environmental Protection (MEP)) reported severe air, water, and soil pollution in its annual reports from 1989 to 2017. At the 2014 Central Economic Work Conference, President Xi Jinping concluded that China is at the limit of its environmental carrying capacity or has even exceeded it. A transformation towards a green, low-carbon, and circular development path is necessary (MEP, 2015a). Fortunately, awareness about environmental protection is growing at all levels, from within governments down to the general public.

International organizations and actors are entering environmental governance in China through cooperation and the active exchange of ideas and technologies with local government. These organizations have established many environmental projects in cooperation with Chinese local governments, particularly municipal governments (Martinot, 2001; Schreurs, 2008; World Bank, 2015; WWF, 2008). Local governments also actively search for international investment in environmental technologies (F. Chen, 2003; Schreurs, 2008). Notably, however, it is difficult for international actors to change local policies.

Global consumers constitute a much more important factor for local green development, through the power of the market. China is an export-oriented economy and Chinese businesses pay close attention to international market trends. As consumers in foreign countries demand more environmentally friendly products from China, they push Chinese firms towards compliance with international environmental standards (Zhu, Sarkis, & Lai, 2007). Thus, green consumerism has significantly impacted governments' environmental policies through these businesses.

The central government continues to encourage local governments to experiment with a shift towards green development, setting energy-saving and emission-reduction targets which it distributed among local governments starting in 2007 (Kostka & Hobbs, 2012; Price et al., 2011; N. Zhou, Levine, & Price, 2010). Even before the NDRC published its comprehensive *Energy Production and Consumption Revolution Strategy (2016–2030)* in 2017, several policies were in place that incentivized the development of renewable energy (e.g., distributed wind, biomass, solar energy, etc.). Yet, although these policies encourage local governments to pursue green development, they are not mandatory for local leaders. The choice to "go green" or not still lies squarely in the hands of local governments—unlike, for instance, satisfactory GDP growth, which is a mandatory goal (A. Wang, 2013).

Local actors, such as environmental NGOs (ENGOs) and local residents, sometimes push for local green development as well, especially through increased public participation in local construction projects with significant environmental impact (Martens, 2006; Ren, 2013; Tang, Tang, & Lo, 2005). The number of ENGOs is increasing rapidly, as is the number of local environmental protests and petitions (Gang, 2009; W. Li, Liu, & Li, 2012; Talamantes, 2014; Tang & Zhan, 2008; G. Yang, 2005). In some cases, these groups have succeeded in persuading local governments to modify or even cancel projects with clear adverse environmental impacts (e.g., chemical plants or waste incinerators), although they are still excluded from the key industrial policy decision-making process (Johnson, 2013a, 2013b; Lang & Xu, 2013; K. Lee & Ho, 2014; H. Lu, 2009; Lv & Zhao, 2009; Wen, 2015). However, blocking large development projects through demonstrations and petitions often causes economic damage to local governments and industries.

Despite the central government's attempts to strengthen its control over local leaders (Landry, 2008), local governments remain essentially authoritarian in China. These leaders still enjoy the authority to manage local cadres and resources and retain high financial autonomy in their respective regions. The central government employs a multi-criteria evaluation system to decide the promotion of political officials, in which GDP growth plays a key role. While environmental performance is becoming increasingly recognized as a criterion in this evaluation, it is still not a top priority.

Global green influences

Formal and official cooperation between international organizations and local governments

When the Chinese central government implemented vast administrative decentralization in the 1990s, it also transferred responsibility for environmental protection to the country's local governments (Zusman & Turner, 2005). At the same time, internationally, the "think globally, act locally" idea shifted greater focus on environmental protection to the local level (Betsill & Bulkeley, 2004). International governmental organizations and NGOs that follow China's environmental issues have realized the importance of local governments in implementing environmental protection, and thus, they frequently seek to cooperate with them (ADB, 2015; Jain, 2006; UNEP, 2015; WWF, 2008).

For instance, in 2015, the United Nations Environment Program (UNEP) entered into a partnership with Hohhot, the capital city of China's Inner Mongolia Autonomous Region (UNEP, 2015). Inner Mongolia is rich in wind energy and Hohhot sought to harness this wind energy for heating. Similarly, the Local Governments for Sustainability (ICLEI) worked closely with Chinese eco-city projects and held a symposium to discuss how cities can make their urban energy systems 100% renewable by 2030. The World Bank gave grants and support to Shenzhen's sustainable policymaking under its City Energy Efficiency Transformation Initiative, led by its Energy Sector Management Assistance Program (World Bank, 2014). The German Energy Agency is actively involved in promoting sustainability with several Chinese cities (German Energy Agency, 2018). At the municipal level, there are hundreds of sister city environmental partnerships between Chinese and foreign municipal governments; there were 251 pairs of sister cities between China and Japan at the end of 2013, and environmental protection has been an area of intense international collaboration (Heyan, 2013; Lam, 2006; Sasuga, 2004).

It must be noted that international aid or cooperation agreements are unequally distributed in China. Among the three cases covered in this book, Shanghai, as an international city, has the most international resources while Wuning, as a rural county, has the least international resources. Baoding has fewer international resources than many cities, such as Beijing and Tianjin, yet it managed to become a frontrunner for low-carbon development. Hence, it appears that increased opportunities for formal and official international cooperation do not necessarily determine the local green development agenda.

Informal and indirect influence from global "green consumers"

Chinese local governments routinely encourage businesses to target the global market, and green consumerism is one global trend that is highly relevant to these firms (K. Guo & N'Diaye, 2009; Rodrik, 2006). Green consumerism indirectly impacts local green development through the intermediary role of local businesses, particularly green businesses.

"Green consumers" are "ordinary people who believe that businesses have a vital role to play in the struggle to preserve the environment" (Straughan & Roberts, 1999, p. 574). Increasingly, consumers in industrialized markets are demanding more transparent information about the environmental impact of the products they use, and the number of green consumers in developed countries is rising (McCormick, 2002; Probe, 1989; Speshock, 2010). This trend is forcing Chinese businesses to raise the environmental standards of their products (Salzman, 1997). Under public pressure for green production, MNCs are also aiming to adopt higher environmental standards when they set up subsidiaries in China (Christmann & Taylor, 2001). In addition, some export-oriented Chinese firms are under pressure due to quasi-green trade sanctions, because many products do not meet international green standards (Hou & Su, 2004; Jun & Yan, 2005; Qiu & Yang 2007). In these ways, Chinese companies are being pushed towards green supply chain management practices that meet environmental standards set by both consumers and MNCs in the global market (Zhu et al., 2007). In response to these international demands, local governments are increasingly supporting local businesses in upgrades of their environmental technologies and facilities.

Likewise, the international demand for renewable energy products has promoted a dynamic green industry in China. Some Chinese entrepreneurs seized the opportunity to establish renewable energy companies when they saw public and government support of green products in Western nations. In fact, Chinese solar companies Trina Solar and Yingli now dominate the global solar photovoltaic (PV) market (IHS, 2015). In 2015, seven of the 10 largest solar module manufacturers were Chinese companies, together capturing 35.4% of the global market (Bloomberg New Energy Finance, 2015). In addition, three Chinese wind companies appear among the top 10 global wind turbine manufacturers in 2017 (*Windpower Monthly*, 2017).

Chinese businesses are central actors in the shift towards green practices in the international market. The leaders of the abovementioned companies have closely observed the requirements of green consumers' growing demands and adapted their production activities accordingly. When determined green entrepreneurs are present in a locality, they can persuade the local government of the significant demand for green products or services in the global market, and of the market opportunities that this demand can provide to their locality. In this way, businesses' activities can influence local officials' decisions to follow a green development strategy—particularly when their green businesses are successful in the global market.

National government's influence

Encouraged but not mandated

The Chinese central government has encouraged local governments to work towards green development by launching numerous pilot projects through which local governments can gain fiscal and policy support. For instance, the NDRC launched low-carbon pilot projects in cities and provinces from 2010 (NDRC, 2010). Similarly, the MEP established ecological economy pilots in provinces, cities, and counties since 2012 (MEP, 2012). The central government's economic stimuli, enacted as a response to the economic slump of 2008, all had strong green investment elements to them. Clean energy and technologies are regarded as high-tech industries, capable of transforming the economy. Therefore, the government invested substantial resources in these industries, particularly during the global financial crisis (J. Y. Lin, 2011). On the other hand, the central government also supports some energy-intensive industries, such as construction and traditional power industries. Most importantly, the

28 China's local green development background

central government's policies are primarily oriented towards economic growth, with environmental sustainability being a secondary goal only.

China's green development is path dependent, dominated by the state, and associated with strong economic interests (Cheng, 1998). The Chinese government has sustained a high investment in the energy sector, and the share of investment in renewable energy within the total investment in energy is increasing (see Figure 2.1). In 2015, for the first time, investment in wind energy surpassed investment in conventional energy (Xiao, 2015). As of 2017, China is the leading investor in renewable energy globally, with its investments reaching $126.6 billion that year—a 31% increase over its investment in 2016 (UNEP, 2018).

The Chinese central government has created a domestic green market in which local governments compete for market shares and subsidies. China's solar and wind energy industries are highly dependent on the central government's policies in several ways. First, wind energy companies benefited from the central government mandatory policy regarding local content requirements since the 1997 Ride the Wind Program; when wind companies got strong, the policy was cancelled in 2010 (Kuntze & Moerenhout, 2013; S. Zhang, Andrew-Speed, & Zhao, 2012). Second, the solar companies confronted trade wars from the US and EU, which led to crisis; the central government started to foster the domestic solar market to help the solar PV companies by launching the Golden Sun project since 2009 (Caprotti, 2015; Yuan, 2011). Local governments support their local renewable energy companies' bids for renewable energy projects from the central government, since these projects can bring economic growth, employment, and political achievements to the locality.

Though the central government's huge investment has encouraged local governments to focus on green development, still only a small number of local governments have turned this investment into local green development

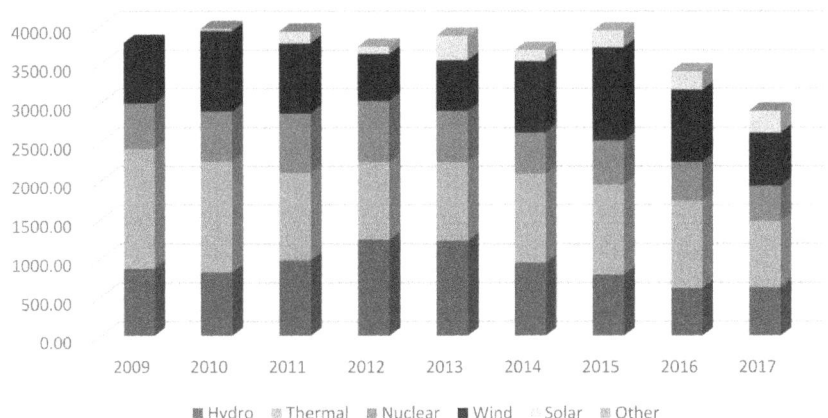

Figure 2.1 Power investment in China from 2009 to 2017 (in billion RMB).
Source: China Electricity Council planning and statistics.

strategies. Further, the survivability of local green businesses that rely on the central government's financial instruments is low (Yuan, 2011). While central government policies can favor green development in a locality, these policies do not constitute a fundamental factor for change in local environmental politics. In addition, the central government has distorted the green market, leading to over-production of green products (Fischer, 2014; Yuan, 2011; Zehner, 2011). Finally, despite stressing the importance of green development, both in rhetoric and project-based policies, the central government still stresses the importance of GDP growth more (e.g., in its cadre management system (Xi, 2018)).

Decentralization

It is crucial to gain an overview of China's administrative structure in order to understand how its local politics function. Many scholars argue that China's environmental problems are caused by its governing system, which is characterized by a decentralization and fragmentation of authority among central and local governments, and the competition between bureaucratic entities (S. Guo, 2012; Jahiel, 1998; Lieberthal, 1997; Lo, Fryxell, & Wong, 2006; Marks, 2010; Mol, 2006; Mol & Carter, 2006; Sims, 1999; Tsang & Kolk, 2010).

For many decades, the Chinese government has decentralized the country's political structure and transferred both rights and responsibilities to local governments (see Figure 2.2). Power in the Chinese political system is distributed to the central, provincial, municipal, county-, town-, and village-level governments. There are two governing principles: one is "the party controlling cadres" (*dang guan ganbu*), which means that the party controls personnel questions within the government system (H. Y. Lee, 1991; T. Lin, 2013); the second principle is "managing only one level" (*xiaguan yiji*), which specifies that the central level supervises the provinces, the provinces supervise the cities, and so on down the hierarchy (T. Lin, 2013).

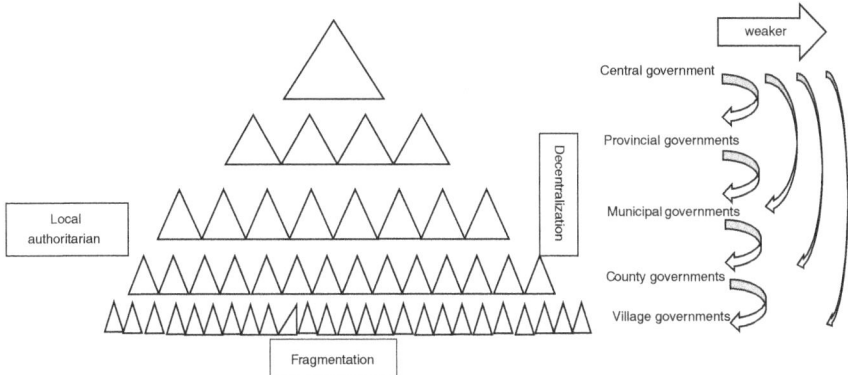

Figure 2.2 Fragmented local authoritarianism in China.

In general, the central government holds stronger control over provincial governments through its personnel power, as the number of provincial-level governments is limited. Most of the studies on central–local relationships focus on relations between the central government and provincial governments, which are at the top level (Breslin, 1996; Chung, 1995). In contrast, the central government's control of municipal, county-, town-, and village-level governments is limited due to the jumps between levels in terms of distance and lack of information, and the vast number of these various entities. From a horizontal perspective, the Chinese governing system is largely fragmented, as it is made up of parallel governments which compete fiercely: provinces compete with other provinces, cities compete with other cities, and counties compete with other counties for national policies, resources, as well as global market share (Jian, Zhang, & Qin, 2007; Montinola, Qian, & Weingast, 1995; Qian & Roland, 1998; Rawski, 1994).

There have been recent efforts by the central government to recentralize the system, but with mixed success (Kostka & Nahm, 2017). The current structure of central–local relationships comprises complicated personnel, financial, and fiscal arrangements that do not allow for rapid change. An important cornerstone of this structure is the economic success of local government experimentation since the 1980s (Zheng, 2007; Zheng & Wu, 1994).

This decentralized and fragmented system created a strong incentive for local government to pursue economic growth, and as such, it is considered a key component of China's successful reform and opening-up, which added to the legitimacy of the ruling CCP (Oi, 1992; 1999; Shirk, 1993; Xu, 2011; S. Zhou, 2007). Some scholars have described the Chinese central–local government relationship during the period after reform and opening-up function as "federalism, Chinese style" (Montinola et al., 1995, p. 52; Qian & Weingast, 1997; Zheng, 2007; Zheng & Wu, 1994). The fierce competition between levels also encouraged China's economic growth and global rise (S. Zhou, 2007).

China's local authorities have high autonomy regarding local economic affairs, and the fiscal reform between the central and local governments created strong local incentives for promoting economic development (Guthrie, 2012, p. 24; Whiting, 2006). Oi (1992) introduced the concept of "local state corporatism" to describe the way in which local government officials steer enterprises in their own territory to promote local economic growth. By comparing local governments to industrial firms, Walder (1995) explains how these governments promote economic development through managing public industries in a market-oriented way (e.g., through competition with other localities).

The Chinese central government has given freedom to local governments to operate in such a market-oriented way (Blanchard & Shleifer, 2000; Montinola et al., 1995; Qian & Weingast, 1997; Shirk, 1993; Weingast, 1995). At the same time, the central government has long used economic growth as a key performance indicator for local leaders (L. Zhou, 2007). In summary, China's current fast and stable economic development is a result of the leadership style of the CCP (Shambaugh, 2008), and it is hard to imagine changing this efficient and effective system with any degree of simplicity or speed.

Conflict between local governments and local people

Growing local petitions and protests

Due to rising environmental awareness, local residents are increasingly willing to protest construction projects that have negative environmental impacts on their area (Deng & Yang, 2013; W. Li et al., 2012; Martens, 2006). Since March 2015, locals at Naiman Banner in the Inner Mongolia Autonomous Region have protested chemical plants seeking to set up locations in the local industrial park (Sina, 2015); just two days after the Tianjin explosion on August 12, 2015, Jiaxing residents protested a PX project in their region (Y. Yang, 2015); and on August 7, 2016, Lianyungang residents protested a nuclear project (BJX, 2016). Through environmental protests like these and others, local citizens deliver strong demands to their local governments to consider the environmental impact of their decisions. It is increasingly likely that local officials may face negative outcomes, and even legal penalties, due to local protests (Dong, Ishikawa, Liu, & Hamori, 2011; Stern, 2013; Van Rooij, 2010). In 2015, Hebei Province sentenced the vice-head of the Environmental Protection Bureau (EPB) in Huangshi City to six and a half years' imprisonment for environmental violations and corruption; this sentence was triggered by a 2013 petition in which 500 villagers in Dawang Township complained about the arsenic pollution to Huangshi's Secretary Zhou Xianwang (Y. Ding & Lei, 2015). Likewise, in 2015, farmers in Linshui County, Sichuan Province, complained online about a coal mining company which limited their access to water and took over their land illegally (Fanfucanglianwangyuanchuangban, 2015). Considering the changing public opinion, green industries have a better chance than ever before of outcompeting traditional polluting industries for local governments' support.

Environmental pollution occurs both in urban and rural regions and has therefore prompted protests from both urban and rural residents against local governments (Jing, 2003; Ren, Shou, & Dong, 2015; Stalley & Yang, 2006; Tilt, 2007; Van Rooij, 2010). Thanks to the support of the media—and especially the new media (e.g., the Internet, SMS, cell phones, social media, microblogging, etc.)—it has become easier and cheaper for individuals to spread their complaints and deliver their opinions on local projects to the central government (Grano, 2015; Shao, Lu, & Wu, 2012; J. Tong, 2015; G. Yang, 2003; Zeng & Huang, 2015; K. Zhao, 2011).

The chart in Figure 2.3 illustrates the growing number of environmental petitions from the public submitted through letters, visits, phone calls, and the Internet. As shown, the number of such petitions increased dramatically after 2000. The chart also reveals that the Internet has become a popular channel for the public to express concerns about environmental pollution.[1]

In addition to making use of the traditional petition system, the Chinese public has sometimes taken more aggressive actions to protest local governments and industries. These actions, called "environmental mass events," are usually characterized by confrontation and conflict between the public and local governments

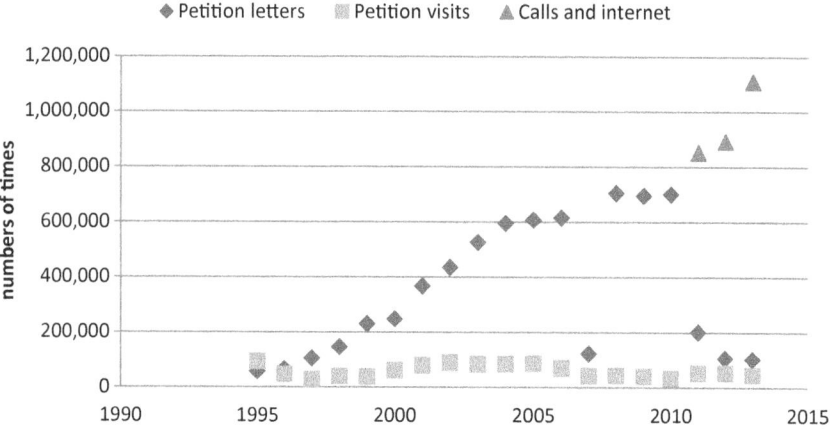

Figure 2.3 Environmental petition data in China from 1994 to 2013.

Source: author calculation from 1994 to 2006 and 2011 to 2013 based on Quanguo Huanjing Tongji Gongbao (Reports on the State of the Environment in China), and from 2007, 2008, 2009, and 2010 based on Huanjing Guanli Zhidu Zhixing Qingkuang (Reports on the Implementation of Environmental Protection in China) from the MEP (now known as the MEE).

and industries (Z. Ding, 2014). Although there is no available data about exactly how many environmental mass events happen each year, one commonly cited statistic is that from 1996 to 2013, the number of environmental mass events grew annually by 29%. This figure comes from Yang Chaofei, vice chairman of the Chinese Society for Environmental Sciences, and Zhou Shengxian, the former Minster of Environmental Protection (Feng & Wang, 2012). Many of these events are related to heavy metals and hazardous chemical contamination in the environment, which has seriously damaged local people's health (Wu & Zhang, 2012). A common public complaint is that the local government and business actors neglect to explain how pollution from new projects may affect local residents (Robbins, 2012).

Some farmers are taking more confrontational and even violent actions against local governments and businesses (P. Zhang & Yang, 2015). For instance, in 2005, thousands of farmers in Zhejiang Dongyang City and Xinchang County fought with local police forces and governments over issues of lead pollution. This event denoted a new level of environmental protest (Yan & Liu, 2014). Later, on December 30, 2014, thousands of farmers in Donghai Township in Xianyou County (Putian, Fujian Province) destroyed government buildings and police cars to protest a chemical factory (Boxun, 2014; S. Gao, 2015). Similarly, people in the Luoding community in Guangdong Province prevented a waste incinerator project through violent confrontations with the local police in 2015 (F. Yang & Wei, 2015). A few months later, in July 2015, another protest against a waste incinerator occurred in Langfang, Hebei Province (NTDTV, 2015).

Along with these rural petitions and protests, mass demonstrations in urban areas are growing as well. One widely publicized case occurred in Xiamen, where citizens protested a chemical PX project, successfully forcing its termination (Huang & Yip, 2012; Shao et al., 2012). Urban Shifang residents organized a mass protest against the construction of a molybdenum and copper plant there in 2012 (Branigan, 2012; H. Wang, 2013). In the same year, residents of Qidong initiated a large demonstration against pollution caused by a Japanese paper factory (Nan, 2012). Protesters in Jiangmen similarly opposed a uranium-processing plant in Guangdong Province in 2013 (*The Economist*, 2013), and citizens in Lianyungang took to the streets in protest when they learned of a proposed nuclear waste project in their area.

As urban residents' living standards rise, they are more likely to protest projects with negative environmental impacts than rural residents. Moreover, they usually take action before the potential environmental damage has been done. Their protests have specific aims—often, to stop or remove certain polluting companies or projects. However, these protests and petitions have yet to force a local government to change its overall developmental policies or strategies.

Changing local green politics

China's environmental politics are locally focused; "[they derive] emotional force from people's attachment to particular places, landscapes, and livelihoods, and to an ethic of communal living that can sustain stable, long-term regimes for the protection of shared resources" (Jasanoff & Martello, 2004, p. 7). Beyond the wave after wave of environmental petitions and demonstrations happening at the local level, the number of ENGOs is growing (Knup, 1997; Morton, 2005; Sun & Zhao, 2008; G. Yang, 2005). ENGOs are involved in local affairs, and they help the public organize environmental petitions, demonstrations, and litigations (Economy, 2005; Ho, 2001). One NGO, the Ocean Protection Commune, helped protesters direct petitions to the MEP and State Oceanic Administration in 2007 (Yan & Xu, 2010). ENGOs also organize locals for anti-dam movements (T.-C. Lin, 2007).

The 2014 Environmental Protection Law grants NGOs the right to pursue legal actions towards environmental pollution generators and to represent the interests of pollution victims and the public (National People's Congress [NPC], 2014). At the end of 2018, there were 40 environmental law suits initiated by Friends of Nature (Friends of Nature, 2018). Another well-known NGO, the Center for Legal Assistance to Pollution Victims (CLAPV), provides free legal assistance and representation to pollution victims. Notably, however, few NGOs pursue litigation because they lack the financial capability, legal expertise, and capacity, or because they face pressure from local governments (Jin, 2015).

Local governments tend to have significant power over local environmental affairs as well as close relationships with industries. The 1994 fiscal reform established a system in which the central government received about 48% of total revenue, while it was responsible for less than 20% of total expenditure.

Consequently, for many years now, local governments have had to remit a large amount of their revenue to the central government even as they carry the responsibility for most expenditure. Thus, these local governments try hard to develop industries to generate fiscal revenue (Wong, 2000; J. Zhang, 1991; Y. Zhang, 2007), seeking out business opportunities which support their own interests (Gong, 2006). The local government is both "a state political agent and a local economic principle," and local officials have more incentives to develop economic agendas, including personal economic gains, than pursue public welfare, like environmental protection (Gong, 2006, p. 85). Just as the local EPBs are under the leadership of local governments, the local jurisdiction is not independent from local governments (Long & Li, 1998).

Any local or social instability which catches the attention of the central or upper-level governments will reflect very poorly on local leaders and will likely negatively affect their political careers (Cai, 2008a; Edin, 2003; Han, 2012; Zhong, 2015). Local protesters and petitioners know this and may use particular protest strategies to gain the attention of central-level authorities, such as petitioning upper-level governments and Beijing to try to stop the construction of projects, or taking to the streets to highlight local environmental affairs (Cai, 2010; L. Li, 2004; O'Brien & Li, 2005). Most people still believe that government administrations are better channels than court proceedings for solving environmental problems (J. Zhang, 2014; Y. Zhou, 2006).

Accordingly, environmental victims prefer to rely on the traditional petition and complaint system, *xinfang*, to gain compensation and support from upper-level governments (X. Chen, 2008; Ying, 2004; Y. Zhou, 2006). For example, as part of the anti-Pengze nuclear power station event, four retired local officials in Wangjiang County wrote a petition letter to the central government questioning the environmental impact assessment of the Pengze nuclear power station (F. Guo & Huang, 2012). Further, the central government is able to deal with local affairs in a top-down way, instead of through the normal time-consuming process that moves from one level to another (J. Zhang, 2014); after the Songhua and the Tianjin environmental disasters, the central government sent working groups to deal with the local affairs of these areas (Xinhuanet, 2015; S. Zhou, 2007).

At the same time, it is not easy to petition or demonstrate, since local governments can suppress protesters with the help of local police power (Cai, 2008a, 2010). Because the number of submitted petition is one important measure of performance for local officials, local governments usually strive to keep this rate low (Ying, 2004; Y. Zhou, 2006). It is therefore common for local governments to send local police to keep order and imprison active protesters in order to deter demonstrations (Van Rooij, 2010).

Community residents and ENGOs are in a weak position to challenge the close relationships that exist between local governments and businesses (Y. Zhang, 2007). As Bryant and Bailey note, "No actor is omnipotent and hence, no actor is completely powerless" (1997, p. 129). Environmental protection is a power-building issue which can bring many people together to protest a local government and upset social stability at the local level. With the help of the Internet, cell phones, and social media, locals are able to bypass local government censorship and prevent local officials from suppressing all such demonstrations (Sullivan & Xie, 2009; Yang, 2003). Although local governments closely monitor netizens' words and messages, they cannot entirely stop the spread of information among citizens because of a lack of time and labor.

As environmental demonstrations spread across different cities, conflict between locals and big industries backed by local governments is intensifying. These demonstrations can be alarming for the central government and have prompted it to seriously consider the public's demands—and even, sometimes, to punish local government officials. Regarding the conflicts between local residents and local government/industries, some scholars, lawyers, and policymakers call for embracing more public participation in supervising local government and industry activities in terms of environmental protection (MEP, 2014a; J. Shi, 2014; K. Tong & Gao, 2013). In this vein, as of 2015, the newly revised Environmental Protection Law allows public participation in environmental pollution protests and in response to ecological crises. More public participation is expected in local environmental affairs; yet, at the same time, some local governments may resist implementing the new law that allows this participation (J. Chang, 2015; MEP, 2015b).

The relationships between local people, government, and industries are changing, as locals increasingly demonstrate that they care about environmental problems and are willing to take action to weigh in on local environmental affairs. Mass demonstrations (or even the possibility of the same) are relatively effective measures to check the behavior of local officials, as they will negatively affect local officials' maintenance of local social stability and also damage their image in the eyes of upper-level governments. Yet, while both ENGOs and protests put pressure on local officials to respond to environmental concerns, neither is effective at bringing about permanent change in local decision-making. Protesters may raise their voices against specific projects with identified negative environmental impacts, but it is hard for them to judge or blame local governmental policies (such as industrial policy) as problematic.

Fragmented local authoritarianism

Although the Chinese central government's authority has been challenged by decentralization and fragmentation, local government remains authoritarian. Hence, instead of seeing China as a centralized and authoritarian system, it is more useful to see it is as consisting of thousands of fragmented local authoritarian units. Xu (2011) describes the relationships between the central and local authorities in China as "a regionally decentralized authoritarian system" (RDA), in which the central government controls the political power through the personnel power while the local government holds economic power.

This book, however, will focus more on the running of local governments within their respective governing regions, using the term "fragmented local authoritarianism" to stress the authoritarian nature of local governments as well as the weakened control of the central government over municipal, county-, town-, and village-level governments. This research considers municipal and county-level governments to be the typical authoritarian unit in the current Chinese political system. Provincial governments, like the central government, face some control issues due to the distance involved, limited information of local context, limited capacity, the size of governing regions, and so on. In this fragmented local authoritarian system, both the central government (top level) and the public (bottom level) are limited in their involvement in local affairs.

Local authoritarianism is made up of several important rights. First, local governments hold the right to be the necessary formal channel between the top central government and the bottom people in the Chinese political system. The central government has given local officials responsibility for maintaining social stability in their jurisdictions; therefore, as noted, local officials often suppress local disagreements (Cai, 2008a). According to the hierarchy of the political system, local people are not able to contact central government officials directly. At the top of this hierarchy is the Central Committee of the CCP; at the bottom is Chinese civil society, which is relatively weak. Opinions from the bottom are very unlikely to reach the top because local governments usually prevent them reaching the central government. The hierarchical system often pressures people to "assume that the intentions of the authorities are good" (T. Shi, 2014).

Second, each local government has the right to manage most of its own local affairs, including environmental affairs. Lieberthal concludes that the authority of local government (*kuai*) is stronger than the vertical supervisory power of the MEP (*tiao*) (1997, p. 5), and this same conclusion applies with respect to legislation, police power, and other administrative areas. This finding suggests that, in general, the central government has limited power in local affairs—except when those affairs become national concerns (e.g., when they result in mass demonstrations or environmental disasters).

Third, local governments are entitled to mobilize local resources. In China, property rights are protected through political support from all levels of local governments, rather than by property ownership or commercial law (Goodman, 2008). As Naughton notes, "With day-to-day control over decision-making, local government leaders have significant authority over both cash flow and decisions about use of land and other assets" (2007, p. 118). Local governments hold those property rights (Cannon, 2000) and they can exchange property in the market when it is argued to be in the interest of the people (Qian, 2002). Local government officials own and run many state-owned companies in place of the central government, especially those related to land and resources (Leng, 2009; Szamosszegi & Kyle, 2011).

Fourth, a local government has the right to make its own development strategies—and, in particular, its own industrial policies—to gain advantages over neighboring regions and provinces (Guthrie, 2009, p. 44). At the lowest level of the governing system, village heads and township officials who act as the representatives of the collective that owns the land frequently take responsibility for business decisions (Cai, 2003). These officials negotiate sales prices and arrange compensation or relocation for displaced farmers (Naughton, 2007, pp. 118–120). They may also compete with one another by advocating for different development strategies. Ultimately, it is up to the local leader to decide which strategies and industries will enjoy preferential treatment.

Fifth, local governments hold the right to appoint and mobilize local officials. Power is in the hands of various levels of party committees (H. Y. Lee, 1991). There has been insufficient research on how the *nomenklatura* system functions within local governments. A local leader stimulates action on the part of local officials through the *nomenklatura* system. The central government gave local government leaders the right to appoint their own local officials, which created a high-quality and efficient local personnel system (Burns, 1989). With cadre management decentralized, local government leadership gained more authority to appoint its own civil servants, rather than having them appointed by the central or provincial party committees (Edin, 2003). Local government leaders are responsible for local economic development and have the power to control officials working underneath them. Local leaders can recruit people with rich local knowledge in order to help develop their localities; these individuals must then compete for promotion within the *nomenklatura* system (H. Li & Zhou, 2005).

The fragmented local authorities are busy competing for better economic growth with little incentive to cooperate; therefore, they are unable to challenge the central authority. Since economic development has long been a pillar of legitimacy for the CCP and a tool for sustaining its political power, it also became the main criterion for the central CCP to decide whether or not to promote local government leaders in the *nomenklatura* system (Burns, 1994; Edin, 2003; Heilmann & Kirchberger, 2000; Landry, 2008; C. Xu, 2011; S. Zhou, 2007).

Conclusions

Many local governments are still following the traditional economic path of chasing growth and neglecting environmental protection. Local governments' fiscal revenue and local officials' personal gains and political careers are all closely related to local economic growth. Yet, public environmental awareness continues to rise, which partially explains why conflicts between the public and local governments have intensified. Environmental reform from the central government has been gradual and met with local governments' resistance because environmental protection is still regarded as a supplementary issue, while economic growth remains central to the legitimacy of the ruling party. In this way, environmental reform will require comprehensive institutional reform; it is not only an issue of environmental administration or laws, but also of political reform (A. Wang, 2013). NGOs' power is heavily constrained in the Chinese political system, which limits their participation in local decision-making processes (Stalley & Yang, 2006; Tang & Zhan, 2008). Protesters and petitioners can help the central government to supervise the actions of local governments, and thus, to maintain social stability. Their actions should not necessarily be interpreted as challenging the political power of the CCP (Cai, 2008b; L. Li, 2004).

China's local green development is occurring within a broader context that includes support from international influences, the central government, and local residents. The international community can provide environmental aid and knowledge about green development. The Chinese central government is promoting favorable policies and regulations to encourage local governments to pursue green development. Local protesters and ENGOs are pressuring local governments to take responsibility for environmental protection via petitions and demonstrations. Although these forces are influential factors in the decisions of local officials and entrepreneurs, they are not enough to change the fundamental behavior of local governments. Power still lies mainly in the hands of local leaders and businesses, as will be discussed in detail in the following three case studies: Shanghai, Baoding, and Wuning.

Note

1 Calls and Internet data pre 2011 are not available.

References

Asian Development Bank [ADB]. (2015, October 24/25,). *Central–local government relations: Fiscal sustainability*. Paper presented at the Central–local Government Relations: Fiscal Sustainability, Wuhan PRC. Retrieved from www.adb.org/news/events/central-local-government-relations-fiscal-sustainability.

Betsill, M. M., & Bulkeley, H. (2004). Transnational networks and global environmental governance: The cities for climate protection program. *International Studies Quarterly, 48*(2), 471–493.

BJX. (2016). Lianyungang "fanhe feiliao" shijian shimo [The full story of Lianyungang's "anti-nuclear waste"]. Retrieved from http://news.bjx.com.cn/html/20160808/759562.shtml.

Blanchard, O., & Shleifer, A. (2000). Federalism with and without political centralization: China versus Russia: National bureau of economic research. *IMF Staff Papers, 48*, (pp. 171–179). Retrieved from www.imf.org/External/Pubs/FT/staffp/2001/04/pdf/blanchar.pdf.

Bloomberg New Energy Finance. (n.d.). Global market share of solar module manufacturers in 2013. In Statista—The Statistics Portal. Retrieved from www.statista.com/statistics/269812/global-market-share-of-solar-pv-module-manufacturers/.

Boxun (Producer). (2014, July 15). Shanghai Pudong qizhen shidi nongmin jiannan de weiquan licheng [A challenging path for farmers from seven townships in Pudong to protect their rights]. Retrieved from www.boxun.com/news/gb/china/2014/07/201407150140.shtml#.VV2vyfmqqko.

Branigan, T. (2012, July 03). Anti-pollution protesters halt construction of copper plant in China. *Guardian*. Retrieved from www.theguardian.com/world/2012/jul/03/china-anti-pollution-protest-copper.

Breslin, S. (1996). *China in the 1980s: Centre-Province relations in a reforming socialist state*. London: Springer Nature.

Bryant, R. L., & Bailey, S. (1997). *Third world political ecology.* London: Routledge.
Burns, J. P. (1989). *The Chinese Communist Party's nomenklatura system: A documentary study of party control of leadership selection, 1979–1984.* New York: ME Sharpe Inc.
Burns, J. P. (1994). Civil service reform in China. *Asian Journal of Political Science, 2*(2), 44–72.
Cai, Y. (2003). Collective ownership or cadres' ownership? The non-agricultural use of farmland in China. *The China Quarterly, 175,* 662–680.
Cai, Y. (2008a). Local governments and the suppression of popular resistance in China. *The China Quarterly, 193,* 24–42.
Cai, Y. (2008b). Power structure and regime resilience: Contentious politics in China. *British Journal of Political Science, 38*(03), 411–432.
Cai, Y. (2010). *Collective resistance in China: Why popular protests succeed or fail.* Stanford: Stanford University Press.
Cannon, T. (2000). *China's economic growth: The impact on regions, migration and the environment.* London: Macmillan.
Caprotti, F. (2015). Golden sun, green economy: market security and the US/EU-China "solar trade war." *Asian Geographer, 32*(2), 99–115.
Chan, C., & Yao, X. (2008). Air pollution in mega cities in China. *Atmospheric Environment, 42*(1), 1–42.
Chang, J. (2015). Xin huanbaofa zaoyu shishi nanti difang zhengfu pubian "buyuan zhifa." Jingji Cankaobao [The Revised Environmental Protection Law (2015) encountered resistance from local governments; local governments are often not willing to implement it]. Retrieved from http://news.xinhuanet.com/legal/2015-04/08/c_12766 5929.htm.
Chen, F. (2003). Between the state and labour: The conflict of Chinese trade unions' double identity in market reform. *The China Quarterly, 176,* 1006–1028.
Chen, X. (2008). Collective petitioning and institutional conversion. In K. J. O'Brien (Ed.), *Popular protest in China* (pp. 54–70). USA: Harvard University Press.
Cheng, J. Y. (1998). *China in the post-Deng era.* Hong Kong: The Chinese University of Hong Kong Press.
Christmann, P., & Taylor, G. (2001). Globalization and the environment: Determinants of firm self-regulation in China. *Journal of international business studies, 32*(3), 439–458.
Chung, J. H. (1995). Studies of central–provincial relations in the People's Republic of China: a mid-term appraisal. *The China Quarterly, 142,* 487–508.
Deng, Y., & Yang, G. (2013). Pollution and protest in China: Environmental mobilization in context. *The China Quarterly, 214,* 321–336.
Ding, Y., & Lei, Y. (2015, February 10). Hubei zuida wuran huanjing ruxing anyishen xuanpan. Zhongguo Qingnianbao [The first trial decisions came out: the biggest environmental pollution litigation in Hubei Province]. Retrieved from http://zqb.cyol.com/html/2015-02/10/nw.D110000zgqnb_20150210_3-06.htm.
Ding, Z. (2014). Nongcun nuanjing quntixing shijian qiujie [Searching for solutions: collective rural environmental actions]. *Renmin Luntan People's Tribune, 10.* Retrieved from http://paper.people.com.cn/rmlt/html/2014-04/11/content_1427891.htm.
Dong, Y., Ishikawa, M., Liu, X., & Hamori, S. (2011). The determinants of citizen complaints on environmental pollution: An empirical study from China. *Journal of Cleaner Production, 19*(12), 1306–1314.
Economy, E. (2005, May 07). China's environmental movement. Testimony before the Congressional Executive Commission on China Roundtable on Environmental NGOs

in China: Encouraging Action and Addressing Public Grievances, 7. Retrieved from www.cfr.org/publication/7770/.

Edin, M. (2003). Remaking the communist party-state: The cadre responsibility system at the local level in China. *China: An International Journal, 1*(01), 1–15.

Fanfucanglianwangyuanchuangban. (2015, May 25). Sichuansheng Shuangpanhe meikuang yanzhong weigui pohuai shengtai huanjing, qunzhong shangfang shinian wuguo [Shuangpanhe coal mining in Sichuan Province seriously damages the environment, 10 years of local complaints in vain]. Retrieved from http://blog.sina.com.cn/s/blog_be40b6ce0102veis.html.

Feng, J., & Wang, T. (2012, November 29). "Kaichuang" qiujie huanjing quntixing shijian ["Open the window" to search for solution for environmental mass incidents]. Retrieved from www.infzm.com/content/83316.

Fischer, D. (2014). Green industrial policies in China—The example of solar energy. In A. Pegels (Ed.), *Green industrial policy in emerging countries* (pp. 81–115). London: Routledge.

Friends of Nature. (2018). Huanjing Gongyi Susong Jianbao [A brief report on public environmental litigation]. Retrieved from www.fon.org.cn/index.php?option=com_content&view=featured&Itemid=105.

Gang, C. (2009). *Politics of China's environmental protection: Problems and progress (Vol. 17)*. Singapore: World Scientific.

Gao, S. (2015). Putian hua gong wei wen bai zhan [Putian chemical industry failed to keep social stability]. *Cai Jing*. Retrieved from http://finance.sina.com.cn/china/dfjj/20150130/120421437668.shtml.

Germany Energy Agency (2014). Eco-Cities in China: erste Pilotstaedte ausgewaehlt [Press release] [Eco-cities in China: first round of pilot cities announced]. Retrieved from www.dena.de/presse-medien/pressemitteilungen/eco-cities-in-china-erste-pilotstaedte-ausgewaehlt.html.

Gong, T. (2006). Corruption and local governance: the double identity of Chinese local governments in market reform. *The Pacific Review, 19*(1), 85–102.

Goodman, D. S. (2008). *The new rich in China: Future rulers, present lives*. Oxon: Routledge.

Grano, S. (2015). The role of social media in environmental protest in China. In H. Kriesi, L. Dong, & D. Kübler (Eds.), *Urban mobilizations and new media in contemporary China* (pp. 101–116). Surrey: Ashgate Publishing, Ltd.

Guo, F., & Huang, B. (2012, March 05). Wangjiangren "fanhe" de santiao lu [Three strategies in Wangjiang's "anti-nuclear protest"]. *Zhongguo Jingji Zhoukan*, 9. Retrieved from www.ceweekly.cn/html/Article/20120305605541321134.html.

Guo, K., & N'Diaye, P. (2009). Is China's export-oriented growth sustainable? (WP/09/172). Retrieved from doi:www.imf.org/external/pubs/ft/wp/2009/wp09172.pdf.

Guo, S. (Ed.). (2012). *Political science and Chinese political studies: The state of the field*. Heidelberg: Springer Science & Business Media.

Guthrie, D. (2009). *China and globalization: The social, economic and political transformation of Chinese society*. New York: Routledge.

Guthrie, D. (2012). *China and globalization: The social, economic and political transformation of Chinese society*. New York: Routledge.

Han, Z. (2012). Liyi biaoda, ziyuan dongyuan yuyi cheng shezhi [Interest expression, resource mobilization, and agenda setting]. *Gonggong Guanli Xuebao*, 2.

Heilmann, S., & Kirchberger, S. (2000). The Chinese nomenklatura in transition. *China Analysis, 1*.

Heyan, Z. (2013, June 26). Jinian zhongri hepingyouhao tiaoyue dijie 35 zhounian jian zhongri youhao chengshi jiaoliu 40 zhounian yantaohui zhaokai [Celebrating the 35th anniversary of the Sino-Japanese Treaty of Peace and Friendship and 40th anniversary of the Sino-Japanese Friendship Cities]. *Clair* 71. Retrieved from www.clair.org.cn/pdf/131226_01.pdf.

Ho, P. (2001). Greening without conflict? Environmentalism, NGOs and civil society in China. *Development and Change, 32*(5), 893–921.

Hou, T. S., & Su, Z. D. (2004). Research on technological innovation effect of China's export industry chain resulted from green trade barrier. *Studies in Science of Science, 4*, 008.

Huang, R., & Yip, N.-m. (2012). Internet and activism in urban China: A case study of protests in Xiamen and Panyu. *Journal of Comparative Asian Development, 11*(2), 201–223.

IHS. (2015). Chinese suppliers continued to lead the solar PV module market in 2014, IHS says [Press release]. Retrieved from http://press.ihs.com/press-release/technology/chinese-suppliers-continued-lead-solar-pv-module-market-2014-ihs-says.

Jahiel, A. R. (1998). The organization of environmental protection in China. *The China Quarterly, 156*, 757–787.

Jain, P. (2006). *Japan's subnational governments in international affairs*. Oxon: Routledge.

Jasanoff, S., & Martello, M. L. (Eds.). (2004). *Earthly politics: Local and global in environmental governance*. Cambridge: Mit Press.

Jian, W., Zhang, J., & Qin, C. (2007). Fiscal decentralization, competition between local governments, and the economic growth of FDI. *Management World*, 3, 002.

Jin, Y. (2015, February 02). Xin huanbaofa manyue xianshi gongyi susong poju huanbao zuzhi youxin wuli [One month after the new Environmental Protection Law went into effect, ENGOs are willing to take public litigation but with limited capacity]. *Xinjingbao*. Retrieved from www.acef.com.cn/news/gndt/2015/0202/17898.html.

Jing, J. (2003). Environmental protests in rural China. In E. J. Perry & M. Selden (Eds.), *Chinese Society* (pp. 222–240). London and New York: Routledge.

Johnson, T. (2013a). The health factor in anti-waste incinerator campaigns in Beijing and Guangzhou. *The China Quarterly, 214*, 356–375.

Johnson, T. (2013b). The politics of waste incineration in Beijing: The limits of a top-down approach? *Journal of Environmental Policy & Planning, 15*(1), 109–128.

Jun, Z., & Yan, L. (2005). A study on the exportation of China's textile clothing trade: Trade barriers and countermeasures. *International Trade Journal, 4*, 021.

Knup, E. (1997). Environmental NGOs in China: An overview. *China Environment Series, 1*(3), 9–15.

Kostka, G., & Hobbs, W. (2012). Local energy efficiency policy implementation in China: Bridging the gap between national priorities and local interests. *The China Quarterly, 211*, 765–785.

Kostka, G., & Nahm, J. (2017). Central–local relations: recentralization and environmental governance in China. *The China Quarterly, 231*, 567–582.

Kuntze, J., & Moerenhout, T. (2013). Local Content Requirements and the Renewable Energy Industry—A Good Match? Retrieved from https://unctad.org/meetings/en/Contribution/DITC_TED_13062013_Study_ICTSD.pdf.

Lam, P. E. (2006). *Japan's relations with China: Facing a rising power*. Oxon: Routledge.

Landry, P. F. (2008). *Decentralized authoritarianism in China*. New York: Cambridge University Press.

Lang, G., & Xu, Y. (2013). Anti-incinerator campaigns and the evolution of protest politics in China. *Environmental Politics, 22*(5), 832–848.
Lee, H. Y. (1991). *From revolutionary cadres to party technocrats in socialist China (Vol. 31)*. California: University of California Press.
Lee, K., & Ho, M.-s. (2014). The Maoming anti-PX protest of 2014. *China Perspectives, 3*, 33–39.
Leng, J. (2009). *Corporate governance and financial reform in China's transition economy (Vol. 1)*. Hong Kong: Hong Kong University Press.
Li, L. (2004). Political trust in rural China. *Modern China, 30*(2), 228–258.
Li, W., Liu, J., & Li, D. (2012). Getting their voices heard: Three cases of public participation in environmental protection in China. *Journal of Environmental Management, 98*, 65–72.
Li, H., & Zhou, L.-A. (2005). Political turnover and economic performance: The incentive role of personnel control in China. *Journal of Public Economics, 89*(9), 1743–1762.
Lieberthal, K. (1997). China's governing system and its impact on environmental policy implementation. *China Environment Series, 1*, 3–8.
Lin, J. Y. (2011). China and the global economy. *China Economic Journal, 4*(1), 213–229.
Lin, T. (2013). *The politics of financing education in China*. London: Palgrave Macmillan.
Lin, T.-C. (2007). Environmental NGOs and the anti-dam movements in China: a social movement with Chinese characteristics. *Issue and Studies, 43*(4), 149.
Lo, C. W.-H., Fryxell, G. E., & Wong, W. W.-H. (2006). Effective regulations with little effect? The antecedents of the perceptions of environmental officials on enforcement effectiveness in China. *Environmental Management, 38*(3), 388–410.
Long, Z., & Li, C. (1998). Lun sifa duli yu sifa shouzhi [A discussion of juristic independence and constraint]. *Faxue* (12).
Lu, H. (2009, December 31). Panyuren: women buyao bei daibiao [Panyuren: We do not want to be represented, we need our civil rights]. *Nandu Zhoukan*.
Lu, Y. (2011, May 13). Dangnian woguo fengdian jingying fazhan wenti ji jianyi [The current problems of and suggestions to China's wind energy economy]. *Nengyuan Pinglun Guojia Dianwang. The State Grid*. Retrieved from www.sgcc.com.cn/ztzl/newzndw/cyfz/05/246972.shtml.
Lv, M., & Zhao, Y. (2009). [Laji zhanzheng] Wujiang jingshi: laji, zhucheng huoshankou? [[War of waste] The Wujiang alarm: waste prompts volcano-like protests]. *Nanfang Zhoumo*. Retrieved from www.infzm.com/content/36872.
Marks, D. (2010). China's climate change policy process: Improved but still weak and fragmented. *Journal of Contemporary China, 19*(67), 971–986.
Martens, S. (2006). Public participation with Chinese characteristics: Citizen consumers in China's environmental management. *Environmental Politics, 15*(02), 211–230.
Martinot, E. (2001). World bank energy projects in China: Influences on environmental protection. *Energy Policy, 29*(8), 581–594.
McCormick, J. (2002). Environmental policy in Britain. In D. Desai (Ed.), *Environmental politics and policy in industrialized countries* (pp. 121–147). London: MIT.
Ministry of Environmental Protection [MEP] (2012). Guojiaji Shengtai Shifanqu [National ecological demonstrations]. MEP. Retrieved from http://sts.mep.gov.cn/stsfcj/mdl/201201/t20120110_222401.htm.
MEP (2014, September 28). Huanjing baohubu juban gongzhong canyu yantaoban [The Ministry of Environmental Protection organized a synposium on public participation]

[Press release]. Retrieved from www.mep.gov.cn/gkml/hbb/qt/201409/t20140928_289663.htm.
MEP (2015a). 2014 Zhongguo huanjing zhuangkuang gonggao [State of the environment report 2014]. MEP: Retrieved from http://jcs.mep.gov.cn/hjzl/zkgb/2014zkgb/201506/t20150605_302991.htm.
MEP (2015b). Huanjing baohu gongzhong canyu banfa [Measures for public participation in environmental protection[(effective)]]. Retrieved from www.mep.gov.cn/gkml/hbb/bl/201507/t20150720_306928.htm.
Mol, A. P. (2006). Environment and modernity in transitional China: Frontiers of ecological modernization. *Development and Change, 37*(1), 29–56.
Mol, A. P., & Carter, N. T. (2006). China's environmental governance in transition. *Environmental Politics, 15*(02), 149–170.
Montinola, G., Qian, Y., & Weingast, B. R. (1995). Federalism, Chinese style: The political basis for economic success in China. *World Politics, 48*(01), 50–81.
Morton, K. (2005). The emergence of NGOs in China and their transnational linkages: Implications for domestic reform. *Australian Journal of International Affairs, 59*(4), 519–532.
Nan, X. (2012). Qidong protest: Another polluting project cancelled. Retrieved from: www.chinadialogue.net/article/show/single/en/5076-Qidong-protest-another-polluting-project-cancelled.
National Development and Reform Commission [NDRC]. (2010). Guojia Fagaiwei guanyu kaizhan ditan shengqu he ditan chengshi shidian gongzuo de tongzhi (fagai qihou 1587(2010)) [NDRC: The notice of launching low-carbon pilot provinces and cities (climate changeNDRC No. 1587(2010))]. Retrieved from http://bgt.ndrc.gov.cn/zcfb/201008/t20100810_498787.html.
National People's Congress [NPC] (2014). Zhonghua renmin gongheguo huanjing baohufa [Environmental protection law of the People's Republic of China]. Retrieved from www.npc.gov.cn/npc/xinwen/2014-04/25/content_1861279.htm.
Naughton, B. (2007). *The Chinese economy: Transitions and growth (Vol. 1)*. Cambridge: MIT Press Books.
NTDTV (Producer). (2014, August 31). Hunan pingjiang wanren dayouxing kangyi xingjian huoli fadiancang [Thousands of people in Pingjiang, Hunan Province demonstrated against a newly proposed thermal power station]. Retrieved from www.ntdtv.com/xtr/gb/2014/09/20/a1139688.html.
NTDTV (Producer). (2015, August 31). Jicun jinfan laji fenshaochang qianjing zhenya shangbairen zhuashu shi [A thousand policemen suppressed a hundred villagers' protest against a waste incinerator in Hebei province]. Retrieved from www.ntdtv.com/xtr/gb/2015/07/03/a1207765.html.
O'Brien, K. J., & Li, L. (2005). Popular contention and its impact in rural China. *Comparative Political Studies, 38*(3), 235–259.
Oi, J. C. (1992). Fiscal reform and the economic foundations of local state corporatism in China. *World Politics, 45*(1), 99–126.
Oi, J. C. (1999). *Rural China takes off: Institutional foundations of economic reform*. California: University of California Press.
Price, L., Levine, M. D., Zhou, N., Fridley, D., Aden, N., Lu, H., … Yowargana, P. (2011). Assessment of China's energy-saving and emission-reduction accomplishments and opportunities during the 11th Five Year Plan. *Energy Policy, 39*(4), 2165–2178.
Probe, P. (1989). *The Canadian Green Consumer Guide*. Toronto: McClelland and Stewart.

Qian, Y. (2002, July 21). How reform worked in China. *William Davidson Institute Working Paper Number 473.* Retrieved from http://libguides.scu.edu.au/content.php?pid=161580&sid=2263819.

Qian, Y., & Roland, G. (1998). Federalism and the soft budget constraint. *American Economic Review, 88*(5), 1143–1162.

Qian, Y., & Weingast, B. R. (1997). Federalism as a commitment to preserving market incentives. *Journal of Economic Perspectives, 11*(4), 83–92.

Qiu, G., & Yang, Y.-w. (2007). The impact of green trade barrier on Chinese forestry products export and countermeasures. *Journal of International Trade, 5,* 004.

Rawski, T. G. (1994). Chinese industrial reform: Accomplishments, prospects, and implications. *The American Economic Review, 84*(2), 271–275.

Ren, B. (2013). Environmental protests and local governance in rural China. In E. J. Perry, H. Rosovsky, & M. Selden (Eds.), *Chinese environmental governance: Dynamics, challenges, and prospects in a changing Society* (pp. 208–226). London: Routledge.

Ren, B., Shou, H., & Dong, L. (2015). Internet and mobilization in China's urban environmental protests. In D. Kübler, H. Kriesi, & L. Dong (Eds.), *Urban mobilizations and new media in contemporary China* (pp. 51–66). Surrey: Ashgate.

Robbins, P. (2012). *Political ecology: A critical introduction (Vol. 16).* West Sussex: John Wiley & Sons.

Rodrik, D. (2006). What's so special about China's exports? *China & World Economy, 14*(5), 1–19. Princeton: Princeton University Press.

Salzman, J. (1997). Informing the green consumer: The debate over the use and abuse of environmental labels. *Journal of Industrial Ecology, 1*(2), 11–21.

Sasuga, K. (2004). *Microregionalism and governance in East Asia.* Oxon: Routledge.

Schreurs, M. A. (2008). From the bottom up local and subnational climate change politics. *Journal of Environment & Development, 17*(4), 343–355.

Shambaugh, D. (2008). *China's Communist Party: Atrophy and adaptation.* California: University of California Press.

Shao, G., Lu, J., & Wu, J. (2012). New media and civic engagement in China: The case of the Xiamen PX Event. *China Media Research, 8*(2), 76–82.

Shi, J. (2014). You gongzhong canyu caineng zhaohui lvshui qingshan—Fang *Guanyu tuijin huanjing baohu gongzhong canyu de zhidao yijian* qicaoren zhi yi, huanbaobu zhengyan zhongxin shehuibu zhuren Wang Hua Boshi [Only with public participation can we restore clean water and green mountains—Interview with Dr. Wang Hua, the director of environmental policy research center of the Ministry of Environmental Protection and one of the drafters of *The guiding opinions of promoting public participation in environmental protection*]. *Huanjing Jiaoyu, 7,* 003.

Shi, T. (2014). *The cultural logic of politics in mainland China and Taiwan.* Cambridge: Cambridge University Press.

Shirk, S. L. (1993). *The political logic of economic reform in China.* California: University of California Press.

Sims, H. (1999). One-fifth of the sky: China's environmental stewardship. *World Development, 27*(7), 1227–1245.

Sina. (2015, March 24). Naimanqi huagongqu qunzong weidu shijian [People in Naiman Banner communities blocked the chemical plants from entering the local industrial park]. Retrieved from http://nmg.sina.com.cn/z/nmwr/index.shtml.

Speshock, C. H. (2010). *Empowering green initiatives with IT: A strategy and implementation guide.* New Jersey: John Wiley & Sons.

Stalley, P., & Yang, D. (2006). An emerging environmental movement in China? *The China Quarterly, 186*, 333–356.

Stern, R. E. (2013). *Environmental litigation in China: A study in political ambivalence.* Cambridge: Cambridge University Press.

Straughan, R. D., & Roberts, J. A. (1999). Environmental segmentation alternatives: A look at green consumer behavior in the new millennium. *Journal of Consumer Marketing, 16*(6), 558–575.

Sullivan, J., & Xie, L. (2009). Environmental activism, social networks and the Internet. *The China Quarterly, 198*, 422–432.

Sun, Y., & Zhao, D. (2008). Environmental campaigns. In K. J. O'Brien (Ed.), *Popular protest in China* (pp. 144–162). USA: Harvard University Press.

Szamosszegi, A., & Kyle, C. (2011, October 26). An analysis of state-owned enterprises and state capitalism in China: Capital Trade, Incorporated for US-China Economic and Security Review Commission. Retrieved from www.uscc.gov/sites/default/files/Research/10_26_11_CapitalTradeSOEStudy.pdf.

Talamantes, M. J. H. (Ed.). (2014). *Energy security and sustainable economic growth in China.* Hampshire: Palgrave Macmillan.

Tang, S.-Y., Tang, C.-P., & Lo, C. W.-H. (2005). Public participation and environmental impact assessment in mainland China and Taiwan: Political foundations of environmental management. *Journal of Development Studies, 41*(1), 1–32.

Tang, S.-Y., & Zhan, X. (2008). Civic environmental NGOs, civil society, and democratization in China. *Journal of Development Studies, 44*(3), 425–448.

The Economist. (2013, July 20). Limiting the fallout. Retrieved from www.economist.com/news/china/21582016-rare-protest-prompts-government-scrap-plans-build-uranium-processing-plant.

Tilt, B. (2007). The political ecology of pollution enforcement in China: A case from Sichuan's rural industrial sector. *The China Quarterly, 192*, 915–932.

Tong, K., & Gao, N. (2013). Yingdui huanjing qunti shijian zhengfu xu zhuanbian juese [The need for changing the role of governments in dealing with environmental mass events]. Retrieved from www.qstheory.cn/st/hjbh/201308/t20130826_264106.htm.

Tong, J. (2015). *Investigative journalism, environmental problems and modernisation in China.* Hampshire: Palgrave Macmillan.

Tsang, S., & Kolk, A. (2010). The evolution of Chinese policies and governance structures on environment, energy and climate. *Environmental Policy and Governance, 20*(3), 180–196.

UNEP. (2015). District energy in cities unlocking the potential of energy efficiency and renewable energy UNEP. Retrieved from www.unep.org/energy/portals/50177/DES_District_Energy_Report_full_02_d.pdf.

UNEP. (2018). Global trends in renewable energy investment 2018. Retrieved from www.greengrowthknowledge.org/sites/default/files/downloads/resource/Global_Trends_in_Renewable_Energy_Investment_Report_2018.pdf.

Van Rooij, B. (2010). The People vs. Pollution: understanding citizen action against pollution in China. *Journal of Contemporary China, 19*(63), 55–77.

Walder, A. G. (1995). Local governments as industrial firms: An organizational analysis of China's transitional economy. *American Journal of Sociology, 101*(2), 263–301.

Wang, A. (2013). The search for sustainable legitimacy: Environmental law and bureaucracy in China. *37 Harvard Environmental Law Review 365; UCLA School of Law Research Paper No. 13-31.* Retrieved from http://papers.ssrn.com/sol3/papers.cfm?abstract_id=2128167.

Wang, H. (2013). *Local governments and policy responses: The case of Shifang protest.* Published mater thesis, the University of Waterloo. Retrieved from https://uwspace.uwaterloo.ca/bitstream/handle/10012/7939/Wang_Hejin.pdf?sequence=1.

Wang, X., & Mauzerall, D. L. (2006). Evaluating impacts of air pollution in China on public health: implications for future air pollution and energy policies. *Atmospheric Environment, 40*(9), 1706–1721.

Weingast, B. R. (1995). The economic role of political institutions: Market-preserving federalism and economic development. *Journal of Law, Economics, & Organization,* 1–31.

Wen, Y. (Producer). (2015, August 29). Shanghai jinshan minzhong wangshang faqi zhoumo fan PX xingdong (shiping) [Local residents in Shanghai launched an online protest against PX]. Retrieved from www.rfa.org/cantonese/news/protest-px-06252015092939.html.

Whiting, S. H. (2006). *Power and wealth in rural China: The political economy of institutional change.* Cambridge: Cambridge University Press.

Windpower Monthly (2017). Top 10 wind turbine makers of 2017. Retrieved from www.windpowermonthly.com/article/1445638/top-ten-turbine-makers-2017.

Wong, C. P. (2000). Central–local relations revisited the 1994 tax-sharing reform and public expenditure management in China. *China Perspectives,* 52–63.

World Bank. (2014, May 14). Helping global cities harness the power of energy efficiency [Press release]. Retrieved from www.worldbank.org/en/news/feature/2014/05/14/helping-global-cities-harness-the-power-of-energy-efficiency.

World Bank. (2015). Promotion of sustainable cities in China. Project ID P147087). Retrieved from www.worldbank.org/projects/P147087?lang=en.

Wu, H., & Zhang, J. (2012). Huanbao Buzhang: Zhongguo huanjing quntixing shijian nianjun zeng sancheng [Minister of Environmental Protection: Environmental mass incidents are growing 30% annually]. Takungpao. Retrieved from www.takungpao.com/news/content/2012-11/13/content_1374496.htm.

WWF. (2008). Low carbon initiative in China. Retrieved from http://en.wwfchina.org/en/what_we_do/climate___energy/mitigation/lcci/.

Xi, J. (2018). Zai qingzhu gaige kaifang 40 zhounian dahui shang de jianghua (Speech on the 40 anniversary of the reform and opening-up). Retrieved from www.xinhuanet.com/politics/leaders/2018-12/18/c_1123872025.htm.

Xiao, Q. (2015, February 09). Woguo fengdian zhuangji yizhan quanqiu sifenzhiyi [China's wind energy installed capacity is one fourth of the global share]. *Zhongguo Nengyuanbao.* Retrieved from http://paper.people.com.cn/zgnyb/html/2015-02/09/content_1532917.htm.

Xinhuanet (Producer). (2015, September 01). Xi Jinping zhuchi zhengzhiju changweihui huiyi bing fabiao zhongyao jianghua [Xi Jinping delivered an important speech at the meeting of the Standing Committee of the Politburo]. Retrieved from http://news.xinhuanet.com/politics/2015-08/20/c_1116319720.htm.

Xu, C. (2011). The fundamental institutions of China's reforms and development. *Journal of economic literature, 49*(4), 1076–1151.

Yan, Y., & Liu, Z. (2014). Fengxian shehui lilun fanshixia Zhongguo "huanjing chongtu" wenti jiqi xietong zhili [Environmental conflicts and their coordinated management in China: Viewed from the perspective of risk society theory]. *Nanjing Shifa Xuebao (Shehui Kexueban)* (3).

Yan, Y., & Xu, Z. (2010). Fanhe zhenxiang: Rushan hedianzhan gezhi zhizheng [The truth behind anti-nuclear protest: the delay and dispute over Rushan nuclear power station]. *Kexue Xinwen* (014), 16–22.

Yang, F., & Wei, S. (2015). Guangdong Luoding cunmin kangjian laji fenshaocang jingmin yidu fasheng chongtu [Luoding peasants in Guangdong Province confronted policemen in a protest against a waste incinerator]. Retrieved from http://news.qq.com/a/20150408/039336.htm.

Yang, G. (2003). The Internet and civil society in China: A preliminary assessment. *Journal of Contemporary China, 12*(36), 453–475.

Yang, G. (2005). Environmental NGOs and institutional dynamics in China. *The China Quarterly, 181*(1), 46–66.

Yang, Y. (2015). Wangchuan Jiaxing jian PX xiangmu huanbao bumen piyao hou you tingzhi gai xiangmu shenpi [Protest broke out online when people were informed that Jiaxiang will build a PX project; later the environmental protection bureau rejected the proposal]. Retrieved from http://news.sohu.com/20150814/n418896822.shtml.

Ying, X. (2004). Zuowei teshu xingzheng jiuji de xinfang jiuji [Remedy of "letter and visit" is a special response to administrative litigations and review]. *Faxue Yanjiu*, 3, 58–71.

Yuan, Y. (2011). Burned by the sun. China Dialogue. Retrieved from www.chinadialogue.net/article/show/single/en/4232-Burned-by-the-sun.

Zehner, O. (2011). Unintended consequences of green technologies. In P. Robbins, D. Mulvaney, and J. G. Golson (Eds.), *Green technology.* (pp. 427–432). London: Sage.

Zeng, F., & Huang, Y. (2015). The media and urban contention in China: A co-empowerment model. *Chinese Journal of Communication, 8*(3), 233–252, DOI: 10.1080/17544750.2015.1036762.

Zhang, J. (1991). Pudong Xinqu tudi pizu jiaga wenti tantao [An exploratory discussion of land leasing prices in Pudong New Area]. *Tansuo yu Zhengming*, (1), 37–39.

Zhang, J. (2014). "Sukuxing Shangfang" nongmin huanjing xinfang de yizhong fenxi kuangjia [Complaint-based appealing: An analytical framework for peasants' environmental petition]. *Nanjing Gongye Daxue Xuebao: Shehui Kexueban, 13*(1), 78–85.

Zhang, P. & Yang, Z. (2015). Jin shinianlai woguo huanjing quntixing shijian de tezheng jianxi (A brief analysis of the features of the environmental mass events over the past decade). *Zhongguo dizhi daxue xuebao (shehui kexueban) Journal of China University of Geosciences (social science edition), 15*(2), 53–61.

Zhang, S., Andrews-Speed, P., & Zhao, X. (2013). Political and institutional analysis of the successes and failures of China's wind power policy. *Energy Policy*, 56, 331–340.

Zhang, Y. (2007). Zhongguo nongcun huanjing ehua yu chongtu jiaju de dongli jizhi: Cong sanqi "quntixing shijian" kan "zhengjing yitihua" [The institutional incentives for environmental degradation and the intensification of environmental conflicts in rural China: Three case studies of environmental mass incidents and the integration of political and economic power]. *Hongfan Commentary* Volume 9. Beijing: Zhongguo zhengfa daxue chubanshe.

Zhao, K. (2011). Boundary-spanning contention: The Panyu anti-pollution protest in Guangdong, China. *Stanford Journal of East Asian Affairs, 11*(1), 17–25.

Zheng, Y. (2007). De facto *federalism in China: Reforms and dynamics of central–local relations (Vol. 7)*. New Jersey: World Scientific.

Zheng, Y. & Wu, G. (1995). Lun zhongyang—difang guanxi [*On Central and Local Relations*]. *Modern China Studies*. Issue 6. Retrieved from www.modernchinastudies.org/us/issues/past-issues/51-mcs-1994-issue-6/327-2011-12-29-11-30-39.html.

Zhong, Y. (2015). *Local government and politics in China: Challenges from below.* London: Routledge.

Zhou, L. (2007). Zhongguo difang guanyuan de jingshen jinbiaosai moshi yanjiu [Governing China's local officials: An analysis of promotion tournament model]. *Jingji Yanjiu, 7*(36), 36–50.

Zhou, N., Levine, M. D., & Price, L. (2010). Overview of current energy-efficiency policies in China. *Energy Policy, 38*(11), 6439–6452.

Zhou, S. (2007). *Jiyu yu jueze: Songhuajiang shijian de shendu sikao* [*Opportunity and choice: indepth research on the Songhua pollution event*]. Beijing: Xinhua chubanshe.

Zhou, Y. (2006). Xinfangchao yu Zhongguo jiufen jiejue jizhi de lujing xuanzhe [The tides of letters and calls of complaints from the people and the path selection of the dispute resolution mechanism of chain]. *Jiannan Xuebao: Zhexue Shehui Kexueban, 1*, 37–47.

Zhu, Q., Sarkis, J., & Lai, K.-h. (2007). Green supply chain management: pressures, practices and performance within the Chinese automobile industry. *Journal of Cleaner Production, 15*(11), 1041–1052.

Zusman, E., & Turner, J. L. (2005). Beyond the bureaucracy: Changing China's policy-making environment. In K. Day (Ed.), *China's environment and the challenge of sustainable development*. (pp. 121–149). New York: ME Sharpe.

3 A run-down city regains competence

Shanghai

Now Shanghai is "the show case of a reformed China" and an international city. Back in the planned economic era, Shanghai was confronted with many problems. Shanghai was left with serious pollution during the planned economic era, as it was the center of many industries. Its contribution to the national economy and its revenue to the nation were huge; it had little money to improve the local living conditions, particularly infrastructure and housing. Shanghai lost its competitiveness on the global level after the elimination of the private business sector in the 1950s. Lastly, throughout the reform and opening-up era, Shanghai started to fall behind Shenzhen (which benefited from preference policies) in terms of domestic competitiveness (Cheng, 2012). This chapter deciphers how a city with so many problems revives.

A city loses itself

Before the nationalization of private firms, Shanghai had a dynamic entrepreneurship and prosperity of private businesses (J. Zeng, 2013). In the 1930s, Shanghai was the finance center of Asia (S. Han, 2000). After 1950, in the planned economic era, Shanghai was transformed into a planned industrial center, shifting its historical role as a symbol of capitalism into "a stronghold of China's command economy" (J. Zeng, 2013). Shanghai's economy was highly planned in the socialist era; it was directly under the leadership of the State Planning Commission and the Shanghai Planning Commission as well (Buck, 2012). At the planned economic era, a large amount of industries were moved into Shanghai; resources were distributed to Shanghai by the Central Planning Commission for Industrial Production and its products were distributed to the whole nation by planning bureaus. Shanghai became the number one industrial city (Yeh, 2007). Shanghai became a key city for the central government for gaining fiscal resources, so that Shanghai was under strict control as the planned economy (Wan & Yuan, 2001). Shanghai was so deeply involved with the planned economy with conservative powers. No private business activities were allowed for years. It became harder for Shanghai to introduce reform and opening policies than Shenzhen and other places which were the pilots at the beginning of reform and opening-up.

Under a planned economy, its two rivers, Suzhou River and Huangpu River were greatly polluted; the water was black and foul-smelling. This pollution was the side effect of the prosperity that came from the regional industries, especially the heavy industries from the 1950s. There was a heavy metal pollution event which highlights the pollution in Shanghai at that time. The farmers living nearby the rivers raised ducks for a living. Around 1975, these farmers discovered that some ducks were behaving abnormally. The staff from the Zhabei district health and epidemic prevention tested the water and found a large amount of cadmium. Cadmium is poisonous and has caused the "Itai-itai disease" in Japan. In a conference held in western Germany in the 1970s, a Japanese scholar Yu Jin Chun suggested President Zhou Enlai should pay attention to Chinese cadmium pollution (Yang, 2001). The pollution of Shanghai caught the attention of the central government from this time. After the reform and opening-up, Shanghai lagged behind the special economic areas, like Shenzhen. This reality pushed Shanghai to make a change.

Local entrepreneurs calling for a better Shanghai

Living conditions in Shanghai deteriorated, and the Shanghainese faced crowded housing, bad public transportation, and serious pollution. A local citizen, Chen Kunlong, who worked at the Huaihai Road as a street official, had the opportunity to observe the city's problems and how they affected its people. He wrote an article to express his ideas for solving these problems, called "Developing in Pudong in a Broad Space" in 1980 (K. Chen, 1980). Chen is considered the first person in civil society to advocate the development of Pudong (Eastday, 2002; G. Wang, 2008). He eventually entered the Shanghai Plan Management Bureau with his ideas about developing Pudong.

Almost at the same time, Wang Ganghuai, who graduated from Tsinghua University in architecture and civil engineering, joined the Environmental Protection Bureau of Shanghai. In 1980, he was appointed as the director in charge of the Huangpu River pollution treatment plan. Through this task, Wang Ganghuai noticed the problems related to Puxi, the historic centre of Shanghai. Later in his career he worked at the Shanghai National Land Remediation Office in 1982. This office was near the Shanghai Plan Management Bureau, and thus he got to know other people with similar ideas about developing Pudong. As Wang Ganghuai worked his way up the career ladder, he carried the idea to develop Pudong with him and made many friends who shared his idea. In 1985, Wang Ganghuai and Chen Kunlong got to know each other and became friends (G. Wang, 2008).

The civil expert association of entrepreneurs has grown as increasing numbers of experts joined its ranks. To encourage this, the Shanghai City Economy Association created many opportunities for expert entrepreneurs to come together and discuss their ideas. Based on these discussions and research, the expert entrepreneurs published several articles to express their ideas on how to build Pudong into a financial and trade center and set up a special economy zone there. People came from different government departments: the Development Research Center of

Shanghai, the Science and Technology Commission of Shanghai Municipality, the Shanghai Academy of Social Sciences, the Tongji University, and the Shanghai Urban Planning and Design Research Institute, and the Shanghai Party Institute of CCP (G. Wang, 2008). They developed their social capital during this process, which contributed trust and willingness to their cooperative efforts.

With these different people in different departments, it was the 1986 Shanghai City Development Strategy Conference which brought them together and led to the decision for the development of a Pudong strategy. More than 10 governmental departments were involved in organizing the conference. There were three primary strategies for how to solve Shanghai's environmental pollution, crowding, and other problems. The strategies were: to go east to develop Pudong; to go south to build a new city in Hangzhou Bay; and to go north to develop Wujiaochang (Long, 2012; G. Wang, 2008). After fierce discussion, the go-east strategy to develop Pudong area won the support of most experts. International experience suggests that cities with rivers tend to keep the old city on one side of the river and build a new city on the other side. Pudong was the obvious choice to build up a new Shanghai and solve some of the problems confronting the old city Puxi, like its high population density (Z. Chen, 1991). Afterwards, Shanghai held a second conference which focused solely on the development of Pudong. The Shanghai Mayor Wang Daohan and Vice Mayor Ni Tianzeng participated in this conference, which meant that the "Develop Pudong" strategy had entered the government agenda.

Local leader's efforts

Wang Daohan was appointed at a critical time in Shanghai, at the beginning of reform and opening-up in 1980. The mayor, Wang Daohan, set a path which Shanghai would follow for decades, even though he had been the mayor of Shanghai for just five years from 1980 to 1985 (W. Zhou, 2007). He suggested developing Pudong, held an Expo, and established Shanghai as a port center which Shanghai still benefits from today (Q. Zeng, 2011). Wang Daohan has an image as an intellectual official and is famous for his love of books (Lan, 1983; C. Wei, 2013). His mind is open for new ideas from the international society and he is a reformer who helped China be more open to the outside world.[1]

When the reform-minded Hu Yaobang president visited Shanghai in 1983 to encourage Shanghai as the pilot in market reform, Wang tried to make specific plans (L. He, 2006). Mayor Wang liked to hold conferences and bring experts together to discuss how to best develop Shanghai. As early as 1983, he held a conference titled "Shanghai 2000" to envision the future of Shanghai. The Shanghai leadership group set a fieldwork day, each Thursday, to explore problems and solutions for the city's development (Zhao & Zhang, 1984). Wang Daohan attended the Shanghai Economic Develop Strategy Discussion Conference. Based on this conference, Wang Daohan agreed to develop Pudong and sent the Shanghai Economic Develop Strategy Report to the central government (Shanghai Difangzhi Bangongshi [Shtong], 2000).

Wang Daohan encouraged the import of foreign economic experience and advanced management ideas to China; he set up the Foreign Economic and Management Magazine (D. Wang, 1985a). Wang sent some young experts to do research in Shenzhen and specially learn about its reform experiences (D. Wang, 1985b). In order to find solutions to financial problems and develop Shanghai, he sent local officials to Hong Kong to learn about banks and finance, especially about acquiring funds for constructing Shanghai (D. Wang, 1987). Referencing the pollution problems at Huangpu and Suzhou rivers, Wang cited the examples set by India, arguing that India got billions of aids from international organizations, such as the World Bank, to solve its domestic problems, why shouldn't China do the same? It was Wang Daohan who first started to use international aid to treat the pollution in Shanghai. The Suzhou River Treatment was the first World Bank project in China; in this way Shanghai gathered knowledge about how to deal with pollution and protect the environment (China review news, 2005; Yang, 2001).

After Mayor Wang decided to support the development of the Pudong strategy, he attempted to use his *guanxi* to gain the approval of central government leaders. Wang and his family have strong *guanxi* with the CCP leaders because Wang's family was one of the creators of the new China. In 1937, his father gave up everything and brought his whole family to Yan'an to join the revolution (Feng, 2006). Later it was Wang who delivered the draft of the developing Pudong strategy to Deng Xiaoping that would win the support of the central government.

Guanxi *in pushing forward "develop Pudong strategy"*

The social capital from bottom-up entrepreneurs who wanted to develop Pudong helped the idea make it onto the government agenda. The local leaders then used their *guanxi* to realize it.

Wang Ganghuai used his *guanxi* to reach the mayor, Wang Daohan; this helped the civil idea to develop Pudong become an official idea of the Shanghai government. Wang Daohan then connected civil experts with officials through associations and conferences. In 1986, he became the director of the China City Economy Association which aimed to find out how to develop a city and solve city problems (W. Liu, 1986).

In 1986, the Shanghai Economy Research Center asked the Jiusan Society to start a research project about developing Pudong.[2] Wang Ganghuai was appointed as the project leader in the Jiusan Society. After a half year of research, the Jiusan society published a report titled "A Brief Blueprint of Pudong New Area Construction," and experts attended the evaluation of the project. Wang Daohan was one of the experts.

Overseas Chinese also participated in the design work of "Develop Pudong" to make it more appealing to the government to search for the *guanxi* necessary to realize it. Wang Daohan invited Lin Tongyan to discuss how to develop Pudong, and Lin was named as the first overseas person to advocate for the development of Pudong. He was a successful civil engineer. To give an example of his expertise, Lin came back to Shanghai to visit his brother and had an idea to build a bridge over the Huangpu River to further the development of Pudong. He put his ideas into real plans and instructed his company to send their bridge designs to the Shanghai government.

Then in 1985, Lin got the chance to meet Wang Daohan in America to express his ideas about Pudong's development. He suggested using the rivers to define the territory of Pudong, building a bridge to raise the value of Pudong's land, and then renting it out to acquire more finance for Pudong's development (Huanqiuwang, 2008). Wang organized a committee to research how to develop Pudong and published a report titled "Develop Pudong, Build a Big Modern Shanghai." At that time Wang Daohan left his position as Shanghai mayor.

These different actors with a shared vision all contributed their social capital to the achievement of their common goal. The experts from different fields expressed their wishes in detailed plans and policies. These experts were concerned with the situation in Shanghai and were open to reform. After Wang Daohan joined them, his connections to the national CCP leaders led to a breakthrough in the development efforts. As explained in the first section, at that time the central government was still not confident enough to open the economic center of Shanghai (D. Dong, 2005).

There were thus still many barriers to reform in Shanghai at that historical moment. Many people thought Wang Daohan's ideas of developing Pudong were not practical. Some people were against his ideas since they believed that Pudong would secede from the rest of Shanghai and absorb the factories and other resources. Furthermore, these critics thought that Pudong was a special area for the central government but not for Shanghai (C. Wei, 2013).

Even though the central government was afraid of opening Shanghai at that time, the experts in Shanghai and overseas were already working to find a strategy for Shanghai's development. Wang Daohan insisted on developing Pudong, but there were many difficulties yet to come. He had just started to put the idea onto the government agenda when he retired.

One key task of the remaining local leaders who supported developing Pudong was to gain the approval of the central government leaders. The next Shanghai mayor was Jiang Zemin; he was recommended by Wang Daohan and had a close relationship with Wang Daohan (Kuhn, 2005). Jiang later became the president of China after the 1989 Tiananmen Square Event.[3] After him, the next generation of the Shanghai leaders put their efforts into persuading the central government to open Shanghai and develop Pudong (Li, n.d.).

The advocacy of government leaders

Collective efforts of the local leadership

Although Wang retired from the mayor's position in 1985, he still had influence on Shanghai's leaders. He remained an advisor to the Shanghai government and led the plan to develop Pudong. This section will explain how successive Shanghai leaders promoted the idea of "Develop Pudong" and how it became a local strategy.

After Wang Daohan, the new, very liberal Shanghai CCP secretary, Rui Xingwen, agreed the plan to develop Pudong and he supported it wholeheartedly (C. Wei, 2013). Secretary Rui, an economist, was a supporter of Zhao Zhiyang, who was a strong reformist president from 1987–1989. Before he came to Shanghai, Secretary Rui was the vice director of the State Planning Commission of China and the Minister of Urban and Rural Construction and Environmental Protection. During discussion of the Seventh Five-Year Plan, he came forth as a supporter of several environmental protection ideas. He advocated putting more responsibility on the shoulders of provincial chiefs, mayors, county chiefs, and factory managers (Z. Chen, 1984). His liberal spirit is also reflected in his attitudes toward limited censorship on authors' works (L. Zhao & Chen, 1986). He was not only a politician but also an economist (Zhong, 2005).

Secretary Rui paid special attention to environmental protection after learning about it during his trip to four European countries, just before he became Party Secretary of Shanghai. Another famous environmentalist and government official wrote an article about this three-week trip to Great Britain, Germany, Denmark, and Sweden with representatives from different departments.[4] Rui met with the four countries' environmental ministers and mayors to talk about environmental protection and city development. He invited the first environmental minister Qu Geping to his home to talk about environmental protection.

All in all, secretary Rui can be characterized as a pioneer and a strong supporter of Deng Xiaoping's reform and opening-up. He paid special attention to the economic and financial experiences of these countries. He considered Hamburg's free port a very important example for Shanghai. He requested to visit a stock market in Great Britain and an insurance company in Germany (Xia, 2008). Under the leadership of Rui, Shanghai set up a city ecological economy association in 1986 (Y. Chen, 1987).

He had some innovative ideas for raising funds to support the development of Shanghai. Rui suggested two strategies: the first was to obtain capital from the society, such as opening a stock market in Shanghai; the second was to obtain capital through land exchange and rentals. At that time, the best places at the Bund were used by different public departments and for storage and factories. Rui suggested the Shanghai government officials make the most of their land resources. He experimented with land exchange, so that those good places at the Bund could be explored as business areas. Rui also appointed several experts to research on renting land usage rights to foreign business and private enterprises. He even convinced the secretary to send people to Hong Kong, in order to study the land auction system (C. Wei, 2013).

Thus, it comes as no surprise that Rui raised many comments about Lin Tongyan's report "Develop Pudong" and sent it to another department for reevaluation. Rui was moved to another position in Beijing in 1987.

After Wang Daohan left office, Jiang Zemin became the mayor of Shanghai and the partner of Rui Xingwen. Wang Daohan had a significant influence on Jiang Zemin and actively supported numerous civic activities for developing Pudong. The idea to develop Pudong was carried out further by the new generation of Shanghai's leadership. There were new local leaders like Jiang Zemin and Zhu Rongji, who continued to develop Pudong and old leaders like Ni Tianzeng who also insisted on carrying out the development programs.

During Jiang Zemin's term, the "Develop Pudong" idea was actively promoted in the government. In October 1986, Shanghai's government gathered two groups of experts to draft a plan for developing Pudong's economy, society, science, and education system. Another group was gathered to develop a plan for construction and transportation (Long, 2012). Under Shanghai's CCP and the Shanghai government, the Develop Pudong United Advising Group was founded. It consisted of domestic and overseas experts. Wang Daohan was the chief advisor, Ni Tianzeng headed the domestic expert group, and Lin Tongyan headed the team of overseas experts.[5]

The domestic group was the first special organization under the Shanghai government for the development. The group invited former Shanghai CCP secretary Chen Guodong, Vice Mayor Hu Lijiao, Wang Daohan, Li Guohao (an expert in bridge construction), and Zhao Zukang to serve as senior advisors. This group was grounded in solid political and social relationships. Furthermore, the group invited 19 experts to research strategies, policies, laws, regulations, and finance through 15 research projects. Based on these projects, the group carried out fieldwork in Shenzhen, Xiamen, and Hainan to gain empirical materials. This group produced several reports which confirmed the possibility of the successful development of Pudong and explored methods like the use of foreign investment (Long, 2012).

In 1988, Jiang Zemin listened to their report and stated that Pudong should be developed as soon as possible. He suggested preparing a group of civil servants to begin working on the development of Pudong and do the necessary research at the same time. He also talked to those experts in person and encouraged their efforts. Another vice mayor who asked many questions about developing Pudong was Huang Ju who later became the Shanghai mayor (J. Li, n.d.).

At that time, the Shanghai mayor was Zhu Rongji, a leader famous for his reform ideas (S. Yuan, 2013). When Ni Tianzeng suggested "Develop Pudong" to Zhu Rongji, Zhu had many specific comments. He said that Pudong is the hope for a new Shanghai and pointed out two crucial factors: infrastructure and transportation. He argued that Pudong should be the most modern area in Shanghai and that Pudong should use foreign capital to develop, build infrastructure, and attract foreign enterprises to do business there (Long, 2012). Zhu Rongji wrote several articles in his memoir, *Shanghai Speech* that supported the idea of developing Pudong (Zhu, 2011).

Within the Shanghai local government, "Develop Pudong" has become a consensus statement among the reform-minded local leaders. They were very well prepared to develop Pudong, but the program faced opposition from supporters of the Chinese socialist way. Critics argued that with the development of Pudong, there would be too many resources transferred to the market, which would not be under the control of the nation. It was a very sensitive topic, since Shanghai was criticized by conservative powers as the symbol of capitalist exploitation of foreign powers during the colonial time. Opening Shanghai to the market could, they feared, lead from socialism to capitalism (Sullivan, 1988). The reintroduction of foreign capital, land renting practices, and the reappearance of foreign powers all recalled memories of old Shanghai and the old society. There were many conservative ideas like this which had to be overcome for Pudong's development to proceed. Therefore, the approval of the central government was necessary.

Two approvals of the central leaders

Even though "Develop Pudong" has become a local strategy for self-development that was studied and advocated by local officials and experts for years, it still needed the approval of the central government to become a reality. Shanghai reveals the struggle between the reformers and anti-reformers, and it is a case study of how much autonomy the Chinese central government is willing to give to its local governments (F. Wu, 2000). There were two approvals of "Develop Pudong" from the central leaders: one was from the reform side but failed; the other was from Deng Xiaoping and succeeded.

It was hard for Shanghai to open itself to the market, because there were many barriers and conservative disapproval. When the Shanghai leader submitted the Pudong development proposal to the central government in 1985, it was approved by the central government, however, Shanghai's implementation for the development strategy was not. This reveals the struggle between reform-minded and conservative politicians and the power relationship between the top leaders Deng Xiaoping and Hu Yaobang (Sullivan, 1988). At that time, President Hu Yaobang visited Shanghai and encouraged Shanghai to be a pilot in reform and opening-up (Peng, 2014). His attitude and words also motivated Shanghai's local officials to take actions towards reform and opening-up. Chen Yun, the former leader of Shanghai and other senior leaders, however, were worried to open Shanghai and said that the number of special economic zones should be limited instead of spreading to other localities, particularly regarding the Jiangsu and Zhejiang region (Y. Chen, 1995; Li, 2011). Deng Xiaoping considered their opinions, and decided it was still not the right time to open Shanghai.

This situation changed after the 1989 Tiananmen Square Event. There is little documentation available about this domestically.

This year was considered the darkest year in China's modern history by the international community as it suggested China was a less free nation than previously assumed, based on China's steady reform and opening-up progress (Naughton, 1996, pp. 273–304). It was a hard time in China's reform. The international community thought China ceased economic reform and restarted political repression (Naughton, 1996, pp. 273–304). Many reform leaders were ousted of their political power and became political prisoners, the reform leader,

Zhao Ziyang, the General Secretary of the CCP was under house arrest (Fewsmith, 2001, pp. 41–87). This event also caused serious economic sanctions from the international community. The US government issued several suspensions regarding high technology and prevented trade with China in many cases, such as delaying new financial investments (Brick, 1989). The Japanese government waved some of its foreign aid towards China (Katada, 2001). China's political leaders had to determine how to change China's image and regain the trust of the international community (Qian & Guo, 2010; Wan & Yuan, 2001).

Nowadays, it is hard to imagine what happened before and after the 1989 event. In 1988, Wang Daohan, Jiang Zemin, and Zhu Rongji went to Beijing to report to the central government officials on the preparation work of "Develop Pudong." The central government agreed to it and gave specific instructions for the continuing work. The central government leader at that time was Zhao Ziyang, and he was considered a reformer. In 1988, under instruction from the central government, Shanghai's government set up the "Develop Pudong leadership group," under Gu Chuanxun. Its office was at the Shanghai municipal foreign investment Working Committee. Some conservatives persuaded Deng that Shanghai's reform was too risky, for it would affect the whole country if it failed.

This situation changed following the year of 1989, after the Tiananmen Square Event, and after the conservatives regained power to control the economy (Naughton, 1996, pp. 273–304). Many Western countries commented that China would give up its reform and opening-up or continue as a less open and free nation (Brick, 1989; Gillies, 1996, pp. 140–173; Naughton, 1996, pp. 273–304)). To save the idea of "Develop Pudong," Hu Lijiao and Wang Daohan used their social capital to contact Yang Shangkun and send their plan to develop Pudong to Deng Xiaoping. This time Deng paid attention to it. The approval of Deng Xiaoping was a key step in turning the idea into reality. Deng was quoted as saying: "some people say we are going to step back from reform and opening-up and turn left in politics. Shanghai's comrades, please think about doing something to prove that we are not going to do that" (Situweizhi, 2012).

Deng's approval came in a step-wise fashion. In 1990, Deng Xiaoping stayed in Shanghai for the traditional Chinese spring festival. Wang Daohan, the senior local leader, and Zhu Rongji, the current local leader, brought up "Develop Pudong" again. Deng clearly agreed with the idea "Develop and Open Pudong." He further suggested Zhu Rongji to tell Jiang Zemin of his plan since Jiang was the president at that time (E. Yuan, 2012; Situweizhi, 2012).

According to Yuan Enzhen, when Deng returned to Beijing in February 1990, he invited President Jiang Zemin and Premier Li Peng to his home and told them about the idea of "Develop Pudong." Later Deng invited senior central leaders to talk about the international situation and explained to them that Shanghai was an easy way to show China's reform to the international society (E. Yuan, 2012, p. 1).

In February, Jiang Zemin and Li Peng appointed Yao Yilin vice premier to Shanghai. Yao listened to the "Develop Pudong" idea (Long, 2012). Yao brought people from different government departments: the State Council Special Zone, the Ministry of Finance, the China's People's Bank, the Ministry of Foreign Trade, the Ministry of Business, and the Bank of China. Before Shanghai had to turn in most of its revenue to the central government and could only retain little revenue for its own development, this group resolved the fiscal burden on Shanghai and agreed that Shanghai could keep a fixed fiscal finance to the central government and keep the rest to build Shanghai Pudong (E. Yuan, 2012).

In April 1990, Premier Li Peng announced that the Central CCP and the Central Government had agreed to develop Pudong on the fifth anniversary of Volkswagen in Shanghai. He further shared that there will be specific economic policies from the central government towards Pudong (Q. Zhao, 2007). After years of work, the idea to develop Pudong had become a reality in Shanghai.

Deng Xiaoping's decision to develop Pudong brought together all kinds of resources and fostered significant consent in the local government. The set-up of Pudong has been under "the will of the CCP and the government, relying on the strong support of the central government" (Qian & Guo, 2010, p. 16). Shanghai was privileged with special financial and trade rights (Y. D. Wei & Leung, 2005; Yeung, Lee, & Kee, 2009; Q. Zhao, 2007), thus gaining the name "the most special zone of all special zones" (Q. Huang, 1995, p. 19; Qian & Guo, 2010, pp. 26–42; Wan & Yuan, 2001). This was part of a national strategy to show to the world the resolution behind the reform and opening-up process after the Tiananmen Square Event (Wan & Yuan, 2001).

Deng came to Shanghai in 1991, and one year after his arrival he declared that Pudong was four to five years late in reform and opening-up and that the delay was his fault (Shen & Yu, 2012; Q. Zhao, 2007). Shanghai was no longer a planned economy; instead, it became a forerunner and reform pilot. In 1991, Shanghai's reform greatly influenced the entire Yangtze River Basin. Shanghai raised hot debates about reform which provided support for further market reform throughout the country, since at that time, there were many voices that opposed further reform (P. Huang, 1991).

Pudong is chosen as a case study of local green development because examining the ideas underlying "Develop Pudong" and the environmental considerations of decision-makers helps us to understand local green development. Pudong has won many awards as an ecological area, as a garden city, and as a most livable city. We will thus examine Pudong as an example of local green development.

"Develop Pudong" as a form of green development

"Develop Pudong" is a local government strategy that caught the attention of the central government at a critical time. "Develop Pudong" was a plan advocated for by local and international experts to address economic and environmental problems in the old Shanghai. Old Shanghai experienced pollution and other problems commonly found in mega cities.

One important aim in developing Pudong was to establish a new city, a new life, and a new mode of development for Shanghai. Pudong is a highly planned area with high aims and standards which come close to those of an "ideal city." Preservation of the environment is one of its aims. This section will focus on green development practices and the process of "developing Pudong."

A new ecological area

As the industries started in Shanghai in the late 19th century, pollution also came to this city. In the 1960s, Shanghai became a planned industrial center. Water, air, noise, and solid waste pollution were reported in the *Shanghai Local Chronicles of Environmental Protection* (Shanghai difangzhi bangongshi, 1998). In 1956, the nationalization of capitalist industry and commerce in the city was finished. During the Second National Five-Year Plan, more than 10,000 factories and enterprises were moved to Shanghai. This resulted in further large amounts of waste water, air pollution, and high energy consumption (Shanghai difangzhi bangongshi, 1998). During the Great Leap Forward, Shanghai participated in steel production to catch up with Great Britain under the call of Mao Zedong. This too caused environmental pollution (Shapiro, 2001).

During the 1980s and the 1990s, Shanghai produced on average 3,866,000 tons of industrial waste water per day of which only 685,000 was treated (Shanghai difangzhi bangongshi, 1998). Dianshan Lake, which used to be known for having the best water quality in Shanghai, started to seriously degrade. Huangpu River was black and foul-smelling for 146 days on average in a year. The water of Suzhou River was so bad, that it was considered to have the worst water quality in the Chinese water measurement system (Shanghai difangzhi bangongshi, 1998). The environment and the people were exposed to high levels of hazardous heavy metals, like mercury, cadmium, and chromium, and there was acid rain caused by SO_2 (Shanghai difangzhi bangongshi, 1998). The people who lived near to the factories suffered from heavy exposure to these environmental hazards (Shanghai difangzhi bangongshi, 1998). Because millions of people relied on the Huangpu River for their drinking water, Shanghai was known as the biggest "cancer village" (Sina, 2013).

At the beginning of reform and opening-up, foreigners who stayed in Shanghai, were afraid to drink the tap water; they preferred to drink mineral water for their health. The living conditions for the local people were very crowded and dirty. Locals living near factories were exposed to serious environmental pollution since in the planned economy system, environmental protection was not a topic of high concern (Eastday, 2002; Shapiro, 2001). The bad environmental quality was the reason why experts noticed the problems of Puxi and raised the proposal to develop Pudong. After visiting his relatives and seeing their poor and overcrowded living conditions, Lin Tongyan was touched by their plight and decided to change the situation (Huanqiuwang, 2008).

Because of occurrences like this, the idea "Develop Pudong" has a strong ecological mission. Pudong was planned as an ecological area. There were several indicators of growing ecological concerns during the development of Pudong. There was an emphasis placed on making sure there would be greenery and that the city would be suitable for people to live in. Attention was given to the creation of local policies to protect the environment. Shanghai with its stricter environmental laws and regulations became a frontrunner for the central government.

During the planning of Pudong, the Shanghai government invited many international experts to design Pudong (Olds, 1997). They brought with them ideas about developing Pudong in an ecological and sustainable way. Pudong was to be internationalized and modernized and the city was to jump out of the "pollution first, treatment later" path and enter the 21st century as an outward, multifunctional, and modern city (Gao, 1991; Y. Liu, 1991; Qiu, 1991; F. Zhao, 1991).

In Old Shanghai, the average greenery was one square meter per person. In comparison, most international cities have over $20\,m^2$ per person. The standards of Pudong were set at $20\,m^2$ greenery per person (Q. Zhao, 1994b). Two parks were designed to be the green lungs of Pudong. One is the green park at the golden area, Lujiazui, which is about $100,000\,m^2$ with a manmade lake in the middle. Before the planning began, this area was a slum of Pudong with 3,000 households. Another green park is the Century Park (*Shiji Gongyuan*), with about 140 acres (X. Wang, 2005). "Develop Pudong" also includes many city reforestation programs, including the import of 80,000 trees from other provinces to create 9,000 acres of ecological forest. Pudong introduced reforestation through the market, so that it did not just rely on government funds. Planners encouraged street units and government departments to adopt green land. Later foreign companies were also included in this adoption system. Pudong won the national award for a garden city district (Q. Zhao, 2007).

In addition to the greenery, modern infrastructure and facilities were constructed to maintain Pudong as a suitable living place. The introduction to the book, *New Century, New Pudong*, says "growth is not development, wealth is not happiness, the 21st century's cities are not decorated with smoke-stacks, and they should be well informed and ecologically harmonized" (Q. Zhao, 1994a, p. 279). "Develop Pudong" considered pollution issues as related to the city's infrastructure and framed the construction of infrastructure as key to reducing pollutants.

Pudong has constructed infrastructure for turning coal to gas. It is one of the city's 10 big projects, the Pudong Gas Company. It includes two storage units for gas and pipelines for gas. The environmental standards of this gas company are much higher than those of the old gas companies at Puxi. Altogether, the investment in environmental facilities accounts for 22% of the total investment in Pudong (W. Ji, 1997). Pudong also introduced a centralized heating and cooling system. Before the development of Pudong, the heating was provided by thousands of small coal boilers, which damaged the environment and public health. Apart from this, heat production also wasted lots of energy. The centralized heating and cooling system located in planned development zones, like Waigaoqiao, Jin Qiao, and Lujiazui (W. Ji, 1997). These experiments also suggested the potential for introducing renewable energy for heating the city, through, for example, waste incineration technology.

Pudong also issued local regulations to protect its environment. At first, Pudong set up an Environmental Protection Office, and wrote the Pudong New

Area Environmental Protection plan and policy frameworks to regulate the industries and environment in its area (W. Ji, 1997). Pudong also adopted market-based methods to reduce pollutants and protect the environment. One of these methods was the fee for waste discharge system which was imported from developed countries and was very popular before it was replaced by the environmental protection tax in 2018. The second method was the ecological compensation fee system, which charged for the use of environmental resources and changed the concept that ecology has no price in the market. These methods helped to resolve the conflicts between ecology users and ecology providers. Pudong has published local regulations *On Trial Implementation with the Method of Ecological Compensation in Shanghai Pudong New Area* (Q. Zhao, 1994a).

The experts and government officials planned to build Pudong as an ecological area to reduce environmental pollution, since Shanghai already showed signs of serious city pollution. They framed ecological protection with the Chinese slogan, *gongzai dangdai, lizai qianqiu*, which means the efforts are made by the current generation, while the benefits are enjoyed by future generations.

Government-led urbanization

Another mission of Pudong was to find a new path for development that differed from the labor-intensive and low-technological models of Shenzhen and Sunan at that time, which resulted in environmentally polluting development. Shenzhen and Sunan opened their industry sectors to the outside world (Wan & Yuan, 2001), while the Pudong model emphasized building modern market institutions (Qian & Guo, 2010).

Deng Xiaoping called on Pudong to turn Shanghai into a financial city like Hong Kong (E. Yuan, 2012; Q. Zhao, 2007). Pudong aimed to open its service sector to the outside world. Pudong has three central sectoral areas, namely finance, trade, and shipping. As all are planned, the industries are grouped area by area; there are four areas that are often mentioned: Lujiazui Finance and Trade Zone, Zhangjiang High-tech Park, Shanghai Waigaoqiao Free Trade Zone, and Shanghai Jinqiao Economic and Technological Development Zone.

As a pilot area, Pudong has enjoyed not only the specific preferential policies of the central government, but also the preferential policies of the other special economic zones. The preferential policies guaranteed industrial growth since they were not allowed to develop in other places (Lin, 1995). The search for a different development model is reflected in Pudong's preferential industrial policies for finance and high-tech industries.

The role of preferential policies is clear in the reconstruction of the finance center under the power of government, the Lujiazui Finance Center (H. Han & Yan, 2010; A. D. Wang, 2013). Finance was not free then, nor is it today. Lujiazui was not a blank paper upon which planners could draw the ideal financial center. There were 50,000 residences, 520,000 m^2 of old buildings, and 430,000 m^2 of factories and storage centers (A. D. Wang, 2013). Lujiazui enjoyed some special policies that allowed foreign banks to settle there. It opened the tertiary industry sector to foreign businesses, for example, supermarkets and later banks and insurance companies. The central government also allowed Pudong to set up a stock market to raise money for the city's development.

The preferential policies are also reflected in the focus on high-technology industries aiming for technology innovation. Pudong simultaneously refused many polluting industries (Q. Huang, 1995). The development of Pudong was in a functional development mode, so several development zones were designated according to their function. Besides Lujiazui as a financial center, there was the Waigaoqiao Free Trade Zone, the Jinqiao Export Processing Zone, the Zhangjiang High-technology Park, and the Sunqiao Modern Agriculture Zone (Q. Zhao, 2007).

As these policies favored high-technology industries, many town and village factories were closed. The government did not make any significant effort to save or change them (Sha, Bao, & Gu, 1999). The government invested huge amounts of capital to build these four sectoral areas to attract foreign investment, capital, and business (L. Xu, 1994; Z. Zhang & Zhang, 1994).

The process of fast urbanization in Pudong has been copied in many localities. According to Fei Xiaotong, a famous social scientist, Pudong's society was the first case in which an agricultural society was connected to one of China's most modern economies and urbanized in such a short time. Its process, its path, and its challenges deserve special attention (Fei, 1997).

Accelerated urbanization

One main issue in "Develop Pudong" is the development of land and the transformation of a rural area into an urban area. Pudong's original urban area was a small area along the Huangpu River; 90% of Pudong was rural (Wan, 1997). From a social change perspective, it is a process of turning a traditional society into a modern society by the state in a short time. Farmers were forced to change their lifestyles. Most of the developers saw this process as an economic process that attracted businesses and industries to settle down in certain areas. This section will analyze the change of land in Pudong and its social and environmental impacts in Pudong, which are neglected or ignored in the major literature about Pudong's economic development.

First, we will look at the loss of local identity and culture during Pudong's development and later in relation to globalization. Pudong is named according to its geographical location. People have lived hundreds of years calling them different names, such as Chuansha (F. Xu, 2013). When the central government declared its plan to develop Pudong, the land was turned from collectively owned land to state-owned land.

Chuansha County was turned into the Pudong New Area, and the entire Chuansha County government was dissolved in 1992. The old Chuansha County chief took charge of keeping stability in Chuansha in order to support the plan to

"Develop Pudong" (Ren, 2013). This step to turn collectively owned land into state-owned land made urbanization possible and was by the order of the central government. From 1990 to 1995, the Pudong New Area government confiscated 79.56 km^2, of which 59.7 km^2 was arable land (Wan, 1997). With this, Shanghai almost doubled its city area. After the land was transformed, the new government started to build infrastructure on it. As described above, the infrastructure was planned by first-rate architects developing the best level of facilities. This infrastructure was largely limited to the specific areas that were included in the government plan (B. Ji & Zhou, 2013). Some villages at Pudong became typical urban villages and kept the old facilities of villages although located in the cities (W. Zhou et al., 2013). As the economy developed, these urban villages become settlements for migrant workers (W. Wu, 2005). Most of the local villagers rely on rent for a living. Because of unequal economic and environmental benefits among local people and the local government, there is a high probability that these villagers will petition for their interests making it important to keep an eye on social justice during the process of land development (Boxun, 2014; W. Zhou et al., 2013; X. Zhang & Lu, 2002).

The Pudong land development model has been praised as an innovative method for urbanization. The specific process followed several steps. First, the government fiscal department signed a check over to the development companies for the value of the land. After this, the development companies used this check to obtain the land use rights from the government land department. Hence, they changed from the former planning procedure in which the local government distributed land according to its plan, to one where the development companies essentially represented the local government. They could then use the land in the market, for example renting it to foreign companies.

Second, based on the concept that land rights are tradable and have a price, the development companies can trade land rights for capital. Pudong set up four development companies as the holders of the land (Wan & Yuan, 2001). Initially, the development companies were without liquid assets. The development of land needs capital, so they started to sell part of their land usage rights to other companies or use land rights usage as a capital resource to cooperate with other companies. They also used land to get capital through the stock market and to get loans from the bank. When the development companies finished the infrastructure work, they started to rent out land to other businesses. The value of the land went sky high during this process (Wan, 1997; Wan & Yuan, 2001). When the value of the farm land rose so enormously during the process of urbanization, how were farmers affected and what compensation did they get? The idea and practices of local people are hardly seen in Pudong's urbanization process.

Third, as most of Pudong's land belonged to farmers, the process of urbanization is also a process in which farmers lost their land and agricultural lifestyles. Some mention the sacrifice of those farmers for a national strategy or dream, still most commentators ignored the rights of farmers to their land. Instead, they justified the loss of land by stating that the land belongs to the nation. "Develop Pudong" has removed thousands of people from their homes to make way for

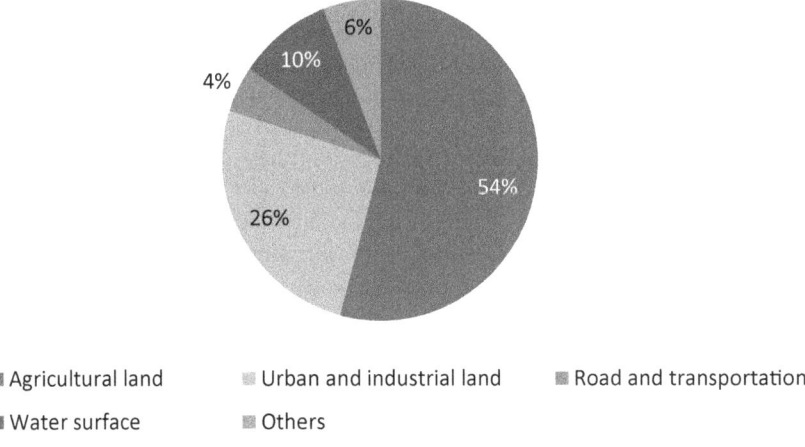

Figure 3.1 1995 Pudong land use structure.
Source: author calculation based on Wan (1997).

the government's plan. As the development companies wanted to pay less for the land, they usually tried to obtain a large area of land, even without having any specific program for the land and before the value of the land rose too much (Q. Huang, 1995). They did this arguing that the wealth should stay in the hands of the nation (Q. Huang, 1995; Wan & Yuan, 2001).

This study is constrained by the information available to the topic about compensation, land issues, and relocation. The data shows the land using structure of Pudong in 1995 (see Figure 3.1).

There were two groups of people in Pudong, one group was made up of Puxi city residents, and the other of farmers. Under the projects of "old and dangerous housing renovation," the city residents were relocated to new resident blocks by the Pudong New Government. In 1995 only, 22,100 households on Dongchang Road and Xiepu Road were moved to New Dongchang villages (Wan, 1997). The area where the farmers lived was the largest source of land for the new government. By 1993, land acquired from villages amounted to 454 km², or 87% of Pudong's total land area of 522.7 km². Most of the people in the development zones were relocated to villages (Wan, 1997). During 1991 to 1995, the government confiscated 79 km² of land (Wan, 1997).

Compensation was changed in form and level over time, with a tendency towards higher benefits the later the land was confiscated. Before the new Land Administration Law of 1998, Pudong had confiscated large amounts of collective land from farmers. According to articles 28 and 29 of the 1986 Land Administration Law, the compensation fee for agricultural land was to be three to six times the average income of the land during the three years before confiscation and the compensation for relocation was to be twice to three times the value of the average income of the land during the three years before confiscation. The total sum of the compensation fees was not to reach over 20 times the average income of the land during the three years before confiscation (Standing Committee of the National People's Congress [SCNPC], 1987).

In 1998, article 47 of the amended land administration law set the compensation level at six to ten times the average income of the land during the three years before confiscation. The relocation compensation was raised to four to six times the average income of the land during the three years before confiscation, the total cap on compensation was not to reach over 30 times the average income of the land during the three years before confiscation; and compensation was added for crops and other things on the confiscated land (SCNPC, 1998). The final compensation for farmers was about 25,000 RMB per mu (a mu is a Chinese unit of area equal to $666.6\,m^2$) of field land (X. Chen, 2015). In the case of Pudong, farmers had little gain from the large future land profits. The compensation was later enlarged to cover job location services and shareholders in collectives' companies to enjoy companies' benefits for landless farmers (Y. Wang, 2011). The big difference in compensation benefits before and after the new laws and regulations were introduced irritated many farmers who had lost their land before the new laws and regulation came out (Zheng, 2001). Also some landless farmers did not enjoy the same insurance that Shanghai Hukou residents received as the local government designed different insurance for small city and township (Boxun, 2014; Ye, 2010). The picture is clear. Many farmers lost their land at the beginning of the process of developing the Pudong area, only to gain limited compensation despite the rising land prices.

The government emphasized that "economic compensation, social insurance, and job services" were to help farmers become Shanghai citizens. Compared with the fast development of the functional industrial areas, there were few changes in the non-planned rural areas of Pudong (Q. Huang, 1995). "Develop Pudong" has brought limited job opportunities for landless farmers since the Pudong government aims for high-tech industries. After three years of developing Pudong, there were 90,000 new jobs and the new government encouraged the TVEs to absorb much of the labor (Q. Huang, 1995).

The Pudong way of development set an example for other cities for how to obtain land from collective villages and how to sell and develop it. The development companies are state-owned companies, public and private at the same time. Pudong is a place which has integrated international, national, municipal, and village-level actors and powers during the "Develop Pudong" process. It is a good example of modernization and urbanization, but also an example that reveals the costs and damages of these processes.

Analysis

The core idea of "Develop Pudong" was to solve the problems that exist on one side of the Huangpu River, by addressing them on the other side of the river. The

"Develop Pudong" strategy is "the miniature modernization of Shanghai"; it has transformed Shanghai's skyline in two decades, and it has won many prizes from national and international society. In one sentence, "it is a miracle" (Q. Zhao & Shao, 2008, p. 10). Pudong New Area has been a window through which we can observe China's rapid development.

Develop Pudong was not directly connected to green development, although the strategy was a response to the serious ecological crisis of old Shanghai and was advocated for by experts and local leaders with high levels of environmental awareness. Its advocates aimed for Pudong to be an ecological district competing with the best cities in the world and the most modern areas. Pudong became a pilot area to experiment with different kinds of reforms. Its mode of development has been copied by many cities. Even though "Develop Pudong" has taken ecological value into consideration, its implementation has not always been good for the local ecology and people.

Powers and actors behind "Develop Pudong"

"Develop Pudong" was conceived by people with an innovative spirit to solve the problems of Shanghai as it transitioned from light industry to heavy industry. These bottom-up entrepreneurs, with rich local knowledge, sought a better future for the city. Though the strategy was confronted with many challenges, with local leaders and entrepreneurs' *guanxi* networks, it became a reality and later a miracle.

They were touched by the damage brought by the planned economy, by the hard life the people were leading, which made Shanghai lose its competence compared with its international counterparts. Compared with other international cities, Shanghai was left behind, especially compared with the Four Asian Dragons, namely Hong Kong, Singapore, South Korea, and Taiwan (J. Zhou & Pan, 1999).

The local leaders accepted the reality and try to reform. Due to the importance of Shanghai in China's economic structure, the reform of Shanghai faced many more challenges in its way to reform and opening-up. As Wang Daohan researched about how to develop Pudong, the reform-minded central government supported the necessary reforms in Shanghai (J. Zhou & Pan, 1999). Pudong's development was delayed by core senior and conservative leaders, as evidenced in Deng's regret that Pudong's development came too late and that this was his fault (E. Yuan & Gao, 2012).

After the Tiananmen Square Event in 1989, Deng decided to insist on moving forward with reform and opening-up. Pudong was chosen to show the international society about the direction that China was heading in. Deng's decision was glorified by many followers, especially implementing officials (Q. Huang, 1993; Q. Zhao, 2000). Under Deng's order, the central government's approval of "Develop Pudong" was decisive and key to putting the idea into practice.

In the Chinese political system, it tends to contribute achievement to the leaders, or the central government. This chapter explains the efforts of bottom-up actors and the local leadership in pursuing a better future for their localities which is easily ignored by scholars.

Who gets what, when, and how?

"Develop Pudong" was an idea invented by civil experts who then gradually formed a social network based on the common belief "Develop Pudong." Later the local government leader picked up the idea and further developed it (Cao, Deng, & Fang, 1990; W. Xu, 1995): local officials used their social relations to make the idea stronger. Just like in the broader political system, the approval of the key leader Deng Xiaoping was necessary to turn ideas into actions. The people involved in the implementation of "Develop Pudong" gained either material benefits or career promotion, or both.

Chen Kunlong, who advocated developing Pudong, died a short time before the government announced its approval of the plan. It is said that he was disappointed at that time of his death as the central government had not yet agreed to development of the region (Tihuhedong, 2007). These people worked for a common idea and were motivated by their knowledge and wish to make Shanghai better.

As Zhu Rongji was the implementation leader during Pudong's development in 1990, he has been praised as the creator of "Develop Pudong" and became its spokesperson (S. Yuan, 2013). Zhu was later promoted to premier of China. Many people who participated in "Develop Pudong" have been promoted to key political positions, as they built Pudong with nothing in hand except for land. Huang Qifan was the mayor of Chongqing from 2010 until 2018, and the development companies who began with four people and little capital have become successful managers, especially in the housing industry, holding huge amounts of capital (Sha, 2000; A. D. Wang, 2013). Pudong is an example of a political achievement. Pudong is continuing to receive many preferential policies from the central government which have guaranteed its image as the window of China.

For local people, Pudong has brought wealth but also the loss of their land and homes. During the modernization of Pudong, local people had a hard time entering the labor market in the finance and high-technology industries. At the same time, the former village and township enterprises were in competition with those big and strong industries, which made it harder for local people to get enough jobs in Pudong.

For the local environment, a large part of the area's farm land was turned into a business areas and high-level residential areas. As Pudong before development was the destination for polluting companies in the Puxi area, it was also highly polluted before "Develop Pudong." The "Develop Pudong" strategy has cleaned many rivers and land (J. Huang, 2005; C. Zhu, 2000). At the same time, "Develop Pudong" has brought chemical industries to Pudong which has had a serious impact on local people and ecology (Shanghai huagong, 1990).

The powerful actors in the process of "Develop Pudong" have gained the most from the area's transition. There are improvements in environmental protection, but there are also new environmental problems.

How green is "Develop Pudong"?

As was explained previously, "Develop Pudong" has a strong environmental protection mission. The inclusion of ecology in the plan, with its aim to reduce pollution, and the industries that were chosen plus the area's implementation process has proved that "Develop Pudong" truly is a green development strategy.

As green development is associated with power and interests, it has a different influence on different actors with respectively different power levels. For Pudong, it was lucky that there were supporters of environmental protection involved in the design plans. Furthermore, during the planning process, the influence of international designers strongly pushed ecological considerations in the plan. Green is also a relative concept; the powerful actors in the planning process decided what is green and what is not green. They considered large open spaces as green, despite that creating it forced thousands of people to move. Unfortunately, this was to be expected, since in the planning phase, the residents had little or no influence and no power to protect their interests.

At the same time, it was not local people who were the target groups for the green facilities. The planners aimed to attract business and talent to settle in Pudong. The Biyun international residence was developed for high-income people, especially international managers working in MNCs. Local people did, however, benefit from the treatment of pollution in Huangpu and Suzhou rivers.

The implementation of "Develop Pudong" also experienced some problems. The government behaved like a businessman in the process of land acquisition, obtaining land from the people cheaply and making the most of profits from the land's conversion. With such a business-oriented development model it is hard to prevent the abuse of land rights. Many ecological resources are also based on land which faced abuse during the process.

The Pudong New Area is relatively greener than other urban areas. As Shanghai had previously experienced an ecological crisis, it adopted international concepts about city ecology. As a special area with attention from the local and central governments, a huge amount of resources flew into Pudong's development.

Conclusion

This chapter has described a historical case study that took place at a critical time in China. "Develop Pudong" continues, it is still a pilot in furthering reform and opening-up. Pudong brought new ideas and policies to the region and to China. The Secretary of Pudong declared that every reform idea that other places are afraid to implement, Shanghai Pudong will happily try out (H. Shen & Ji, 2008). The previous leaders of Shanghai have proved their creative and reform spirit throughout Pudong's history. Wang Daohan, Chen Kunlong, Wang Ganghuai, and many others realized Shanghai's environmental problems and were far-sighted enough to try to avoid similar problems in the planning of Pudong.

Shanghai is now also a pioneer in green development in China. This case has selected its historical change from a city with heavy industries and pollution issues to an international city. I think the moment of "Develop Pudong" strategy is the beginning of a green development path of Shanghai. It is widely neglected by the public. The efforts of local leadership and entrepreneurs in the 1980s should be pointed out; they have laid out a long-term sustainable development path for Shanghai. It is a bottom-up strategy which gained the approval of the central government.

As an economic reform strategy, Pudong developed its land into valuable land; it is now some of the most expensive land in the world. Through the globalization process, the land that belonged to Pudong's farmers' collectives has been turned into lands of the nation or industrial land. Pudong's land economy has also been a miracle within the Chinese economy. The idea of developing land has since been advocated by local innovators and implemented by local officials in other areas.

As a political mission, "Develop Pudong" reflects the speed of urbanization and modernization under the government's leadership. The approval of the central government was key to the development of Pudong; later the Chinese government mobilized huge amounts of resources to support the building of infrastructure, the financial center, and shipping center. The ongoing justification for land nationalization has been a central issue that reflects the distribution of political power in the Chinese system—a strong local government and a weak local people.

As a social strategy, "Develop Pudong" has transformed Pudong's society in a short time. The government planned their urbanization and farmers were urbanized passively during the process. Since "Develop Pudong" has attracted many international businesses to Pudong, it started a migrant worker run to Shanghai Pudong.

Lastly, as an ecological process, "Develop Pudong" shows the power of humans to change their impacts on the environment. Pudong's efforts to place the environment in harmony with economic and social development have influenced many other cities. The lack of public participation or local involvement means only a few experts decided which part of the environment is worthy of protection. Their lack of local knowledge has put their decision and judgment in doubt.

In summary, green development has been advocated for experts and through the "Develop Pudong" strategy. It has been implemented by politicians, while the environment and the local people have had to accept these green development ideas from the top. The powerful actors in Pudong have decided what green development is and how to have green development; the weaker actors had to make way for green development.

Notes

1 Wang's former chief is Gu Mu who is a reformer and the person in charge of the Foreign Expert and Investment Management Committee. Wang was the vice director of it before he went to Shanghai, and another vice director became the mayor of Shenzhen. Wang has also recommended Jiang as the vice director (Kuhn, 2004).

2 The Jiusan society is a democratic party that has existed in China since 1946. It is made up of people who work in science, education, health, and culture. It had 132,000 members by the end of 2012. For more information see www.93.gov.cn.
3 At that time, the CCP demanded that officials should be younger and more professional. It required that older officials retire from their jobs and leave them for the younger generation. As such, Wang recommended Jiang as the next Shanghai Mayor.
4 He worked his whole life for environmental protection and his blog is called "Green for a life." He is a diplomat and has written a book titled *Environmental Protection Foreign Affairs*.
5 Ni Tianzeng was also an important local leader. He supported and helped to realize the "Develop Pudong" idea. He graduated from Tsinghua University and majored in architecture.

References

Boxun (Producer). (2014, May 21). Shanghai Pudong qizhen shidi nongmin jiannan de weiquan licheng [A challenging path for farmers from seven townships in Pudong to protect their rights]. Retrieved from www.boxun.com/news/gb/china/2014/07/201407150140.shtml#.VV2vyfmqqko.
Brick, A. B. (1989). *Reform in China after Tiananmen Square (Vol. 203)*. Heritage Foundation.
Buck, D. (2012). *Constructing China's capitalism: Shanghai and the nexus of urban-rural industries*. New York: Palgrave Macmillan.
Cao, P., Deng, R., & Fang, Z. (1990). Shanghai Pudong kaifa juece qianhou [Before and after the decision-making of "develop Pudong"]. *Kaifang Shidai, 1*, 012.
Chen, K. (1980). Xiang Pudong guangkuo diqu fazhan [Developing in Pudong in a broad space]. *Shehui Kexue, 5*, 010.
Chen, X. (Producer). (2015, May 21). Difang zhengfu zhengdi yao baozhang nongmin liyi [Local governments should protect farmers' rights when they confiscate their lands]. Retrieved from http://znzg.xynu.edu.cn/Html/?23036.html.
Chen, Y. (1987). Shanghaishi shengtai jingji xuehui chengli [The Shanghai Ecological Economy Association is established]. *Shehui Kexue, 1*, 022.
Chen, Y. (1995). *Chen Yun wenxuan (di san juan)*. Beijing: Renmin Chubanshe.
Chen, Z. (1991). *Pudong kaifa kaifang jianlun [A brief history of opening and developing Pudong]*. Shanghai: Fudan Daxue Chubanshe.
Chen, Z. (1984). Rui Xingwen buzhang zai Zhongguo huanjing zhanlue wenti yanjiu ban tan "qiwu" qijian huanbao fangzhen weile cujin shengzhang, shizhang, xianzheng, cangzhang deng geji lingdao dui huanjing baohu gongzuo de zhongshi, Rui Xingwen tongzhi zancheng bufen tongzhi de jianyi: Guojia dui cangzhang jinxing kaohe, yao xiang Shenyagnshi nayang you huanjing baohu de neirong [Minister Rui Xingwen: A talk about raising the environmental awareness and responsibility of local leaders, such as province chiefs, mayors, county chiefs, and managers, during the Seventh Five-Year Plan period in a symposium on China's environmental strategy]. *Huanjing Baohu, 10*, 000.
Cheng, L. (2012). Globalization and Shanghai model: A retrospective and prospective analysis. *Journal of International and Global Studies, 4*(1), 59–80.
China review news (2005, December 25). Zhuzheng Shanghai shouti kaifa Pudong [Wang Daohan: Governor of Shanghai proposed "develop Pudong" first]. Retrieved from www.chinareviewnews.com/crnwebapp/search/allDetail.jsp?id=100076268&sw=%E8%89%AF.
Coble, P. M. (1986). *The Shanghai capitalists and the nationalist government, 1927–1937*. USA: Harvard University Asia Center.

Dong, D. (2005). Pudong kaifa kaifang 15 zhounian Zhao Qizheng tuikai Pudong luoji de lishi zhi men [After 15 years of "open and develop Pudong," Zhao Qizheng opens the door to history: the logic of Pudong]. Retrieved from www.china.com.cn/chinese/2005/Apr/841219.htm.

Eastday (Producer). (2002, October 01). Pudong zhonguo de mengxiang [Pudong: the dream of China]. Retrieved from http://bbs.sjtu.edu.cn/bbsanc,path,%2Fgroups%2FGROUP_9%2FDistrict9%2FDBE80124D%2FDAF6D58CB%2FDA7761201%2FD550AAF05%2FD573FD938%2FD5B7EA93A%2FD628DFF83%2FM.1030082514.A.html.

Fei, X. (1997). Zhebian wenzhang zhiyou Zhongguoren ziji lai xie—Fei Xiaotong weiyuanzhang tan Pudong kaifa kaifang zhong de nongmin wenti yanjiu [Chinese people have to write this article themselves—Fei Xiaotong's opinions and researches on the farmer issues during the process of "develop and open Pudong"]. *Pudong Kaifa, 7*.

Feng, L. (2006). Wang Daohan de chuanqi rensheng [Wang Daohan: A legendary life]. *Zhongshan Fengyu, 2*, 012.

Fewsmith, J. (2001). *Elite politics in contemporary China*. Oxon: East Gate Book.

Gao, Y. (1991). Pudong Xinqu huanjing baohu guihua de shexiang [Pudong New Area: Policies, planning, and design of environmental protection]. *Shanghai Huanjing Kexue, 10*(1), 15–18.

Gillies, D. (1996). *Between principle and practice: Human rights in north-south relations*. Quebec: McGill-Queen's Press.

Han, H., & Yan, Y. (Eds.). (2010). *Pudong zhi Lu, jinrong fazhan jingyan yu zhanwang [The path of Pudong: Experiences and outlook on financial development]*. Shanghai: Shanghai Renmin Chubanshe.

Han, S. S. (2000). Shanghai between state and market in urban transformation. *Urban Studies, 37*(11), 2091–2112.

He, L. (2006). Wang Daohan wenhe er youli de gaigezhe [Wang Daohan, a benevolent and strong reformer]. *Zhongguo Xinwen Zhoukan*, (1), 62–65.

Huang, J. (2005). Lv: Shengtai Pudong zhudase [Green: The dominant color of an ecological Pudong]. *Pudong Kaifa, 12*, 006.

Huang, P. (1991). 1991 nian huang fuping wenzhang [1991 series of article by Huang Fuping]. *Jiefang Ribao*.

Huang, Q. (1993). Jingji gaige he fazhan de guanjian shi gaohao jinrong xuexi Deng Xiaoping wenxuan disanjuan youguan jinrong zhanlue zhishi yougan [The key for economic reform and development is the finance industry; a book review of Deng Xiaoping's work, volume 3: Guidance about financial strategy]. *Shanghai Jinrong, 12*, 000.

Huang, Q. (1995). *Tan Pudong kaifa de zhanlue zhengce ji guanli [The strategy and management of "develop Pudong"]*. Shanghai: Shanghai Renmin Chubanshe.

Huanqiuwang. (Producer). (2008, October 15). Pudong kaifa [Develop Pudong]. *Huanqiu Lishi*. Retrieved from http://history.huanqiu.com/txt/2008-12/331168_5.html.

Ji, B., & Zhou, W. (2013). Chengzhongcun chengshihua zhong de jieduan tezheng yu pojie lixing yi Shanghai Pudong xinqu Gaoqiaozhen Xibangtou wei li [Village in a city: Temporary features and breakthrough reasoning during urbanization—the case of Gaoqiaozhen Xibangtou in Shanghai Pudong]. *Shanghai Chengshi Guanli (4)*, 70–75.

Ji, W. (1997). *Chengshi jianshe lun [Urban development]*. Shanghai: Shanghai Yuandong Chubanshe.

Katada, S. N. (2001). Why did Japan suspend foreign aid to China? Japan's foreign aid decision-making and sources of aid sanction. *Social Science Japan Journal, 4*(1), 39–58. ng. *Huanqiu Lishi*. Retrieved from http://history.huanqiu.com/txt/2008-12/331168_5.html.

Kuhn, R. (2004). *The man who changed China: The life and legacy of Jiang Zemin.* New York: Crown Publishers.

Lan, Y. (1983). Yi yige shenghuo cemian lai fanying renwu [From one perspective to reflect a figure's character]. *Xinwen Jizhe, 5,* 024.

Li, J. (n.d.). Huigu Pudong Xinqu de guihua he jianshe [A review of the planning and construction of Pudong New Area]. *Shanghai Committee of Chinese Political Consultative Conference.* Retrieved from http://news.eastday.com/epublish/gb/paper167/2/class016700001/hwz322627.htm.

Li, Z. (2011). Deng Xiaoping, Chen Yun de gaige sixiang bijiao [The comparison between the reform ideas of Deng Xiao ping and Chen Yun]. *Anhui shixue (Historical Research in Anhui), 4,* 58–64.

Lin, N. (1995). Local market socialism: Local corporatism in action in rural China. *Theory and Society, 24*(3), 301–354.

Liu, W. (1986). Zhongguo chengshi jingji xuehui choubai huiyi zai jing zhaokai [The establishment of China's Urban Economy Association held in Beijing]. *Caimao Jingji, 6,* 016.

Liu, Y. (1991). Pudong Xinqu huanjing baohu zhengce chutan [An investigation of Pudong New Area's environmental protection]. *Shanghai Huanjing Kexue, 1,* 007.

Long, H. (2012, February 03). Pudong kaifa kaifang qianqi yanjiu he yunniang [The research and preparation for opening and developing Pudong]. *Pudong Shizhi.* Retrieved from http://szb.pudong.gov.cn/pdszb_pdds_dsyj/2012-02-03/Detail_411714.htm.

Naughton, B. (1996). *Growing out of the plan: Chinese economic reform, 1978–1993.* Cambridge: Cambridge University Press.

Olds, K. (1997). Globalizing Shanghai: The "global intelligence corps" and the building of Pudong. *Cities, 14*(2), 109–123.

Peng, K. (2014). Hu Yaobang erfu Shanghai diaoyan [Hu Yaobang did fieldwork in Shanghai twice]. Retrieved from http://blog.sina.com.cn/s/blog_a3f2f5990102v78p.html.

Qian, Y. & Guo, L. (2010). *Pudong zhi lu chuangxin fazhan 20 nian zhi huigu yu zhanwang [The path of Pudong: a reflection and outlook for 20 years of innovative development].* Shanghai: Shanghai People's Publisher.

Qiu, X. (1991). Pudong Xinqu huanjing baohu zhengce de yanjiu [Pudong New Area: A study of environmental protection policies]. *Shanghai Huanjing Kexue, 1,* 008.

Ren, S. (2013). Wending Pudong kaifa de baozhang [The promise of "develop Pudong": Social stability]. *Pudong Kaifa.* Retrieved from http://gov.pudong.gov.cn/pudong-News_JS_201306/Info/Detail_476442.htm.

Sha, H., Bao, Z., & Gu, Z. (1999). Pudong chengshihua jincheng zhong de nongmin wenti yanjiu [Research on peasant problems during Pudong's urbanization process]. *Mao Zedong Deng Xiaoping Lilun Yanjiu, 1.*

Sha, L. (2000). Zuo Pudong kaifa kaifang detuohuangniu [Be a pioneer in opening and developing Pudong]. *Shanghai Renda Yuekan,* (4), 14–15.

Shanghai Difangzhi Bangongshi [Shtong] (2000). Pudong kaifa kaifang [Open and develop Pudong]. Retrieved from www.shtong.gov.cn/node2/node2247/node4590/index.html.

Shanghai Difangzhi Bangongshi. (1998). Shanghai huanjing baohuzhi [The history of environmental protection in Shanghai]. In Shanghai huanjing baohuzhi bianzhuanweiyuanhui (Ed.), *Shanghai Difangzhi.* Shanghai Difangzhi Bangongshi.

Shanghai huagong (1990). Jiakuai kaifa Pudong diqu huadong nongyao bade touchou [Chemistry and pesticide industries are forerunners in "develop Pudong"]. *Shanghai Huagong, 3.*

Shapiro, J. (2001). *Mao's war against nature: Politics and the environment in revolutionary China*. Cambridge: Cambridge University Press.
Shen, H., & Ji, M. (2008, April 18). Zhongguo gaige kaifang paitoubing Shanghai Pudong Xinqu queli weilai luxiantu [The pilot of China's reform and opening-up: Shanghai Pudong New Area]. *Xinhua News*. Retrieved from http://news.xinhuanet.com/newscenter/2008-04/18/content_8003599.htm.
Shen, X., & Yu, M. (2012). Dao Pudong qu de, doushi zhuangshi [Pioneers in Pudong]. *Zhongguo Xinwen Zhoukan*, (1), I0015-I0017.
Sina (Producer). (2013, March 20). Huangpujiang zhiwushi: quanguo zuida "aizhengchun" de chuxian he xiaoshi [The history of controlling pollution in Huangpu River: the existence and disappearance of the biggest "cancer village"]. Retrieved from http://green.sina.com.cn/2013-03-20/192226590993.shtml.
Situweizhi (2012). Deng Xiaoping paiban pudong kaifa [Deng Xiaoping decided to develop Pudong]. *Dongfang Pinglun*. Retrieved from http://pinglun.eastday.com/p/20120122/u1a6325272.html.
Standing Committee of the National People's Congress [SCNPC]. (1987). *Zhonghua renmin gongheguo tudi guanlifa (1986) [Land administration law (1986)]*.
Standing Committee of the National People's Congress [SCNPC]. (1998). *Zhonghua renmin gongheguo tudi guanlifa (1998)[Land administration law (1998)]*.
Sullivan, L. R. (1988). Assault on the reforms: Conservative criticism of political and economic liberalization in China, 1985–86. *The China Quarterly, 114*, 198–222.
Tihuhedong (2007). Qinshen jingli xianwei renzhi de Pudong kaifa lishi neimu [Personal experience: The inside story of "develop Pudong"]. In Tihuhedong (Ed.), *Tihu Hedong (Vol. 2013)*. Retrieved from Sina.blog.
Wan, Z. (1997). *Tudi jingji lun [Land economy]*. Shanghai: Shanghai Yuandong Chubanshe.
Wan, Z., & Yuan, E. (2001). *Toushi Pudong sisuo Pudong [A lens through which to look and think about Pudong]*. Shanghai: Shanghai Renmin Chubanshe.
Wang, A. D. (2013). Chengzai guoji jinrong zhongxin shiming de Lujiazui [The mission to be an international financial center: Lujiazui]. Retrieved from www.pdtimes.com.cn/html/2013-04/11/content_6_1.htm.
Wang, D. (1985a). Wang Daohan Shizhang de hexin [A congratulation letter from Wang Daohan mayor]. *Waiguo Jingji yu Guanli, 1*, 018.
Wang, D. (1985b). Wang Daohao shizhang tan Zhongguoshi xiandaihua guanli [Mayor Wang Daohan speaks about the Chinese model of modern management]. *Guanli Xiandaihua, 2*.
Wang, D. (1987). Wang Daohan Tongzhi zai Shanghai zijin shichang chengli dahui shang de jianghua [Wang Daohan's speech at the opening of capital market conference in Shanghai]. *Shanghai Jinrong [Shanghai Finance]*, 5–6.
Wang, G. (2008). Huiyi Pudong kaifa [A review of "develop Pudong"]. Retrieved from www.tsinghua.org.cn/alumni/infoSingleArticle.do?articleId=10016213&columnId=10016199.
Wang, X. (2005). *Dudong Pudong Pudong shiwunian kaifa jilu [A record to help understand 15 years of "Develop Pudong"]*. Shanghai: Shanghai Renmin Chubanshe.
Wang, Y. (2011). Jingji buchang + shehui baozhang + jiuye fuwu—Shanghai Pudong pojie shidi nongmin wenti de xin tansuo [Economic compensation + social insurance + job services—Shanghai Pudong's new exploration for farmers who have lost their land]. *Xiandai Nongye*, (5), 122–124.
Wei, C. (2013). Shuchi Wang Daohan [A bookworm: Wang Daohan]. Retrieved from www.21ccom.net/articles/rwcq/article_2013091892218.html.

Wei, Y. D., & Leung, C. K. (2005). Development zones, foreign investment, and global city formation in Shanghai. *Growth and Change, 36*(1), 16–40.

Wu, F. (2000). The global and local dimensions of place-making: Remaking Shanghai as a world city. *Urban Studies, 37*(8), 1359–1377.

Wu, W. (2005). *Migrant settlement and spatial transformation in urban China: The case of Shanghai.* Paper presented at the World Bank Third Urban Research Symposium, April 4–6. Retrieved from http://siteresources.worldbank.org/INTURBANDEVELOPMENT/Resources/336387-1269364699096/6892630-1269364758309/wu.pdf.

Xia, K. (2008, January 26). Wo pei Rui Xingwen fang Ouzhou siguo [Rui Xingwen visited four European countries]. *Lvse Yisheng (Vol. 2013).* Retrieved from http://xiakunbao.blog.sohu.com/77659767.html.

Xu, F. (2013). Shanghai yanjiang kaifa yu jindai Pudong shijiao jingji fazhan shulue [The development of Shanghai along the river and the economic history of Pudong suburban areas]. *Anhui Nongye Kexue, 41*(14), 6518–6520.

Xu, L. (1994). Kuaguo gongsi yu Pudong kaifa [MNCs and "develop Pudong"]. *Shanghai Caishui, 12,* 012.

Xu, W. (1995). Kaifa kaifang Pudong de juece shimo [The decision-making model for "develop and open Pudong"]. *Zhongguo Ruankexue, 7.*

Yang, H. (2001). Zhonggu diyitiao bei wuran heliu de xinsheng [The rebirth of the first polluted river]. Retrieved from www.people.com.cn/GB/huanbao/56/20010929/572937.html.

Ye, X. (2010). Pudong chengshihua jingjian [Lessons and experience from Pudong's urbanization]. *Zhongguo Gaige, 9.*

Yeh, W.-h. (2007). *Shanghai splendor: Economic sentiments and the making of modern China, 1843–1949.* California: University of California Press.

Yeung, Y.-m., Lee, J., & Kee, G. (2009). China's special economic zones at 30. *Eurasian Geography and Economics, 50*(2), 222–240.

Yu, Y. (1992). *Shanghai xingge ji mingyun dangdaiShanghai jingji jishi [The character and destiny of Shanghai].* Shanghai: Shanghai Wenyi Chubanshe.

Yuan, E. (2012). Xiaoping sudu: 60 tian diaoding—"Pudong kaifa kaifang" zhezhang "Zhongguo wangpai" shi zenme da chulai de? [Deng Xiaoping: Deciding to "open and develop Pudong" in 60 days—How did he play out this card?]. *Nanfang Zhoumo.* Retrieved from www.infzm.com/content/75057.

Yuan, E., & Gao, Y. (2012). Deng Xiaoping qiaoding "Pudong kaifa kaifang" neiqing [The inside story of Deng Xiaoping's decision of "develop and open Pudong"]. *Dangzheng Luntan, 14,* 8–8.

Yuan, S. (Producer). (2013, October 08). Zhu Rongji Pudong tuozhi 12 nian zuoguo fada guojia 100 nian de lichen [Zhu Rongji has taken only 12 years to explore and build Pudong, a process in which industrialized countries took more than 100 years]. Retrieved from http://sh.eastday.com/m/20130813/u1a7588777.html.

Yuan, X. (2013). Fada guojia duihua yuanzhu bu shouruan [Industrialized countries changed their attitudes towards aid for China]. Retrieved from http://view.163.com/special/reviews/aidtochina1219.html.

Zeng, J. (2013). *State-led privatization in China: The politics of economic reform.* London: Routledge.

Zeng, Q. (2011). Wuxian de sinian [Warmest thoughts]. In Shanghai Shuhua Chubanshe, *Wang Daohan jinian yingxiang [Wang Daohan film and photo album].* Shanghai.

Zhang, X., & Lu, D. (2002). Kaifaqu tudi kaifade quyu xiaoying ji xietong jizhi fenxi [An analysis of regional impacts and coordinating institutions for land use in development zones]. *Ziyuan Kexue, 24*(5), 32–38.

Zhang, Z., &, Zhang, D. (1994). Pudong kaifa yu Shanghai maoyi zhongxin he chongjian ["Develop Pudong" and the rebuilding of Shanghai as a trade center]. *Pudong Kaifa, 12*.

Zhao, F. (1991). Lun kaifang Pudong huanjing baohu ying jianchi de yuanze [Discussion of the principles of environmental protection in "Develop Pudong"]. *Shanghai Huanjing Kexue, 10*(1), 43–44.

Zhao, L., & Chen, M. (1986). Rui Xingwen yu zuojia ersanshi [Several stories between Secretary Rui Xingwen and writers]. *Liao Wang, 38*, 007.

Zhao, Q. (2000). Deng Xiaoping lilun shi Pudong kaifa kaifang de zhilu mingdeng [Deng Xiaoping's theory is the lamp to light the road of "Develop Pudong"]. *Pudong Kaifa, 4*, 005.

Zhao, Q. (1994a). Dier zhang de tiandi zhi duhou Pudong de dili dimao ji renwen jingguan [The second chapter: The geographic, landscape, and cultural history of Pudong] (Zhao, Q., Trans.). In Q. Zhao (Ed.), *Xin shiji xin Pudong* (pp. 19–50). Shanghai: Fudan Daxue Chubanshe.

Zhao, Q. (Ed.). (1994b). *Xin shiji xin pudong [New century, new Pudong]*. Shanghai: Fudan Daxue Chubanshe.

Zhao, Q. (2007). *Pudong luoji Pudong kaifa yu quanqiuhua [The logic of "Develop Pudong" and globalization]*. Shanghai: Shanghai Sanlian Chubanshe.

Zhao, Q., & Shao, Y. (2008). *Pudong Qiji [Pudong miracle]*. Beijing: Wuzhou Chuanbao Chubanshe.

Zhao, Q., & Zhang, G. (1984). Shanghai shiwei shujimen de diaocha yanjiuri [A day set for fieldwork: Shanghai's party committee members]. *Liao Wang, 26*, 003.

Zheng, H. (2001). Zhongguo nongdi zhengyong de zhidu huanjing fenxi—Yi Pudong Xinqu wei yanjiu ge'an [An institutional analysis of agricultural land confiscation in China—A case study of the Pudong New Area]. *Zhanlue yu Guanli, 4*, 86–94.

Zhong, P. (2005, July 08). Shezhe: Rui Xingwen [Shi Zhe: Rui Xingwen]. *Cai Jing*.

Zhou, J., & Pan, A. (1999). Huimou Pudong kaifang na yi chui [The moment of "Develop Pudong"]. *Shi Ji, 2*.

Zhou, W. (2007). Zhanlue zhihui yinling Shanghai shiji kuayue—Jinian Wang Daohan laoshizhang shishi yizhounian [Governing Shanghai with strategies: The old mayor Wang Daohan]. *Zhongguo Gaige, 1*, 26–28.

Zhou, W., Ji, B., & Liu, S. (2013). Pudong chengzhongcun gaizaode sikao yu lujing [Some thoughts and proposals for transforming Pudong's urban villages]. *Pudong Kaifa, 6*, 40–43.

Zhu, C. (2000). Lvse kaifa Pudong kechixu fazhan biyou zhi lu [Green "Develop Pudong" for sustainable development]. *Pudong Kaifa, 12*, 012.

Zhu, R. (2011). *Zhu Rongji Jianghua Shilu (Di Yi Juan) [Zhu Rongji Memoire, "Shanghai Speech 2"]*. Beijing: Renmin Chubanshe.

4 A polluted city's path towards low-carbon pioneering

Baoding

Baoding is known as a low-carbon city in the international community (Y. Li, 2012; Rasmus, 2008). How and why has a poor and anonymous city become a key advocate of low-carbon development? This chapter narrates Baoding's story, following key actors who have promoted green development for years and finally defined it as a local development strategy.

A city struggle with environmental and economic problems

Local context is key to understanding a place's green development. On the one hand, it highlights the ecological crisis in the Baiyangdian Lake and the serious air pollution in the city. On the other hand, it describes the local officials' willingness to change the reality of poverty and pursue better economic development with high-tech industries. The ecological crisis and economic development problems have triggered conflicts which have led to cooperation among local officials and entrepreneurs.

A city near the capital

Baoding is a city with a history of more than 4,000 years (Hu & Liu, 2008). It is about 150 km away from Beijing. Both lie on the middle of Northern China Plain.[1] Traditionally, Baoding is the southern door to Beijing; it has been the capital city of the province of Hebei several times before Shijiazhuang became the capital in 1968. These geographical and historical factors serve as both advantages and disadvantages for Baoding.

On the one hand, as a city near Beijing—the political, economic, and cultural center of China—Baoding has greater access than other cities to certain resources of the central government. On the other hand, it is outcompeted by Beijing and Tianjin (another provincial-level city) for many resources, such as young talents. As a local state, Baoding's economy lags far behind that of Beijing and Tianjin. In 2017, the per capita GDP of Beijing was four times that of Baoding and the per capita GDP of Tianjin was 3.87 times that of Baoding (BaodingGov, 2018; Beijing Statistical Bureau, 2018; Tianjin Statistical Bureau, 2018). Similarly, in the political hierarchy, it is lower than Beijing and Tianjin.

The impact of this lower ranking could be observed during the 2008 Olympic Games in Beijing; Baoding had to close down many of its polluting factories and enterprises in order to assure a "*lantian*" or "blue sky" for Beijing (Qian, Ge, Wu, Qiu, 2013, C. Zhang, 2008).[2] All in all, Baoding stands in the shadow of the other two cities.

Baoding has administrative control over many counties surrounding the city, which means it has a vast countryside and most of its population is made up of farmers. This study will focus on not only its central city area, but also the countryside that is impacted during the expansion of the city. The farmers are human resources for industrial development in Baoding. Baoding also has several universities which provide the work force for Baoding's development. One of them is the North China Electric Power University (NCEPU), which is the leading Chinese university in the fields of power generation and electricity engineering. The NCEPU has dense social connections to their university graduates who later become the managers in Chinese energy sectors.[3]

From an interviewee, who is an entrepreneur in Baoding, Baoding's economic structure can be generalized as "Southern car, Northern electricity, Eastern textile, Western green and city culture."[4] Culture is often pointed out as an important factor in Baoding's development (interview 5). Baoding has many historical heritages. In the old city district, there is "*Dacige*" (Great Mercy Tower), a Buddhist symbol; there is "*Gu lianhuachi*" which was the famous "lotus" school in the late Qing dynasty; and "*Zhili zongdufu*," which was a historic provincial-level government office building in the Qing dynasty.[5] The rich culture of Baoding is the reason why the locals are generally proud of their heritage and this serves as a rich social connection for locals. Ma Xuelu, a key advisor for the local leaders as discussed below, is a keen promoter of green development and actively gathered local stories and edited books about local culture.

Ecological crisis at the Baiyangdian Lake

Ecological crises can be strong signals to urge humans to change their behaviors and consider the ecological impact of economic development. Baoding is well known for the heavily polluted Baiyangdian Lake in its territory. The pollution is a result of Baoding's traditional fur, feather, and dyeing industries (Zhao & Wu, 2010).[6] The Baoding municipal government is in charge and responsible for the protection of the Baiyangdian Lake and thus responsible for its pollution. Baiyangdian Lake and its wetland have frequently been used as a case for many water pollution studies and ecological protection studies (C. Chen, Pickhardt, Xu, & Folt, 2008; Dou & Zhao, 1998; Y. Li, Cui, & Yang, 2004; M. Xu et al., 1998; Yang, Li, Wang, Gui, & Shang, 2005).[7]

The pollution of Baiyangdian started quite early, even before the reform and opening-up. Research on its pollution control program started in the 1970s (Lv & Gao, 2007). Baiyangdian then entered a cycle of "treating and polluting." One significant phenomenon is the mass death of fish in the Baiyangdian Lake. It occurs almost every year, but it peaked in 2000 and 2006 (*China Daily*, 2006; Saiget, 2006). The domestic and international media reported on the serious pollution which has attracted worldwide attention. The people around Baiyangdian Lake are fishermen and their interests are hurt by the pollution. There are several arguments about the reason why fish are dying, but to the people in Baoding it is obvious; the fish die after Baoding's periodical discharge of waste water. Baoding has built several reservoirs to hold waste water and then discharge it into the lake at certain times (Gao, 2006). Complaints against this practice are common in Baoding. People complain to the city government or complain over the Internet to gain support. The scale of these complaints has become so big that the central government became involved in 2006 and punished several local officials (H. Xu, 2006).

Awareness of these ecological crises has reached the Baoding government through complaints by local people, the media, and the central government. When the pollution happened in 2006, it was also the time the new mayor, Yu Qun, was appointed to Baoding.[8] He did not have any choice; the only way to solve the pollution problem was to close hundreds of small-scale polluting factories. This was not only a great shock to the local economy, but it also bruised Baoding's reputation in front of the whole world. Yu Qun made up his mind to transform Baoding's economic structure and shifted his focus to the Baoding National Hi-tech Zone (HTZ).

Creator of national HTZ at Baoding

In the 1980s, Baoding's economy developed rapidly, such as the booming of TVEs and private businesses (Baoding Policy Research Center, 1989). These businesses mainly rely on natural resources and are labor intensive (Tian, 1987). In 1991, the director of policy research under the Baoding CCP committee, Ma Xuelu, wrote a report to develop high-tech industries in Baoding which aroused a hot debate among Baoding's leadership (F. Ma, 2009; interview 3). It is going to provide some answers to a general puzzle about how a relatively poor and medium-sized city could be able to develop high-tech industries compared with big cities like Beijing and Tianjin.

Mr. Ma wrote an application for national HTZ to the Ministry of Science and Technology (MoST) and, with the same aim to start a new technology revolution, Baoding HTZ was approved by the MoST in 1992 (interview 3; MoST, 2001; Zhou, 2010).[9] And Mr. Ma became the director of Baoding HTZ. The Baoding HTZ management committee received about 12 km^2 of land and enjoyed preferential policies (Xiao, 2004). It thus became a new area with a management committee in charge of its development. In 1995, Baoding National HTZ Development Co., Ltd was set up to manage the development of HTZ. To an extent, these industrial development zones are like enterprises in the name of the national push for science and technology innovation.

Ma is a reform-minded local official. He won the attention of central economic reformers because he was the first person who published an article about enterprise mergers and acquisitions in 1988 (F. Ma, 2009; X. Ma & Shi, 1988). When the approval from the central government arrived, Mr. Ma claimed he got the land and a small sum of money (4,000 RMB), but little direction from the central government. Indeed, from 1992 to 1997 he had no clear idea which industry to develop, since the requirements of the central government were very abstract at the time (interview 3). Everything was in an experimental stage then. The Baoding HTZ management committee attempted to build the infrastructures, and, as Ma called it, turned the raw land into flourishing landscape (*shengdi biancheng shudi*). In developing the area Ma followed the trends of other high-tech industrial zones; with little adoption of practices suited to local conditions, the development did not go well (Zhou, 2010). Ma left the HTZ in April 1998 and worked as the director of the government department of economic research until 2000. During this time, Ma was concerned about the development of the HTZ and gained more information and knowledge about Baoding's industrial and economic development conditions (F. Ma, 2009). At the end of 2000, the HTZ received a yellow card from the MoST because of its poor performance (Zhou, 2010). Baoding HTZ did not differ itself from Baoding's other areas, it was still labor-intensive and had businesses without high technologies (Shin, 2017). At this point, Ma was called back to the HTZ as the director of the management committee. With his renewed involvement, the Baoding HTZ survived and even increased its size to 60 km^2. The next section will explain this surprising turnaround.

Now, Baoding's National HTZ is more modern than the rest of the city, with broader roads and higher buildings. A local, who is an entrepreneur and familiar with Baoding, said that Baoding HTZ is for high-tech industries with high-class residences and has a Central Business District with luxury hotels. It gave a strong "yes" answer to the question whether a small and medium-sized city is able to develop its own high-tech industries.

Local leaders' search for an alternative and suitable development path

The saviors of the Baoding National HTZ are Miao Liansheng and Mr. Ma. Miao is a local entrepreneur who first had the idea to develop solar energy and created the first solar company in Baoding. Mr. Ma is a local official who first had the idea to build HTZ in Baoding. Both are very innovative persons and they have been friends for a long time (interview 3). As already mentioned, at first as the leader of Baoding HTZ, Mr. Ma did not know which industry would be suitable to develop in Baoding's HTZ; it was Miao who delivered his ideas to Mr. Ma through a talk that lasted for three days and nights (interview 3; Zhou, 2010). It is a common problem of the local leaders that they usually held certain important resources, such as land and capital, but they did not know how to use these resources to develop high-tech businesses in their governing regions. It is usually the entrepreneurs who are creatively searching for suitable industries according to the local context.

80 *Baoding*

In this account, we see the innovative role of Miao as an entrepreneur and his utilization of his social capital to gain the support of Ma, the key leader of HTZ. This section will describe how entrepreneur Miao chose the solar energy industry and why he came to director Ma to share his ideas about solar energy. Was Miao not afraid that Ma would reveal his business ideas to other entrepreneurs or start his own company?

Innovative ideas of entrepreneurs on solar energy

Miao Liansheng was the first person to suggest solar energy for Baoding National HTZ. Miao's company, Yingli, is a leading solar PV company and has customers all around the world. Miao has successfully seized the "green" opportunity and set up firms to develop a foothold market. Miao Liansheng's story is well covered in the media, and other interviewees were able to answer many questions about him. His experiences demonstrate the innovative role of entrepreneurs and their dependency on local officials.

Miao was one of those "jumping into the sea" (*xiahai*), a cadre-entrepreneur (Guo, 2011), who were members in the stable government system and later became entrepreneurs in the market. These *xiahai* entrepreneurs have displayed their talents in the market after the introduction of the reform and opening-up policies. Miao was demobilized from the army in the 1980s, which was regarded as a good work place or "*danwei*" (unit) which guarantees welfare and a stable life. Broadly, the army is also an important place for nurturing social capital because of the significant trust established between soldiers. As an entrepreneur, Miao was full of the entrepreneurial spirit that was able to move on from the old socialist institutions and he took risks in new ways to gain more wealth.

In 1987, Miao created his company, Yingli, and became involved in different businesses, like cosmetics and "green" vegetables. Many of them were successful, but Miao did not think they were strategic industries. He read an article about the promising future of solar energy from the *Economic Daily*, and soon after that he tried his best to get all the information available about solar energy, attending international conferences and ultimately becoming an expert himself (P. Chen, 2010).[10] With his knowledge, Miao turned this business idea into action.

First, Miao imported a production line from Japan to produce solar neon light. As an entrepreneur, he took a risk in developing his solar energy industry. In 1993 he gave up his other businesses and invested all his money in the startup Yingli Green Energy (He, 2007). This was the first step in a business attempt full of risks.

Miao's company suffered from the imperfection of the market at the beginning of reform and opening-up, but also enjoyed the advantage of social capital with local officials. Miao's Yingli was a private firm and lacked the quality to gain loans from banks at that time. In 1996, Miao saw opportunity in a solar project in "Western Development." This project was funded by the Chinese National Development Bank. As a private firm, Yingli's chances of getting into the project were small (He, 2007). Thus, Miao had to gain the support of the local government and became a "red hat entrepreneur," (i.e., closely related to the communist party). He decided to find a local official with whom he could establish mutual trust. He used his social capital or *guanxi* to connect with Ma Xuelu.

Local officials supporting green development

As Ma was worried about the fate of Baoding's National HTZ, his meeting with Miao gave him new ideas to save the HTZ that he had created and hopes to realize the aim to develop high-tech industries in a relatively poor and medium-sized city.[11] Ma acclaimed it was his first time to hear about solar energy from Mr. Miao. Miao's talk of solar energy illuminated a clear way forward for Baoding's HTZ. The HTZ could be the first to develop renewable industries. Ma picked up this innovative idea and started to gather information about solar energy and other renewable energies. Ma can be interpreted as an entrepreneur, not in the market, but in the political sphere. As a political entrepreneur and local official, Ma can obtain more information and resources regarding renewable energy development and policies. With a clear blueprint of HTZ's strategy of renewable energy industries, Ma tried his best in his ability to mobilize resources to realize it.

He started to attract renewable energy companies to the area and supported innovative entrepreneurs. It is important to note that Ma is a highly educated and open-minded official, and eager to learn ideas from the outside world. He is a scholarly official who likes reading and writing articles about economics, science, and technological development (interview 3).[12] Baoding HTZ purposely made connections with central government institutes, scientists, national labs, as well as industrial associations related to renewable energy (Shin, 2017). It is widely known that Baoding HTZ clearly supports renewable industries and differed itself from other national HTZs. The Baoding HTZ became famous for its special focus on renewable energy industries and received recognition from the central government and the MoST.

In creating the industry, Ma and his team at HTZ grasped the opportunities to visit Western countries and learn about their renewable energy practices. At the same time, he was chosen as a delegate of China to attend conferences about renewable energy around the world (interview 3). Through these experiences he came to know more about renewable energy and became more confident in it. As the leader in charge of the Baoding National HTZ, he began to divert all those preferential policies with principles to support the local renewable energy industry (Renminwang, 2011).

Ma also had a high environmental awareness when he made industrial policies. When he directed the Baoding HTZ in 1992, he put three principles forward: first, to try to import high-tech industry; second, to not permit polluting industries; and third, to try to become an innovation center to nurture new and primary technology and put them into production (Hu & Liu, 2008). It is easier for Ma to accept the ideas of renewable energy due to its close relationship with climate change as well as environmental protection. He clearly argued that China should not follow the Western industrial way and should instead find its own road. His stance was supported by his knowledge of the history of Baoding; he advocated for maintaining the traditional agricultural and forest civilization rather than realizing an industrial civilization fully. Ma specifically expected a better future for his hometown.

Ma trusted Miao's idea and helped him with full support. Miao and Ma's talk was a talk between two friends with trust and appreciating each other's ideas for a better future of Baoding, which led to concrete cooperation between them to develop the renewable energy industry.

Close cooperation with deep trust between local officials and entrepreneurs

The following section is about how local officials and entrepreneurs cooperated on the development of solar energy in Baoding. To recap, Miao encouraged Ma to support his idea to develop solar energy and they formed a coalition to promote solar panel productions. In 1998, Ma mobilized his resources to support Miao's plan; with his support Miao was able to reconstruct Yingli to a public enterprise by selling a 60% share to the Baoding HTZ Development Company investment branch. At that time, Ma said Yingli was only worth about one million RMB, and even though the Baoding High-tech Development Company invested 600,000 RMB, 60% of Yingli, Yingli was "nationally owned but privately managed" (*guoyou konggu minying jizhi*). This means that Baoding High-tech did not intervene in the actual running of Yingli Green Energy, and the power of Yingli was still in the hands of Miao. Ma just sent one young graduate to Yingli to represent the role of Baoding HTZ (interview 3).

Miao applied for and planned to buy a production line for the Solar Program in Sichuan Aba for the Western Development project in 1999. This project was approved but later Miao had a shortage of capital. At this critical moment, the Baoding HTZ invested additional resources, in the form of capital and land in Yingli; doing so helped Yingli to get into the national high-tech industry pilot program to build up solar power in rural areas. Yingli received 20 million RMB in subsidies from the NDRC and a 50 million RMB loan from the Provincial Economic and Technology Financial Guarantee Company (J. Wang, 2009). This financial investment gave Miao the resources to continue developing the Yingli Green Energy Company.

Yet, another business risk soon tested Miao and Ma's cooperation. In 2001, Ma's HTZ Investment Company which is the guarantee for Yingli, was sued for double guarantee with the same company by the Trade and Industry Management Bureau for bad assets of about 80 million RMB (interview 3). Ma's HTZ Investment Company eventually won the case, but at the time it made it difficult for Yingli Green Energy to allocate enough capital. The cooperation between Miao and Ma was in crisis.

To overcome this crisis, Ma utilized his *guanxi* to introduce Ding Qiang, the chief of the old and large state-owned Tianwei Group, to Miao. Tianwei is a leading state-owned enterprise manufacturing power transformers and equipment. In 2001, Tianwei Baobian was listed in the Shanghai Stock Exchange market as a strong company (He, 2007). In 2002, Ding Qiang bought Baoding HTZ Investment Company's Yingli share, and Yingli Green Energy became Tianwei Yingli in 2001, still under the management principle, nationally owned but privately managed (*guoyou konggu minying jizhi*).[13] Tianwei Yingli grew stronger with the help of the stronger state-owned company. Tianwei brought new capital, human labor, and technology to Yingli. An interviewee said that Tianwei also has a close relationship with German companies. Tianwei introduced Yingli to the German solar energy technology and market. What is more, many talented people changed from other parts of Tianwei Group to the solar energy company Tianwei Yingli. With this support and help from Tianwei, Tianwei Yingli rapidly developed its solar PV industry.

Besides Yingli, Ma independently cooperated with other entrepreneurs in the renewable energy industries as well. Ma started to support and give preferential policies to renewable energy. As he wrote, "under the face of resource depletion and ecological crisis, the replacement of traditional energy by renewable energy is an inevitable choice" (X. Ma, 2007). In 2001, Ma started to promote the Zhonghang Huiteng Wind Energy Company. In 2000 this company patented an invention from the Baoding Huiyang Aviation Propeller Factory, a 600kW large-scale wind turbine blade. With Tianwei Yingli and Huiteng in the Baoding HTZ Ma applied for the MoST's call for the renewable energy and energy equipment manufacturing base in 2002. That is how Baoding HTZ got its name as the first base for renewable energy and energy equipment; this made it different from other high-tech parks.

Ma explained that although the renewable brand did not bring any concrete funds or other material benefits, it did open a window for Baoding to contact the outside world. Since 2002, Ma has had many opportunities to attend domestic and international exhibitions and conferences; he also visited some forerunner countries to observe their progress in renewable energies. Gradually Ma entered the renewable energy field and developed a corresponding social network domestically and in the international community.

Ma also organized and connected several renewable energy magazines and associations. He has connections to the national governmental official—Shi Lishan, a key figure in China's renewable energy development.[14] In 2003, China's Guodian Corporation Group entered the Baoding HTZ and established Guodian United Power, a state-owned high-tech company focusing on the green energy industry and a leading supplier of total solutions of wind turbine generator systems.

Despite these early successes, the coalition's consensus on renewable energy was very controversial within Baoding's local government and even within the national government. The Baoding HTZ was the first pioneer and the future of renewable energy was not clear at that time. Many local government officials did

84 *Baoding*

not treat the renewable energy industry seriously. The resources, capacity, and power that Ma could mobilize were limited without the support of the local government. This situation began to change in 2006, because of Baoding's new mayor, Yu Qun.

Pulling resources for one industry

Before 2006, there were disagreements and different opinions from some leaders in the Baoding municipal government and even from members of the Baoding HTZ management team (Tang, 2009). All the projects happening in Baoding HTZ were only a part of Baoding's economy, Baoding's other industries included automobile and textile industries; the renewable energy industry was not the central industry as defined by the Baoding local government. After an ecological crisis—pollution in Baiyangdian Lake—the Baoding local government has shifted its position on renewable energy. When the crisis happened, Yu Qun was the new mayor; he visited the lake and talked to local people about the changes he would make for Baiyangdian. Yu then adopted Ma's suggestion and pushed for a strong local development strategy in the form of the Electric Valley of China (EVC). This was followed by many innovative policies in Baoding, which also resulted in a rapid development process for Baoding HTZ.

Recognition of the local leader

Yu Qun was elected as mayor on January 14, 2006 by Baoding's local people's congress. Yu had seen the pollution in person and concluded at the Baiyangdian Lake Pollution Integrated Treatment Emergency Mobilization Conference that "only caring about the short-term economic interests, neglecting the ecological environment and people's interest lead to the pollution problem. This behavior displayed a failure and dereliction of duties or even a criminal act" (Xinjingbao, 2006). In order to fight pollution in Baoding, Yu closed about 400 factories, which lowered the region's GDP by 2%. In 2006, Yu also signed a responsibility contract called "Baoding's responsibility for main pollutant amount reduction in the 11th Five Year Plan" at a provincial-level environmental protection conference (C. Zhang, 2006).[15] The costs of environmental pollution had made all of Baoding's municipal governmental officials aware of the problems in the old economic structure (Lovins & Cohen, 2011).

As Yu Qun searched for an alternative long-term economic growth pathway for the region, the Baoding HTZ caught Yu's attention. It had achieved obvious progress in solar PV and windmill productions by 2006. Ma specifically suggested that Yu concentrate on renewable energy industries since they are more environmentally friendly than traditional industries as well as some potential high-tech industries, such as the automobile industry, and have a brighter economic future (Tang, 2009). Furthermore, Baoding can differentiate itself from other cities by supporting renewable energy industries.

In 2006, China's Renewable Energy Law had just been published, but it was not clear how long renewable energy development would take to have real applications. Renewable energy overall was very controversial. Seeking to learn more about renewable energy, Yu visited Great Britain, Spain, and Germany, which were, at that time, the leading countries in renewable energy and environmental-friendly technologies (Baodingwaishiban, 2006). After this trip, Yu concluded that the application of renewable energy would be broader than what was currently being considered in China and the world. Yu also got support from his former leader, the provincial CCP secretary, Bai Keming (Tang, 2009). All these factors strengthened Yu's will to develop renewable energy in Baoding.

Yu's devotion to or belief in renewable energy was also reflected in his articles and speeches; since 2006, he has become nationally known as the renewable energy mayor. He gave a powerful voice to renewable energy and declared that 21st century is the age for China's ecological civilization, the nation was waiting for a renewable energy revolution, and it was a development opportunity that was more relevant than ever before (Shi, 2008). He also gave a speech titled "Renewable Energy Industry Under Crisis" at the Tsinghua University and encouraged his audience to respect nature, be grateful to nature, and live with nature in harmony (W. Chen & Wang, 2009). He has written articles to explain his belief in the promising future of renewable energy. Yu published an article in the *Economic Daily* stating that renewable energy will be the main source of the next cycle of economic growth, the fourth industrial revolution (Yu, 2009).

His core concept for the development of Baoding was that the old mode "first development and then clean up" from the reform and opening-up period is wrong; he further argued that pollution should be avoided altogether, highlighting how Baoding could be different from Beijing, Tianjing, and Hebei Zone (C. Zhang, 2008). His management of Baoding was widely reported in the media for his appreciation of innovation and science. In 2007, Baoding became a solar city.

Yu Qun's addition to the renewable energy industry coalition has helped to mobilize more resources for the renewable energy development in Baoding.[16] Miao was able to mobilize resources in the market, Ma could gather resources around the HTZ, and finally Yu was able to mobilize many different resources from the local government to support renewable energy. As the local leader of Baoding, Yu's decision to commit to supporting the development of renewable energy had a significant impact.

Baoding's green development strategy: Electric Valley of China

In 2006, the Baoding municipal government issued its development strategy, which called for the development of the EVC, and a focus on the new energy sources and equipment necessary for it, such as solar energy and wind energy (F. Wang & Wang, 2008). This project was defined as the most important area of focus in Baoding's Eleventh and Twelfth Five-Year Plan development and industrial program. How did Baoding realize and support the EVC?

86 *Baoding*

First, Baoding promulgated local favorable policies for renewable industries. On November 21, 2006, the local government issued a notice titled "Several Regulations on Encouraging Investment in the EVC" to all city departments and the Baoding HTZ (BaodingGov, 2006). It contained 16 articles which explicitly described policies to support the EVC. The notice clearly defined what are the industries in the EVC: wind, bio-fuel, and other new energy storage materials, power transmission, automation, and high-efficiency power manufacturing enterprises. All enterpriscs were registered with Baoding HTZ management and enjoyed the national high-tech zone preference policies, as well as the favor of local policies. One key feature of these local regulations was to reduce local financial interests and return to the enterprises. Baoding also actively generated resources for the EVC. One way it did this was through the supply of land. The city gained and distributed land usage rights through skillful land transfers from farmers to entrepreneurs.

Second, this approach to promote EVC was complemented by the governmental incentive system for implementation of renewable industries. This policy not only stipulated an incentive system in the local government to reduce resistance and dissent among Baoding's government officials, but also described how the responsibilities and work are distributed among different government departments and appointed key officials. Baoding's local CCP Party Committee and city government together issued an article titled "Opinions about Speeding-up and Advancing Baoding's EVC Construction and Implementation" (Baoding-GOV, 2006). It discussed about the urgency of developing the EVC.

The mayor, Yu, was primarily involved in making the EVC successful on a broader basis, getting all the local officials to work as if they were part of a political movement or enterprises with a clear aim rather than an administrative body. The EVC's main ideas and strategies were organized around energy conservation, sustainable development, and the implementation of recycling as well as keeping up with new power generation technology and equipment. It identified six industry groups all related to renewable energy and energy efficiency, namely solar energy, wind energy, energy-saving, energy storage, power transmission, and automatic equipment.

The EVC further lays out a policy to help entrepreneurs to obtain land for these businesses. One important land transfer was to change the place where the Datang Coal Power Station dumps its soot and dust, to the wind park industrial zone. This change improved the local environment and was praised by local people.

In article five, the role of advertisement was stressed. The proposed slogan was "Let China know EVC, let the world be aware of EVC, let projects settle down in EVC, let EVC go outside to the world." In article six, the ways to accumulate capital for EVC were explained.

The article which follows is about how to build a solar city, and how to encourage EVC to define the new local culture. Baoding set up an EVC Construction and Promotion Committee, led by the party secretary and mayor. Under the Committee were four groups: a coordination group, a project plan group, a land plan group, and an advertising and business attraction group. Each group included almost all of the government departments or institutional resources that Baoding could command. The notice also stressed the Baoding government's responsibility and set up incentives and punishment institutions.

Various resources have been mobilized to invest in EVC. Two main resources are used as indicators, namely land and capital. Land is a physical indicator which describes the pattern of local development and ecological impact. Baoding HTZ has grown from a size of 12 km^2 to 120 km^2 after the EVC, 10 times larger than before. The Baoding HTZ as an enterprise receives more land resources because of the EVC policy. Consequently, it can support the enterprises in its zone by providing cheap land to them.

As land is publicly owned, it is quite difficult for an entrepreneur to get land without the support of the local government. Take the Yingli Green Energy Group as an example; Yingli has received 500 mu (about 33 hectares) to start its third project which expanded its production ability to 500 MV.

In terms of capital, the Baoding local government cooperated with China South Industries Group Corporation (CSIGC) a strong nationally owned enterprise which annexed Tianwei Group and signed a contract to build EVC in partnership. The details were laid out initially by the Eleventh Five-Year Plan, which stated that the investment should reach 12 billion RMB; in the Twelfth Five-Year Plan, the target investment in CSIGC was set even higher, at 30 billion RMB (G. Xu, Wang, & Xu, 2007). In the process of obtaining capital for Yingli, the Baoding government decided to step back from the company and allow Yingli to go to the New York stock market to raise capital in 2007.[17] The Baoding government also held an EVC promotion in 2007 in Hong Kong to raise capital; it was widely reported on by the media in Hong Kong and secured seven projects (Y. Zhang, 2007). With this initial success, it soon became an annual promotion event.

These efforts demonstrated Baoding's commitment to supporting renewable energy industries as its strategic long-term development strategy. But how, exactly, are their efforts being realized in the Baoding HTZ?

Development of renewable energy industries

Baoding's early engagement in renewable energy paid off. Not only did Baoding, as a first mover, profit from the international demand, but it also profited from national policies. The demand for renewable energy products in the national market rose significantly after the central government issued regulations to raise the share of renewable energy in the national energy production mix. These regulations included the Renewable Energy Laws, the Medium- and Long-term Plans for Renewable Energy, and other supplementary policies. As a result, the EVC has benefited in the market, politics, and society.

From the market perspective, the Baoding HTZ had a rapid development period and is now a successful model for a renewable energy industry group (Rasmus, 2008; L.-Y. Zhang, 2015). Despite the financial crisis, Baoding HTZ had a growth rate of over 50% from 2006 to 2009. The Baoding HTZ is at the top of the list in Baoding, and even Hebei Province, in tax revenue, added industrial value, export volume, and actual utilization of foreign capital. The income from products sold and the foreign exchange earned both doubled from 2006 to 2007 (Dong & Gu, 2008a). Yingli in 2008 had a global share of 12%, making it one of the biggest companies in solar PVs. Yingli has also been competitive in domestic solar projects; Yingli offered the lowest bidding price to the Dunhuang solar PV project with 0.60 RMB/kW (Yingli, 2009). Yingli is also actively involved in the Golden Sun Project.[18]

As of 2010, there were more than 200 renewable energy companies settled in Baoding. The region has become a manufacturing base combining with wind power, solar power generation, power transmission equipment, and new energy storage devices. Among these industries, more than 60 companies are related to solar energy, such as the Baoding Tianwei Solar-film, the Dazheng Solar Photoelectric Equipment Manufacture Company, and Victory. In the wind-power industry, there are more than 76 wind-power generation equipment manufacturers which cover everything from wind-power generators, wind blades, control systems, towers, and supporting services. The wind energy sectors are dominated by state-owned companies, such as Guodian United Power, the AVIC Huiteng Wind-power Equipment, and CSIGC. Their achievements have been widely reported on by the domestic and international media. These companies raised Baoding's reputation and changed Baoding's image as a polluting region to a sustainable region.

In terms of politics, the Baoding HTZ has been praised by the central government. In 2007, it was branded as a "national solar energy production integrated application pilot city" and a "national renewable energy industrialization base" by MoST. In 2008, it was chosen as a "national high-tech industry—renewable energy industry base" by the NDRC, the Ministry of Business and Trade, and MoST. In 2010, Baoding was included in the national low-carbon pilot program which included five provinces and eight cities.[19] It appears that Baoding is a pioneer in low-carbon development and a rising political star which has taken up the central government's call for scientific development. Now, Baoding receives many projects from the central government to help realize its EVC development and help it to become a low-carbon city. In 2017, the eastern part of Baoding became the Xiong'an New Area which made Baoding's green development more influential. The EVC strategy has also changed the local society in certain ways.

Baoding received a new brand name for its renewable energy (Tang, 2009). The names of solar companies, wind companies, and of course, Yingli, have become the names of streets and bus stops. Renewable energy as a concept is familiar to many in this middle-sized city compared to the rest of China, since many local people work in the renewable energy companies. The local government has also set up vocational-technical schools to train workers for the renewable energy companies. NCEPU has set up the first renewable energy college to meet the new work force demands. The removal of the dust from coal power factories has improved the quality of the environment in Baoding and the strong advertising campaign by the Baoding government has made a deep impression on the local people as projects that improve the local environment (interviews 6 & 7).

The EVC strategy is essentially an industrial strategy aimed at the transformation of the old local economy from textile and automobile to renewable energy industries and the increase in its competitiveness in the external market (Lovins & Cohen, 2011). Baoding's government has not limited its development strategy to its industrial policies. It has also strongly advocated for the application of renewable energy products and the concept of low-carbon development within the region.

Green city projects

After Baoding focused its development strategy on the EVC in 2006, it subsequently began to build the first solar city. Ultimately it advocated for becoming a low-carbon city. The previous section described the EVC strategy as an effort to improve renewable energy production. This section will focus on the application of these renewable energy products in the city itself as an effort to realize a low-carbon city with low-carbon lifestyle.

The solar city

Baoding started planning a solar city in 2007, to promote the applications of solar energy in lighting, hot water, and heating. Officially, this policy was aimed at realizing energy conservation and emissions reduction goals.

The initiatives to build a solar city are reflected in the government document "Baoding's Government's Opinions about Implementation of Constructing Solar City" (BaodingGOV, 2007). This document discusses the importance of solar energy to Baoding's future and offers some guiding thoughts. In planning a solar city, Baoding aimed to be a frontrunner and model for application of solar energy technology. The local government document precisely describes the application areas and which products are to be used. The application sites are primarily governmental buildings and departments. Like the EVC strategy, plans for solar city development mobilized the Baoding government resources to reach key goals.

These plans were also carried out in the rural areas of Baoding as ecological village building projects. Public facilities, some government-affiliated enterprises, and working units, "*danwei*," are also included. To guarantee proper implementation work, Baoding has set up a coordination group (Dong & Gu, 2008b; Zhu & Zhu, 2006). Baoding's government has also held a promotion conference aimed at all governments and their governing bodies. At this conference, the local leader announced his plan to account for 30% of the region's energy demand with solar energy by 2030; and replace 50% of conventional energy used by 2050. The plan gave numerous examples of how industrialized countries use light emitting diodes (LEDs) instead of conventional light bulbs; it advocated for the potential of solar energy as "a thousand times" more than that of the Three Gorges Dam, the world's largest hydropower station; and it defined the economic and ecological benefits of solar energy to the people (Baodingribao, 2007).

In Baoding there are solar PVs up on the traffic lights along the streets. These are one part of the Solar City project. In-depth reports about some pilot programs mention the Jinjiang EVC hotel which is covered with solar PVs (Dong & Gu, 2008c). This project demonstrates the application of PVs on buildings, namely the Building Integrated Photovoltaics (BIPV) technology. There are several other projects following the same principles. Many factory buildings in the Baoding High-tech Zone now also have integrated BIPV.

Another application of the Solar City project is in a residential area. The New Century Residence has adopted a solar street-lighting system with LEDs and 500 solar thermal devices to reduce overall carbon emission (K. Wang & Yan, 2008). In response to growing awareness of climate change, this program has developed beyond its ambitious 2006 targets.

The low-carbon city

In 2008, Baoding was highlighted by the WWF for its low-carbon city initiative pilot program to reduce carbon emissions (WWF, 2008). Baoding has been recognized as a carbon-positive as it exports renewable products to help the world to reduce carbon emissions (Lovins & Cohen, 2011; WWF, 2012). This cooperation with WWF has been actively cultivated by the Baoding local government. The WWF is regarded as an international partner who has brought global attention to Baoding.[20] To support this relationship, Baoding has attended the WWF low-carbon city initiative since 2007. Since then, Baoding has adopted low-carbon concepts which are much broader than the Solar City program and which have captured the essence of the EVC strategy and Baoding's renewable energy industry.

Baoding is the first Chinese city to have proposed its own carbon reduction targets and to have its own low-carbon city plan. These targets are written into the local government regulation titled "Baoding's Government's Opinions about Constructing Low-carbon City (for trial implementation)" on December 23, 2008 (BaodingGOV, 2008). The local government claimed, by 2020, the carbon emission intensity of GDP was reduced by 35% compared to 2010 emissions levels, the per capita carbon emission will be under control with 5.5 tons, and the value of industrial output of renewable energy industries will reach 25% of the total.

In this document, Baoding advocates restructuring the energy mix, developing a low-carbon industry, raising the research and development (R&D) of low-carbon technologies and its application, boosting the recycling industry and clean production. In order to realize a low-carbon society, Baoding aims to raise awareness of the importance of a low-carbon lifestyle and a low-carbon city construction; in order to realize low-carbon management, it stresses the importance of energy conservation and emission-reduction tasks in the rural areas, industries, buildings, transports, and trade within its jurisdiction.

There are seven key projects to carry out these tasks, namely the EVC, the solar city, the ecological city, the office building low-carbon running pilot program, the low-carbon residence pilot program, and the low-carbon traffic integrated system. This document does not mention the responsibilities for each sector. It is more abstract than the EVC and solar city documents.

In 2010, Baoding's Party Committee and Baoding government promulgated another document titled "Baoding Guidance Opinions about Low-carbon City Construction" (Baoding Shiwei & BaodingGOV, 2010). At this time the targets shifted so that the carbon-emission intensity of the GDP will be reduced by 35% by 2015 and by 48% by 2020 compared to 2005 emissions levels. Public participation and private neighborhoods are included in these targets as well. The low-carbon industries will be expanded to include modern manufacturing, the service industry, agricultural production, and the automobile industry. This document also does not specify the distribution of work, nor was there a promotion conference held on how to build the low-carbon city described in the document. Despite the expansion of low-carbon industries in this year's guiding document, the leading role of renewable energy seems to be shifting in Baoding.

During the fieldwork for this book in 2012, the slogans and advertisements about low-carbon development in Baoding city disappeared. One civil service member in the Baoding CCP mentioned that the slogan disappeared when the last leader Yu, left office. Yu left Baoding and joined the Ministry of Culture at the central government in 2009. Ma has also retired from the position as the director of Baoding HTZ in 2009. After several strategic wrong decisions, Miao also stepped down from the Chief Executive Officer (CEO) of Yingli in 2016, Yingli is now still in fiscal crisis. With the loss of the key leaders and their efforts in green development in Baoding, Baoding's green development is in shadow.

Baoding's green development strategy did not solve the city's serious pollution problem (L.-Y. Zhang, 2015). It is often listed as the city with the worst air quality by the MEP. This greatly challenged its image as a low-carbon city.

Guanxi and actors in Baoding's green development

Baoding's former leader, Yu Qun, learned from ecological crisis, and led the construction of the EVC, the solar city, and the low-carbon city. Baoding's entrepreneurs and local officials' efforts were reflected in the numerous innovative industrial policies, their search for partners, and their utilization of their social capital to spur resources investment to Baoding's green development. Some interviewees disagree that Baoding is a green city given its high energy inefficiency and energy-intensive industries. Even some scholars in Baoding doubt the green development efforts; they have concluded that Baoding is a fake low-carbon city, and that real low-carbon cities exist only in industrialized EU countries (interview 9). As a relatively poor city with a large agricultural population, and a disadvantaged position in high-tech energy, Baoding's efforts in green development should not be judged by ideal low-carbon cities, but taking the local context into consideration, the city is astonishing.

Decisive factors for Baoding's low-carbon strategy

Miao's role as a local entrepreneur sparked the renewable energy industry in Baoding, as he had sensed the promising future of solar energy in the global market. His devotion to solar energy made Yingli's success in the market possible. As a Chinese entrepreneur in the 1990s, only his *guanxi* got him the resources necessary for success in his solar energy business. Solar energy is an industry with lots of governmental policies or interventions. Miao's entrepreneurship and *guanxi* helped him to overcome many problems.

Miao's connections helped his company survive the "winter" of solar energy in 2012. During this time other solar companies, like the Sun-tech solar company in Wuxi, went bankruptcy (Z. Wang, 2013).[21] Miao is described as a typical Chinese businessman. He also likes China's army drama and said that he always thinks of himself as a "soldier" (Xue & Kuang, 2010). He has said "when others do not do it, I will do it first; when all others do it, I will not do it" (P. Chen, 2010). Miao is very familiar with the political culture and *guanxi* network and excels in using it to his advantage. His company is one of the backbones of Baoding's low-carbon city.

Miao's spark spread to Ma, a local official, who is not only an entrepreneur in the market but also an innovator in industrial policies. Ma was a local official who has rich knowledge about local conditions which helped him to find the right industrial and entrepreneurial support for the development of Baoding's HTZ. Ma has expanded solar energy, wind energy, and other renewable energy industries. He has used his *guanxi* in setting up the renewable energy industry in Baoding HTZ. By using his access to market resources, political resources, and social resources in his *guanxi* he has nurtured the coalition of renewable energy industries in Baoding HTZ. His love for local culture and Chinese culture and his strong feelings toward ecological degradation have greatly influenced his acceptance of renewable energy. He has a competitive awareness and a long-term perspective towards economic development; he has worked closely with MoST in its "Torch Program" which plans for China to become a technologically advanced nation, instead of remaining a labor-intensive and resource-export nation. Ma has sophisticated knowledge about industrialization, and he does not totally accept industrialization.[22] All those values held by Ma are reflected in his territory, the HTZ.

The third important person in Baoding's decision to become a low-carbon city was Yu. Yu was the mayor and had the power to command many more resources than Ma did in the Chinese political economy context. Yu's acceptance of renewable energy had been fostered by the ecological degradation and Baiyangdian Lake pollution crisis. Local people's complaints were reported in the media and caught the attention of the central government, since Baiyangdian Lake is also near Beijing. The threat of punishment and orders from the central government had Yu not taken action, greatly influenced his political career. After the crisis, the old ways of economic development had been closed and Yu had to search for an alternative economic development mode. Yu had been persuaded by Ma and his own investigation of the future of renewable energy products in the markets of industrialized countries.

In the Chinese context, the export market is an important decision factor for local governments to choose which industry to support. As mayor, Yu had the ability to command resources in Baoding's territory; he managed the region more like a firm so as to benefit the local economy. The Baoding EVC has shifted many different resources into the renewable energy industries. With these efforts, Baoding's renewable energy industries became very competitive not only in the global solar market but also in the domestic wind market.

The EVC is still far from a low-carbon strategy; indeed, it is more like an industrial strategy. It is a common issue of Chinese government low-carbon development that they are made of industrial policies. The fact that Yu decided to build a solar and low-carbon city is based on his desire to support the renewable energy industry. Primarily, he wanted to promote the application of renewable energy products in the market. One of the best ways to do this was to apply these products initially at Baoding; as such, the application of renewable energy products was widely encouraged in Baoding. The policies that supported this can be interpreted as a case of local protectionism.

The second source of motivation is that renewable energy has been emphasized by the central government, and Baoding wanted to be a trailblazer in this new area. The central government had identified renewable energy as a new high-priority technology and put in place some regulations which aimed to raise the percent of renewable energy.

Third, the low-carbon city concept was readily accepted by Baoding's local society. The advantages of a low-carbon city were apparent and interpreted positively by the people. It is environmentally friendly; it helps bring economic growth to Baoding; and it brings special recognition to the city. Many Baoding netizens have been proud of Baoding's competitive spirit which brought glory and attention to this old city once again.

To conclude, the driving force in Baoding's low-carbon city development is the local entrepreneurship and political power, represented by Miao, Ma, and Yu, and their social capital. They collectively mobilized a vast amount of resources to invest in low-carbon city construction. The three entrepreneurs and politicians used their talents in the market, the political positions, and their social capital to realize their goals.

Who gets what? When and how?

Baoding's exploration of green development reflects the core ideas of political ecology in which powerful actors decide what green development is and how it is to be realized. Different powers in a dynamic relationship with one another determine economic and political gains and losses in terms of political economy, but also in terms of ecological gains and benefits. In the following section, the influence of green development, and social and environmental justice issues will be described, in terms of the market, politics, and the environment.

Miao's early recognition of the global green demand for renewable energy products has made him a billionaire and a successful businessman in the global market. Associated with Baoding's positive image, his products are sold to Western countries. The production process for these green products is energy intensive and polluting (Pan, Zhuang, & Zhu, 2006).

For local people, the renewable energy industries provide job opportunities. Yingli has about 10,000 workers; other renewable energy companies and supporting factories have also created jobs for local people. The income of Baoding's local government has also increased to new levels. In terms of market output, it appears to be a win-win situation for all involved.

The huge amount mobilization of local resources into renewable energy industries and little public participation also caused different voices from the local people. The application of renewable energy products is pushed by the local government and not necessarily initiated by local people. Through interviews, many local people think that they have little to do with renewable energy application and low-carbon city; rather they just follow the actions of the government. Some even complained about the darkness of the solar lights, saying that they caused security problems in the city. Baoding's investment of resources in the renewable energy industries has not been very well recorded in China's economic data.

In terms of politics, Baoding green development got the support of the central government and the provincial government. In 2009, Yu was promoted to the central government because of his innovative policies at Baoding. Miao closely cooperated with the Chinese government in the field of solar energy and has since gained many projects from the central government for Baoding, from solar power stations to solar R&D projects. Ma's HTZ has been praised as an innovative example for other high-tech parks and he has won a reputation for his work. After Ma retired in 2009, he became a strategic advisor for Yingli and he continues to represent the company in climate change negotiations.

Baoding HTZ became an example for other industrial parks.[23] There are more and more local governments who now encourage the use of their industrial parks for renewable energy industries. As of 2010, there were more than 100 renewable energy parks.[24] Some entrepreneurs send proposals for setting up renewable energy companies to gain preferential industrial policies and resources, like land, from local governments. They may not really run renewable energy businesses, but instead use the resources they receive for other purposes, such as real estate development. One such case was a fake renewable industrial park, set up to get resources such as land from the collective property and loans from the local bank (Huang, 2012).[25]

Local people who lost their land for economic development are compensated, but the compensation is usually at much lower than market value.[26] To accommodate a relocation of houses at Baoding HTZ, numerous high-rise buildings are under construction. To the farmers, EVC, solar city, and low-carbon city have become new reasons for local governments to urbanize their farmland in a cheap way. In terms of the Chinese context, it is hard to tell if some of the land dedicated to renewable energy development is being used for other purposes, particularly for real estate. The website of Baoding's HTZ advertises land transfers to estate developers.

The usage of political resources is not so transparent, given the low levels of public supervision. The coalition of renewable energy companies and local government officials is a standard of the nature of the Chinese political context. There was a big discussion in Wuxi's Sun-tech and Jiangxi's LDK solar company about whether the local government should retreat from solar companies and let them go bankrupt or use local fiscal resources to continue supporting them.

Finally, the resources used in renewable energy industries are part of the environment, so green development's ecological impact must be considered. First, a significant amount of farmland is developed into industrial parks. The rapid expansion of Baoding HTZ means a rapid process of land loss as well.[27] Second, for the solar PV industry, the process of production is not energy efficient, despite the products being "green." Yingli has been a black sheep that has stopped the Baoding HTZ from reaching the energy-saving and emission-reduction targets set by the Mayor (Q. Wang & Chen, 2010).[28]

The conflict in energy consumption between the local government and Miao was reflected in the Six and Nine silicon material factory. Miao believes in the future of solar energy but his company's competitiveness in the global market was more important to him as an entrepreneur. He was strongly driven by profit-chasing and competition in the market. In order to get cheap silicon material for his solar PV, he has set up the Six and Nine silicon factory at Baoding. This factory has caused problems for other groups in Baoding. Its environmental impact assessment report has not been accepted by Baoding's local government in 2009 (interview 3).[29,30] All local government officials discouraged him from building the Six and Nine at Baoding HTZ, but Miao used his *guanxi* to cut across the Baoding local government and obtain the permit from the provincial government (X. Li & Yang, 2010).

This factory is upwind of Baoding which greatly influenced the environmental quality of the city. After it began production, there were many complaints from local people. One local moaned in a Baidu chat room that the Six and Nine has polluted the primary school of the HTZ; another posted on Tianya, one of the most famous Internet social networks, that Six and Nine has significantly affected the health of local people (Zeilanengnao, 2010). The pollution also negatively impacted housing prices in the area.

As one of the interviewees said, Baoding's HTZ would like to welcome other industries that are more environmentally friendly than the Six and Nine and turn its orientation away from solar energy. She mentioned that the exchange of resources for development is not sustainable and used a very harsh word to conclude it: *duanzi juesun*, which means "die without future generation." The key actors in politics left the Baoding local government, which means the coalition for renewable energy dissolved. It is uncertain if the new local leaders will promote renewable or other industries rather than the solar energy industry. The new leadership considered that the EVC was the political achievement of the last leaders and the new leadership needs new polices and achievement. Another reason is that solar PV production is also energy intensive which makes it difficult for local leaders to meet energy-saving and emission-reduction tasks. In 2009, Ma retired from his position and Mayor Yu was appointed to the central government. What is the future for low-carbon development in Baoding?

How green is Baoding's development?

In international society, Baoding is famous for its strong renewable energy base, which is widely reported on by journalists and researched by scholars. This is exactly the reason why it was chosen by WWF as one of the low-carbon initiatives; such a designation strengthens Baoding's status as an exporter of renewable energy products (WWF, 2008). It is a "carbon-positive city" but it has consumed lots of local energy and resources to support the global renewable energy market.[31] Yingli's success is due to the low price in the market; it is nicknamed a "price butcher" (*jiage tufu*) (C. Wang 2014; Liang & Zhu, 2012). On the one hand, the fast growth of the world's renewable energy has contributed to global green development and the fast growth of Baoding's renewable industries. On the other hand, Baoding's renewable energy is highly dependent on the global market. In this respect, Baoding has done much better than other cities and it is greener than it used to be.

Baoding has supported many wind-power facilities during the period of fast development of wind power. Originally, the NDRC had a "localization" provision requiring that 70% of the components of wind turbines must come from domestic companies in order to receive subsidies in 2005 (Q. Wang, 2010). From 2006 to 2009, the wind companies had a good income, but in 2010, the price of wind facilities lowered, and there were too many products in storage that could not be consumed by the domestic market. To add to this challenge, Baoding continues to face more and more competitions in the domestic market. Still, Baoding has contributed significantly to the renewable energy development. Baoding is included in the low-carbon city and other pilot programs by the central government. In its eyes, Baoding's practices are still green.

Many residents of Baoding do not care about the renewable industries' competition in the world market; they care more about the environmental issues related to these companies and their production. Chatting about Yingli with locals on the train from Baoding to Beijing, many asked me about Yingli's environmental impact. In this respect, many of the green practices advocated by the local government were not sustained after the initial green campaign ended.

While the decision-making process did not include the locals, we can speculate that they would have used those resources for purposes other than solar PV traffic lights. Many locals said these projects are done just for the favor of local officials. One interviewee stated that: Solar PV looks nice on the surface as it produces electricity from sunlight, and thus, it creates a good image for local governments. For these green development projects, local governments are very generous with local public spending (interview 6). On top of this, it seems people know the price of solar PV and they think it is too expensive for Baoding. They think it would be better to use these investments for other public goods, like education.

As this section demonstrated, the low-carbon and solar city projects are green in the eyes of advocates, but not necessarily local people. Still, the efforts by the local renewable energy coalition have made Baoding different from other cities and have made an impact on the city's population.

Conclusion

This case study reveals how a normal city strived to become a low-carbon city. It is an example of how a Chinese city, even a poor one, can invest huge amounts of local resources to transform its traditional industries to renewable industries.

This study highlights the importance of entrepreneurs from different angles. The entrepreneurs are crucial in economic growth, as well as in renewable industries. The industrial countries' green demand has been very important for the Chinese entrepreneurs. They are highly dependent on the global renewable energy market. As the anti-dumping laws and tax increase took effect, many companies entered a difficult period and closed, particularly small and middle-sized companies. From the slogan of Yingli that they will produce solar PV available to the people, there is still hope that the renewable energy industries will focus on the domestic demand.

Second, this study emphasizes the political power of local officials, especially the local leader, in making change in Baoding. The solar city and low-carbon city programs do not concentrate only on the production, but also on consumption. The retirement of Ma and the resignation of Mayor Yu have greatly influenced the entrepreneurs' ability to put resources into green development. We saw the importance of local officials, like Ma and Yu; this suggests that it is very important to influence the local officials on their ecological values. The local officials have the power to mobilize local resources for their aims and projects, which in the case of Baoding changed the appearance of the city in a short time. Local people were removed, and their farmland was urbanized. Local people's opinions had little weight in the decision-making process.

Third, this study has highlighted the possible social and environmental conflicts with green development. The local government justified the confiscation of large amounts of land in the name of its green development strategy and used a large part of local revenues for green development projects. There was a group of farmers who protested the government for unfair land compensation when the fieldwork was carried out. Since there are so many renewable energy industrial parks and low-carbon cities, the real ecological and social impact should be carefully evaluated and checked in order to find improper justifications of green development. In this evaluation, the weaker social groups in local society must have a voice in the green development discourse. As we know, farmers, fishermen, and the environment are particularly vulnerable in the process of green development.

Notes

1 The Northern China Plain is a fertile land and a main place to produce foods. And there are few barriers, such as mountains and rivers, so that Baoding is an important military point to protect Beijing.
2 Interviewee 5 said that, after the Olympic Games, the air quality got worse. The governmental administration methods are not a sustainable policy to curb air pollution.
3 In interview 5, a local interviewee said that the son of former premier Li Peng, Li Xiaopeng, studied at NCEPU. Later he became the leader of Huaneng—an important SOE in the energy sector. And through this relationship there are many electric power companies in Baoding.
4 In interview 5, here green means countryside which is lacking behind the others and only has agriculture.
5 Here there are many mottos by officials in history, like, to serve the people, be fair and be frugal and so on.
6 One county, Li, was the biggest fur and feather market in China in 1991. And at that time the pollution started.
7 Baiyangdian Lake is an important lake in the Northern China Plain and a famous sightseeing place for its beauty, and it is the pearl of the North in China. Instead of one lake with people living on its shores, Lake Baiyangdian Lake is composed of 143 small lakes, with more than 70 fishing villages.
8 Yu Qun is a scholar-type official who became a strong advocator of renewable energy at the national congress, he gave a speech to address the low-carbon development. And at that time he got the support of Bai Keming, the CCP secretary of Hebeijing Province, who was the secretary of the local CCP. Now, Yu is in the National Ministry of Culture.
9 There were 25 High-tech Zones in 1992, now there are 105 in China. For more information please visit www.MoST.gov.cn/gxjscykfq/.
10 *Economic Daily* was published in 1983 by the State Council and the name was given by Deng Xiaoping.
11 Ma was called back to this position, because it was his idea to set up a high-tech zone and he should take responsibility for it. Ma is very open and he has given interviews to researchers and the media.
12 He mentioned he has the opportunity to read many magazines and newspapers which were not so common at that time.
13 Tianwei Group (Baoding Adapter Factory) was established in 1958. In 1995, through the company law, it became a big high-tech concentrated company. For more information please visit www.btw.cn/ljtw/index.htm.
14 Shi Lishan is responsible for the renewable energy association and he was the secretary of energy in NDRC.
15 The main pollutants are CO_2 discharge and SO_2; the targets are that by 2010 the total amount of CO_2 discharge was to be 54,100 tons which would be 18% less than 2005, for SO_2 the discharge total amount would be 77,400 tons which would be 10% less than 2005. Yu also distributed the responsibility to the counties and key enterprise and signed responsibility contracts with those local leaders. And if they could not reach the targets, they were fired.

Baoding 99

16 Yu Qun left Baoding in 2009 and joined the national cultural ministry. The common character trait of Ma and Yu that both of them emphasized culture may be the reason that they appreciated each other and worked on the renewable energy together.
17 Interview 11. There is a struggle between national-owned and private capital; many people said that Yingli, as private capital, has made good use of the national resources through its relationship with Tianwei, obtaining capital, human resources and other relationships, but later those national resources became private resources. It created a loss of national resources.
18 Golden Sun Project uses Chinese central government subsidies to support solar energy in China. There are many problems around it as it is a one-time subsidy, and the supervision of the implementation is not good. It is seen as a saving fund for many solar energy companies in China, especially after the "double anti" of anti-dumping and anti-subsidy from the global market.
19 The five provinces are Guangdong, Liaoning, Hubei, Shanxi, Yunan, and the eight cities are Tianjin, Chongqing, Shenzhen, Xiamen, Hangzhou, Nanchang, Guiyang, and Baoding. There are five tasks of a low-carbon pilot province or city. (1) a low-carbon development plan; (2) complementary policies to support low-carbon green development; (3) speed up to build low-carbon character industries; (4) establish an emission database and management system; (5) advocate low-carbon green lifestyle and consumption.
20 Interview 3. When Baoding searched for an international partner, Green Peace and WWF were both in consideration, but Green Peace too radical which was regarded as not proper for Baoding, and WWF was chosen.
21 Sun-tech is set up by Shi Zhengrong, who has a PhD in solar technology and came back in 2001 with a solar business plan. He was accepted by his hometown city Wuxi to set up Sun-tech together. Later Sun-tech become a no. 1 solar PV company in China. He became the richest man in China.
22 Ma said that he will develop a civilization theory and write a book about three different civilizations, from industrial to forestry and agriculture and he said these three should exist in harmony. Nowadays, there is too much emphasis on industrial civilization which defrauds the other two civilizations.
23 Baoding Jingjiang hotel was busy with visitors and learners from other local governments. There are classes and exhibitions for them, but these are not open to the public.
24 There is a competition about renewable energy industrial parks run by an energy newspaper, China Economic Development Research Institution, and China Energy Economy Research Institution in 2010, and the 100 strongest have been published online.
25 This event has been reported in detail by a reporter, including many interviews with villagers. Later there was another news report by *People's Daily* which said the former report was wrong, and this reporter interviewed the local officials.
26 There was a protest by the local people in front of the municipal government office. One local said it was about a land dispute (personal observation).
27 In the fieldwork, I have noticed there are still two small fields for crops, and that wheat was planted. There are village committees in the relocation residence. The future of that wheat land is that it will also be developed as an urban area.
28 Energy-saving and emission reduction is a national policy to guide energy and environmental issues in China. It sets aims and measures for local leaders' performance.
29 In the process of producing silicon material, some pollutants will be produced which are harmful to people and the ecology. Even though Miao said that his technology is good, experts know that his technology is still new and not very stable.
30 Interview 3 said that all the local officials have refused to pass the Six and Nine project. But Miao said he has more relationships in Hebei provincial and the central

government, so Baoding has to pass it. Later when the provincial CCP secretary Zhang Qingwei visited Baoding, he has pointed out the pollution issue of the Six and Nine.
31 The city reduced the carbon emission "below zero." The amount that Baoding's renewable products have helped other places to reduce carbon emission is higher than that in Baoding.

References

Baoding Municipal Government (BaodingGOV). (2006). *Guanyu touzi "Zhongguo Diangu" jianshe de ruogan guiding (Baoshizheng [2006] 196 hao) [Provisions for investments in "electric valley of China" construction No. 196 (2006)]*.

Baoding Municipal Government (BaodingGOV) (2007). *Baodingshi Renmin Zhengfu guanyu Baoding jianshe "taiyangneng zhi cheng" Shishi zhi Yijian [Opinions on implementation the Baoding People's Government on constructing a "solar city"]*.

BaodingGOV. (2008). *Baodingshi Renmin Zhengfu Guanyu jianshe ditan chengshi de yijian (Shixing) [Opinions of the Baoding People's Government on constructing a low-carbon city (for trial implementation)]*.

Baoding Policy Research Center (1989). Jinkuai ba geti jingji he siying jingji naru fazhi guidao_ Baodingshi geti(siying) jingji diaocha [Embracing the individual economy and private economy in to the rule of law as soon as possible: Research of Baoding's individual (private) businesses]. *Jingjiguanli (Business Management Journal), 12*(04), 12–16.

Baodingwaishiban (Foreign Affairs Office of Baoding Municiple Government). (2006). *Yu Qun shizhang suaituan chufang Ouzhou chengguo xianzhu [Yu Qun Mayor's EU trip yields impressive achievements]. Baoding Ribao*. Retrieved from www.heb.chinanews.com/todaybd/news/bdxw/2006-06-06/755.html.

Baodingribao. (2007, March 26). Rang "yangguang" zhaoliang Baoding rang "yangguang" wennuan Baoding nuli jianshe jieneng huanbaoxing chengshi—zai quanshi jianshe taiyangneng zhi cheng dongyuan dahui shang [Let "sunshine" light up Baoding, let "sunshine" warm up Baoding, strive to become an energy saving and environmentally friendly city— The promotion conference on constructing a "solar city"]. *Baoding Ribao*. Retrieved from http://zhuanti.bdinfo.net/bdrb/bdrb_info/news_info.asp?news_id=2351.

Baoding shiwei & Baodingshizhengfu (BaodingCCP & BaodingGOV) (2010). *Zhonggong Baoding Shiwei Baodingshi Renmin Zhengfu guanyu jianshe ditan chengshi de zhidao yijian [The guiding opinions of the Baoding CCP Committee and the Baoding People's Government on constructing a low-carbon city]*. Retrieved from http://he.xinhuanet.com/zfwq/2010-11/02/content_21290494.htm.

Beijing Statistical Bureau (2018). Beijingshi 2017 nian guomin jingji he shehui fazhan tongji gongbao [Statistical Communique of Beijing on the 2017 Economic and Social Development]. Retrieved from www.bjstats.gov.cn/zxfb/201903/t20190320_418991.html.

Chen, C., Pickhardt, P., Xu, M., & Folt, C. (2008). Mercury and arsenic bioaccumulation and eutrophication in Baiyangdian Lake, China. *Water, Air, and Soil Pollution, 190*(1–4), 115–127.

Chen, P. (2010, October 27, 2010). Guangneng yu mengxiang [Solar energy and dreams]. *Jin Xiu 2010, 10*. Retrieved from http://blog.ifeng.com/article/8298209.html.

Chen, W., & Wang, X. (2009, March 24). Baoding Shizhang Yu Qun Qinghua fabiao yanjiang changdao shengtai wenming [Baoding Mayor Yu Qun delivered a speech at

Tsinghua University to support ecological civilization]. Retrieved from www.tsinghua. edu.cn/publish/news/4205/2011/20110225232235734101283/20110225232235734101 283_.html.
China Daily. (2006, April 04). Schools of fish killed by pollution in Baiyangdian Lake. Retrieved from www.china.org.cn/english/travel/164527.htm.
Dong, Z., & Gu, X. (2008a). Pianzhang yi: Zhongguo diangu Baoding gouxiang—cong chanye gainian dao zhengfu yizhi [Chapter one: Electric valley of China, the innovative idea of Baoding, from an industrial concept to a government goal], *Jianshe Keji, 7*, 51.
Dong, Z., & Gu, X. (2008b). Pianzhang san: Zhongguo diangu Baoding zhi guang cong guangdian jishu dao taiyangneng [Chapter three: Electric valley of China, the light of Baoding, from solar technology to solar energy]. *Jianshe Keji, 7*, 51.
Dong, Z., & Gu, X. (2008c). Pianzhang si: Zhongguo diangu Baoding dibiao cong Zhongguo shouchuang dao shijie lingxian [Chapter four: Electric valley of China, the landmark of Baoding, from a pioneer in China to a global leader]. *Jianshe Keji, 7*, 51.
Dou, W., & Zhao, Z. (1998). Contamination of DDT and BHC in water, sediments, and fish (Carassius auratus) muscle from Baiyangdian Lake. *Acta Scientiae Circumstantiae, 18*(3), 308–312.
Gao, M. (2006). Baiyangdian juejing [The hopeless situation of Baiyangdian Lake]. *Xinjingbao*. Retrieved from http://news.163.com/06/0403/05/2DOR3CQH0001124J.html.
Guo, R. (2011). *An introduction to the Chinese economy: The driving forces behind modern day China*. Singapore: John Wiley & Sons.
He, Y. (2007, November 08). Tianwei Yingli: Xiangzuo haishi xiangyou? [Tianwei Yingli: Which way to go, left or right?]. *Zhongguo Qiyejia., Sina Caijing.* Retrieved from www.chinavalue.net/Media/Article.aspx?ArticleID=16662.
Hu, Q., & Liu, W. (2008). "Zhongguo diangu—ditan Baoding" yangfan yuanhang—Fang Baoding Guojia Gaoxin Jishu Kaifaqu Guanweihui Zhuren Ma Xuelu ["Electric valley of China—Low-carbon Baoding"—An interview with Ma Xuelu, the director of Baoding National High-tech Park]. *Zhongguo Keji Touzi, 7*, 49–53.
Huang, S. (2012, November 27). Guangxi guangfu zhi du guren biaoyan shangban [The solar city in Guangxi hired people to fake production]. Retrieved from www.21so.com/HTML/zgzqb/2012/11-27-503.html.
Li, X., & Yang, H. (2010, October 12). Liu Jiu Guiye wuran lvzao toushu Yingli Xinengyuan xiangmu shexian weigui [Six and Nine Silicon company was often sued and complained about by the public, Yingli's new project involved illegal transfers]. *Zhongguo Shangbao*. Retrieved from http://finance.ifeng.com/news/20101012/2697700.shtml.
Li, Y. (2012). Environmental state in transformation: The emergence of low-carbon development in urban China. In W. G. Holt (Ed.), *Urban areas and global climate change* (Vol. 12, pp. 221–246). Bingley: Emerald Group Publishing.
Li, Y., Cui, B., & Yang, Z. (2004). Influence of hydrological characteristic change of Baiyangdian on the ecological environment in wetland. *Journal of Natural Resources, 19*(1), 62–68.
Liang, Z., & Zhu, Z. (2012, March 15, 2012). Yingli de dijia luoji: Guipian huan zujian moshi chulu [The logic of Yingli's low prices: The model for changing silicon wafers to solar modules]. *21 Shiji Jingji Baodao*. Retrieved from http://tech.sina.com.cn/it/2012-03-15/02526838213.shtml.
Lovins, L. H., & Cohen, B. (2011). *Climate capitalism: Capitalism in the age of climate change.* New York: Macmillan.
Lv, Z., & Gao, X. (2007). Zhongguo juzi zhiliao "huabei zhi shen" Baiyangdian jiuzhibuyuwuranzheng [China invests huge amounts of capital to treat "the kidney of

North China," Baiyangdian Lake's long-lasting pollution problems]. Retrieved from: http://env.people.com.cn/GB/5385499.html/.

Ma, F. (2009). Ma Xuelu: Wo ba yisheng xiangeile huoju shiye [Ma Xuelu: I dedicated my whole life to the "Torch Program"]. *Zhongguo Gaoxin Jishu Chanye Daobao.* Retrieved from http://blog.sina.com.cn/s/blog_6276b5e60100g8op.html.

Ma, X. (2007). Goujian guojia xinnengyuan chanye fazhan zhanlue pingtai [Establishing the strategic platform for developing renewable energy industries]. *Jianzhu Keji, 18,* 40–42.

Ma, X., & Shi, Z. (1988). "Jianbing"—Gaohuo qiye de you yizhao qi [Mergers and acquisitions—Another measure to invigorate enterprise]. *Jingji Guanli, 3,* 015.

Ministry of Science and Technology, MOST (2001). *Guanyu guojia gaoxin jishu chanye kaifaqu shinian fazhan qingkuang de baogao [Report on 10 years of development of the national high-tech industrial parks].* Retrieved from www.most.gov.cn/gxjscykfq/gxjstjbg/200203/t20020315_9004.htm.

Pan, J., Zhang, G., & Zhu, S. (Eds.). (2006). *Ditan chengshi: Jingjixue fangfa, yingyong yu an'li yanjiu [Low-carbon cities, economic evaluation methods and case study].* Beijing: Shehui Kexue Wenxian Chubanshe.

Qian, H., Ge, J., Wu, M., Qiu, L. (2013, January 21). Wuzhao wumai [Smog after smog]. *Liaowang Xinwen Zhoukan.* Retrieved from http://news.ifeng.com/listpage/29861/111/list.shtml?cflag=1&prevCursorId=21680815&cursorId=21420756.

Rasmus, R. (2008). *A global "electric valley" for sustainable energy production? A litmus test for the world's commitment to renewable energy.* World Wide Fund for Nature China Programme Office, April.

Renminwang. (2011, December 21). Baoding Gaoxinqu xinnengyuan zhuanxing zhi lu [The transition of Baoding High-tech Park]. Retrieved from http://kfq.people.com.cn/GB/236326/236481/236612/16669832.html.

Saiget, R. J. (2006). Pollution slowly choking North Chinas largest lake to death. Retrieved from www.terradaily.com/reports/Pollution_Slowly_Choking_North_Chinas_Largest_Lake_To_Death.html.

Shi, C. (2008, March 13). Yu Qun, dazao Zhongguo Diangu jianshe ditan Baoding [Yu Qun, creating Electric Valley of China, constructing low-carbon Baoding]. Retrieved from www.cenews.com.cn/xwzx/dh/200803/t20080313_222964.html.

Shin, K. (2017). Neither centre nor local: Community-driven experimentalist governance in China. *The China Quarterly, 231,* 607–633.

Tang, Y. (2009, December 10). Ditan chengshi—Baoding paifa xinmingpian [Baoding's brand new low-carbon city]. *Nanfang Zhoumo.* Retrieved from www.infzm.com/content/38513.

Tian, F. (1987). Guanyu shishi zhongxiao chengshi fazhan zhanlue de jige wenti—Jianlun baodingshi fazhan zhanlue [A few questions regarding the development strategies of small and medium sized cities—Research of Baoding's development strategy]. *Jingji shehui tizhi bijiao (Comparative Economic and Social System),* August 29, 61–64.

Tianjin Statistical Bureau. (2018). Tianjin 2017 nian guomin jingji he shehui fazhan tongji gongbao [Statistical Communique of Tianjin on the 2017 Economic and Social Development]. Retrieved from www.tj.gov.cn/tj/tjgb/201803/t20180312_3622447.html.

Wang, C. (2014). Transition from a revolutionary party to a governing party. In K. G. Lieberthal, C. Li, & Y. Keping (Eds.), *China's political development: Chinese and American perspectives* (pp. 73–102). Washington DC: Brookings Institution Press.

Wang, F., & Wang, H. (2008). Baoding qingli dazao "Zhongguo diangu" [Baoding wholeheartedly created "the electric valley of China"]. *Zhongguo Jingji Zhoukan, 9.*

Wang, J. (2009). Peiyu he dazao juyou quanguo jingzhengli de gaozengzhang chanyequn de silu ji celue—Baoding "Zhongguo diangu" de chansheng yu fazhan dailai de qishi [The idea and strategy to nurture and create nationally competitive industrial clusters—The implications of Baoding's development of "the electric valley of China"]. *Keji Xinxi, 18*, 343–344.

Wang, K., & Yan, J. (2008). Wuda xitong gaizao chengjiu yangguang shenghuo—Baoding xinshiji huayuan taiyangneng yingyong sifan [Five systematic reforms support the "sunshine" life—Baoding New Century Garden community demonstration of solar energy products]. *Chengshi Zhuzai, 5*, 28–29.

Wang, Q. (2010). Effective policies for renewable energy—The example of China's wind power—Lessons for China's photovoltaic power. *Renewable and Sustainable Energy Reviews, 14*(2), 702–712.

Wang, Q., & Chen, Y. (2010). Energy saving and emission reduction revolutionizing China's environmental protection. *Renewable and Sustainable Energy Reviews, 14*(1), 535–539.

Wang, Z. (2013). Shu Rongbin kexia Pudong kaifa de nianlun [Shu Rongbin: The years of "develop Pudong"]. *Shanghai Guozi, 1*, 97–98.

WWF. (2008). *Low carbon initiative in China*. Retrieved from http://en.wwfchina.org/en/what_we_do/climate___energy/mitigation/lcci/.

WWF. (2012). Baoding—Carbon positive in the "Green Electric Valley." Retrieved from http://wwf.panda.org/what_we_do/footprint/cities/urban_solutions/themes/energy/?204378.

Xiao, J. (2004). Quanli dazao Zhongguo xinnengyuan zhi du—Fang Baoding Gaoxinqu Guahnweihui Zhuren Ma Xuelu xiansheng [Creating the renewable energy city of China—An interview with Ma Xuelu, director of the Baoding High-tech Park]. *Dianqi Shidai, 6*.

Xinjingbao (2006). Liangbuwei liancha baiyangdian siyu sihjian wuran he queshui cheng sijie [Two ministries research about Baiyangdian dead fish event, polluted water and shortage of water are a dead knot]. Retrieved from http://env.people.com.cn/GB/1073/4263364.html.

Xu, G., Wang, X., & Xu, H. (2007). 300 yiyuan jiang "kongjiang" zhongguo diangu: bingzhuang jituan chongzu baoding tianwei chengai luoding [30 billion RMB will locate in EVC, China South Industries Group Corporation restructure Tianwei is solved]. *Hebei Ribao (Hebei Daily)*, September 26.

Xu, H. (2006, March 26). Hebei Baoding siming guanyuan yin Baiyangdian wuran shijian shou chuli [Four officials in Baoding, Hebei Province were punished because of Baiyangdian pollution]. *Zhongguo Qingnianbao*. Retrieved from http://news.eastday.com/eastday/node81741/node81762/node125890/userobject1ai1938294.html.

Xu, M., Zhu, J., Huang, Y., Gao, Y., Zhang, S., Tang, Y., Yin, C., … Wagn, Z. (1998). The ecological degradation and restoration of Baiyangdian Lake, China. *Journal of Freshwater Ecology, 13*(4), 433–446.

Xue, K., & Kuang, D. (2010). Miao Liansheng: Shijiesheng yiyechengming [Miao Liansheng: Famous overnight because of the World Cup]. *Nafang Renwu Zhoukan, 22*.

Yang, Z., Li, G.-b., Wang, D.-w., Gui, H.-m., & Shang, T.-z. (2005). Pollution and the potential ecological risk assessment of heavy metals in sediment of Baiyangdian Lake. *Journal of Agro-Environment Science, 24*(5), 945–951.

Yingli. (2009). Yingli tan Dunhuang xiangmu zhongbiao shimo [Yingli talks about the whole story of the Dunhuang bidding project]. Retrieved from https://news.solarbe.com/200907/03/5089.html.

Yu, Q. (2009, May 13, 2009). Xinnengyuan chanye jiang chengwei xialun jingji zengzhang zhouqi de zhicheng [Renewable energy will become the core of the next round of economic growth]. Retrieved from www.ccchina.gov.cn/Detail.aspx?newsId=11252&TId=57.

Zeilanengnao. (Producer). (2010, December 28, 2014). Liujiu guiye haisiren [Liu Jiu Guiye pollution]. Retrieved from http://bbs.tianya.cn/post-263-8682-1.shtml.

Zhang, C. (2008, April 07). Baoding shizhang Yu Qun: Zou juyou Baoding tese de shengtai wenming fazhan zhi lu [Baoding Mayor Yu Qun: the road to ecological civilization with Baoding's characteristics]. *Baoding Ribao*. Retrieved from www.heb.chinanews.com/todaybd/news/xyjj/2008-04-07/28551.html.

Zhang, C. (2006, July 03). Sheng di qi ci huanbao dahui zhaokai Yu Qun daibiao Baoding qianding zerenshu [Yun Qun represented Baoding in signing a responsibility contract at the 7th Environmental Protection Conference of Hebei Province]. *Baoding Ribao*. Retrieved from www.heb.chinanews.com/todaybd/news/bdxw/2006-09-01/2764.html.

Zhang, L.-Y. (2015). *Managing the city economy: Challenges and strategies in developing countries*. Oxon: Routledge.

Zhang, Y. (2007). Zhongguo nongcun huanjing ehua yu chongtu jiaju de dongli jizhi: Cong sanqi "quntixing shijian" kan "zhengjing yitihua" [The institutional incentives for environmental degradation and the intensification of environmental conflicts in rural China: Three case studies of environmental mass incidents and the integration of political and economic power] *Hongfan Commentary* Volume 9. Beijing: Zhongguo zhengfa daxue chubanshe.

Zhao, J., & Wu, Y. (2010, August 20, 2010). Baoding lixian zhengtuo pige de shufu chongsu chanye mingpian [Baoding transformed its industrial structure from a fur industry to a renewable energy industry]. *Hebei Ribao*. Retrieved from www.people.com.cn/GB/192235/197037/12493458.html.

Zhou, F. (2010). Yizhang huangpai cuisheng "Zhongguo diangu" [A yellow card was responsible for "China electric valley"]. *Zhongguo Jingji he Xinxihua*. Retrieved from http://finance.sina.com.cn/roll/20100927/10108710049.shtml.

Zhu, C., & Zhu, H. (2006). Caizheng zhuli dazao Zhongguo diangu [Fiscal policies support the development of "China electric valley"]. *Zhongguo Caizheng, 12*, 24–25.

5 A poor county's green leap forward

"Green Rising-Up" in Wuning

Introduction

Wuning is a small and poor county in southern China, one of thousands of similar counties. It lies deep in the mountains, but it aims to be one of the most beautiful small cities or townships in the world. After the reform and opening-up period, Wuning's resources were integrated to the global market, its natural resources were exported, and its young people became migrant workers who contribute to the "world's factory." Unlike many counties, during the industries shifting from coastal areas to inland China, Wuning selected industries according to its green development strategy. This chapter describes a poor county's efforts to protect its environment in pursuing economic development.

Wuning's city has changed significantly following the implementation of its green development strategy; the old city has disappeared along with the old houses, while new and modern houses are sprouting across the city. The whole city became a sightseeing place. There are green slogans along the highway to Wuning; there are other slogans on the street which relate to green ecological concepts, like the "Green Rising-Up," the ecological county and the livable county. These slogans are similar to ideas found in more developed countries, where there is an emphasis on ecological, livable, and happiness. How can a poor county deep in the mountains have such ambitious and avant-garde aims and strategies?

A poor inland county—Wuning

Wuning is in the north of Jiangxi Province and in the middle part of the Yangtze River. The county has a history that spans 1,300 years. It covers 3,506.6 km^2 (Wuning County Party Committee & Wuning Government, 2010) and there are 407,048 people living in this county as of 2016. Among them 174,706 live in the city, and the rest of the population lives in the countryside. The income of farmers is only 12,897 RMB per year, while the income of city dwellers is 27,859 RMB (Wuning County Party Committee & Wuning Government, 2018). Seventy percent of Wuning is covered by forest; one of the four key forest counties in Jiangxi Province. Economic data reveals that Wuning is a county with poor farmers, many of them forest farmers, since it lacks arable land. The forest farmers have limited land scattered along the rivers. Only 6.76% of the land in Wuning is arable (Wuning Government, 2010a).

Like many other counties, Wuning is in the process of industrialization and urbanization. Wuning's farmers are expected to move into the city in the future. To encourage this, Wuning attempted to start industrial activities. About 14.2% of Wuning's economy is in the primary sector, 49% in the secondary sector, and 36.8% in the tertiary sector. Industry is now the biggest component of the economic mix. Industries in the county include coal, cement, fine medicinal capsules, marble, energy-saving lamps, and textiles (Wuning County Party Committee & Wuning Government, 2012). Most of these industries rely on the area's natural resources for production.

A county with rich mountain and water resources

In 2007 Premier Wen Jiabao visited Wuning to track the progress of forest rights reform.[1]

His visit made a strong impression, as he was the first national high-level official to visit this remote county. During his stay, the Premier praised the beautiful ecology, calling the county "Mountain and Water Wuning." This phrase has become a new brand name for Wuning. The forest reform attempts to leave forest rights in the hands of farmers rather than in the hands of the collective as was the case before. Wuning represents one small story of forest reform. The relationship between people and mountains is "*shan ding quan, shu ding gen, ren ding xin*" in Chinese. This translates roughly as: Having clear rights to the forests allows farmers to truly "root" (as if they were trees) to settle and grow in the land. This vividly captures the importance of clearly defined forests rights to local people (Lin & Wang, 2007; Zhongguowang & Zhang, 2011).

The mountains and the waters have brought wealth to Wuning, both in terms of a valuable ecological reputation and material wealth. Wuning has been recognized as a national ecological pilot county by the MEP since 2005. There are trees on the mountains which produce wood, and fruits like bamboo shoots, chestnut, wild kiwi, and mushrooms. There are also many precious plants and animals that live in these mountains and waters, such as the Chinese Yew trees. Underneath the mountains, there are all kinds of minerals, such as lead, wolfram, and mercury. There are also non-mineral materials of value, particularly stones for construction and white earth for porcelain (Wuning Government, 2010a).[2]

The county has 603 rivers, which together are 1,983 km long, cover 3,586 km^2 and have an average annual runoff volume of 2,952.7 million m^3 (Wuning Government, 2010b). As of 2018, there were 104 small hydropower stations in Wuning (Jiujiang Municipal Government, 2018). According to the statistics from the small hydro association at Wuning, only two of these power stations are nationally owned, and the rest are privately owned. All the privately owned hydropower stations have been built by farmers under the leadership of rich locals (S. Ke & Yuan, 2002).

As mentioned above, waters and mountains are the main characteristics of Wuning's environment. Its culture has developed around these resources and Wuning's people respect nature since they rely on it for survival. Wuning is also a highly self-sufficient society.[3] These mountains and waters were not able to prevent the spread of the influences of modernization and industrialization. Many of Wuning's young people now do not want to live a traditional farmer's life in the mountains. Instead they rush into the big cities in the coastal areas to find jobs. Some of them became successful in big cities which became a rich source of capital, knowledge, and entrepreneurship for Wuning.

An immigrant county

Because Wuning has a vast area and a low population density, Wuning has become a popular reservoir resettlement place. There are voluntary immigrants who came into the deep mountains a long time ago, usually due to war and natural disaster, and there are new immigrants who have relocated because of dam projects, especially those in Zhejiang Province.[4] The old town of Wuning was flooded and is now sunk beneath the water for the Zhelin Power Station, while the new town retreated to higher ground near the Zhelin Lake. As of 2012, at least 86,000 people were dam immigrants (Z. Ke & Chen, 2012).[5] Half of the population of Wuning, 180,000 people, are immigrants (J. Ke, 2013). The construction of Zhelin Reservoir flooded 15,000 mu (10 km^2) rice fields and displaced 85,000 people from their homes (Mu, 2010).

These immigrants have brought different cultures and values. There are many Zhejiang people who have moved to Wuning, as Zhejiang Province is neighboring Jiangxi province. As Zhejiang Province has been a pioneer in economic development after reform and opening-up, many Zhejiang people have gone back to their original hometowns. Others became entrepreneurs in the province. While Wuning is still a poor county, many locals have learned from the Zhejiang people's entrepreneurship and have started their own businesses. Moreover, social relations with the Zhejiang people helped the Wuning people to develop their own economy. Zhejiang Province became a key source of capital and business for Wuning.

In the era of industrialization and urbanization, a new wave of immigrants has appeared. This wave is related to the resettlement projects that aim to move people who live in the mountains to the towns and cities. These projects serve the "Green Rising-Up" strategy by boosting the local development (Y. Wang, 2013). The local government propagates the opening of the silent county to the outside world, aiming to create a happy life for the local people (County Party Committee & Wuning Government, 2009). The local government has ambitious dreams to build the most beautiful county (Y. Wang & Tong, 2013).

Rise of entrepreneurs and local officials

Entrepreneurs appeared in Wuning after the period of reform and opening-up and they set up TVEs based on local resources (Wuning Archives Bureau,

2013a). The reform and opening-up policies greatly influenced this mountainous county where there is little available farmland. This has led to two main trends. One is the exodus of many young people who have left to find jobs elsewhere. The second is the effort to find ways to make use of the abundant forest and fish resources in the region; conditions are prime for local entrepreneurs to set up their own businesses. Thus, while some farmers went to other places as migrant farmers, others set up TVEs in Wuning.[6]

As many of the young people found work in other places, fewer and fewer people were left in the county. Some learned technical skills used in production processes and about technologies in other places and started their own businesses back home. Since the 1990s, the local government has endeavored to keep young people in Wuning to contribute to local development. With the opening of special economic zones in southern China, even more local young people began to go outside instead of staying at home. At the beginning of the 1990s, the local government aimed to raise the income of forest farmers and support local TVEs' development (Wuning Archives Bureau, 2013b). In 1991, the Wuning County CCP committee and government organized a trip to southern Jiangxi and Guangdong Province to learn from their experiences (Wuning Archives Bureau, 2013c). The county chief, Cai Dingxin, was responsible for the reform and opening-up, business attraction, and investment group in 1993 (Wuning Archives Bureau, 2013a).

In 1994, Song Yuqin raised the suggestion that Wuning should pursue industrial development instead of focusing on the agricultural sector. In 1996, the local leaders put industrial development as a key task for local officials and Song Yuqin became the group leader for industrial development (Wuning Archives Bureau, 2013d). It was a major transition when Wuning's government started to emphasize the importance of industrial development in addition to agricultural development.

Long search for environmentally friendly industries

There are many local entrepreneurs who have tried to get rich in the reform market. The private sector in Wuning has developed very well and Wuning now is a leader in the Jiujiang regional economy. At the time of the reform and opening-up, most local entrepreneurs started firms which relied on local ecological resources. With capital they accumulated from these ventures, they went out and started other enterprises, such as construction businesses.

Professor Li Dingfu was invited by the Wuning local leaders to give a speech about liberating thoughts and accelerating the development of private businesses in 2001. Professor Li Dingfu is an expert on Wenzhou economic development in Zhejiang Province, which is characterized by dynamic private businesses development (Wuning Archives Bureau, 2013e). Later, Wuning's government held a study group of local officials to learn about this development model. This implied a change of attitudes toward private businesses and industries and reveals how Wuning local leaders became determined to attract businesses.

The Wuning local government, just like other local governments, set up an industrial park to attract entrepreneurs and capital in 2001: Wanfu industrial park. It became a provincial industrial park with a public-private partnership. The first plan foresaw development in an area of 15 km^2 (4000 mu), which belonged to two nearby villages. The park is only 3 km from the center of Wuning city. This park was designed by architects from Tongji University, a first-level university in city planning (Wanfu Industrial Park, 2003).

Initially efforts to attract businesses to Wuning had poor results. Wanfu industrial park was set up under the leadership of the county government, but due to an unfortunate location surrounded by dams and poor infrastructure for businesses, it failed to attract entrepreneurs. Only a few factories initially settled in the park, and several of them failed. One example of this is the local government's efforts to work with an entrepreneur who returned from Wenzhou, a famous small business center. A relatively successful businessman in Wenzhou, this entrepreneur is knowledgeable about shoemaking. He was persuaded by the local government to start a new business in his hometown. Despite having land, his factory did not open because of high costs, including the high cost of transportation. This is one of the many failed attempts of entrepreneurs in Wanfu.[7] Failed projects like this contributed to the slow development of the area.

Wanfu then shifted its development strategy to energy-saving industries. This idea came from a Zhejiang entrepreneur, who set up the first energy-saving lamp factory in Wanfu. In 2001, Xu Huoxing from Zhejiang Province set up the Xingcheng Electric Device Company. The company mainly produces energy-saving lamps and other energy-saving electric devices (Huang, 2013). Due to various reasons, this factory went bankrupt in 2002 (Rao, 2011).

There was no further development for many years, and Wanfu continued to concentrate on resource factories. As a poor and remote mountain county, Wuning's competence in the market was very weak. Local officials concentrated on encouraging successful entrepreneurs to invest back in their hometown. One indicator of their success is the local infrastructure and the construction of roads, schools, and small hydropower stations. These efforts satisfied local basic demands and served as good investments for entrepreneurs. Most of the private small hydropower stations have two responsible agents: the entrepreneurs and the local township government.

Entrepreneurs tried different businesses in Wuning; the development situation did not change until the success of the second energy-saving lamp company in Wuning.

One successful entrepreneur's pull effect

The entrepreneur Zhu Chenghua from Zhejiang Province was attracted to Wanfu by the Wuning local government's industrial policies. His hometown, Lin'an, is famous for its energy-saving lamp industry (B. Li & Yang, 2013). As a peasant entrepreneur, he was not dissuaded from investing in Wuning by Xu's failed attempt. In 2003, he signed a contract with Wuning's government and started the

Chenyang factory in Wanfu. At that time, the local government promised a "one station service" for Zhu which reduced many barriers to start his company, such as finding a suitable location, relocating the local farmers, and securing a stable supply of water, electricity, and road infrastructure necessary to support the Chenyang factory. The county government could make this guarantee since many of these services are run by government-owned companies or the local government itself. After the success of this energy-saving lamp company, the government established particularly preferential regulations for the energy-saving lamp industry, favoring it, for example, with lowered costs for electricity, land, and taxes.

Zhu's success in energy-saving industries in Wanfu was an example for other entrepreneurs. In 2004, three other Zhejiang Lin'an entrepreneurs followed Zhu and started their own businesses in Wanfu. By 2006, there were more and more entrepreneurs returning and setting up their own energy-saving lamp businesses (B. Li & Yang, 2013). The park has been sanctioned by the Jiangxi provincial government as a Jiangxi Energy-saving Lamp Industry Base and Jiangxi Province Green Lighting High-tech Pilot Park. By the end of 2010, there were over 100 energy-saving lamp companies at Wuning Wanfu Park. The scale of the companies grew as well. After 2011, there were 28 investments of 0.1 billion RMB. By the following year, 9,123 people were employed at Wanfu (Industrial Park Research Group, 2012).

At that time, Wuning government's regulations had already offered support for the energy-saving lamp industry. In the 2007 document "Some Regulations about Preferential Policies to Encourage Foreign Investment," the electricity price is set for only 0.43 RMB/kW and water price is set as only 80% of the market price (Wuning County Party Committee & Wuning Government, 2007).[8] The government also published the "Implementation Opinion on the Vigorously Developing Energy-saving Lamp Industry" and invited experts to make a "Ten Year Plan for the Energy-saving Lamp Industry" in Wuning (Industrial Park Research Group, 2012; Wuning Government, 2008). This plan specifies that there will be no land rental costs for entrepreneurs who start companies for producing energy-saving lamps. There are also special land rental prices for large companies (Industrial Park Research Group, 2012). These preferential policies are attractive for entrepreneurs in coastal areas, where the land and labor prices are higher. More and more energy-lamp companies settled in Wanfu Industrial Park. The government support that has made this possible was implemented by the local CCP secretary as is described below.

CCP secretary's reform ambition for Wuning

Shen Yang came to Wuning in 2008 as the local government chief. Since the beginning of his term, Wuning changed significantly. In 2009, he organized a meeting with energy-saving entrepreneurs in Zhongshan's Old Town, Guangdong Province, an important center for energy-saving lighting industries, advertising Wuning's preferential policies towards companies producing energy-saving solutions. In this meeting he promised access to 2.7 km² land in Wuning industrial park, adding "today you sign, tomorrow your company will start, [...], there is no minute's wait, one station service, no charge, no fees and green passes for companies" (*Zhongshan Daily*, 2009). He did the same in Zhejiang, Jiangsu, and other provinces (Wuning Business Bureau, 2009). As the local government leader, he has the power to preferentially allocate resources to select industries to attract entrepreneurs.

Before being appointed as Wuning's local government leader, Shen Yang was responsible for Hukou's Tourism Office. Hukou is a Chinese county at the mouth of the Poyang Lake, the largest freshwater lake in China. In numerous speeches and articles Shen expressed his intention to focus on green development. He used his local regulatory power to create an incentive system in order to implement his development blueprint.

In 2008, Shen gave a speech at the Garden County and Township Conference, organized by the Ministry of Housing and Urban-Rural Development (MHURD), stating that Wuning's environment is its greatest resource. In order to serve Wuning and its future generations there is a need for sustainable development (Shen, 2008). The same year, he opened the Minsheng Blog at the Wenming Net, through which local people or netizens can contact him directly. There are thousands of messages on his blog; most of them are complaints or suggestions for local development. Shen has given detailed answers in response.[9]

There are several typical problems that appear in these messages related to land rights or forests rights transfer problems, the concerns of politically weak social groups, the needs of disabled people, and the local medical system. One woman complained that she could not get the same subsidies from the government as her brothers, to which Shen replied that all people should be treated equally and told her which specific department or person should take responsibility for this issue (Shen, 2009b). Many users reported that their problems were solved through the blog. There are tens of thousands of visits to Shen's blog. There is also a Minsheng Hotline for locals on the Wuning government website.

Shen's blog demonstrates his government values: accountability, efficiency, and clear aims. On the blog he publishes speeches held at local government meetings. In an entry describing the conference of the three local government levels, county, township, and village level, he cites the Confucian proverb "*yan bi xin, xing bi guo, zhi bi de*," (words must believe, actions must be realized, aims must be reached) (Shen, 2009a) as the best way to achieve a "Mountain and Water Wuning" that is a livable and a travelable county. The saying is from the Confucian book *Lunyu*. Shen is very good at writing and public speaking, which are important skills for politicians. There is a saying that those politicians who are good at writing are also ambitious and able politicians. This was true in traditional China, which was ruled by writers and not generals.

He elaborates on these three principles. First, to underline that government should be accountable or credible, he cites two famous Chinese stories: *Hanxin Limu* and *Fenghuo Xi Zhuhou*. The story *Hanxin Limu* tells how Hanxin, a minister in the Qin dynasty, hung notices on the doors and walls which said those who will move to another place will be greatly rewarded. His goal was to win the people's support for reforms. At first, no one believed the notices; those who moved were rewarded. This is a famous example in China's political culture used to educate people. The story *Fenghuo Xi Zhuhou* tells us how Xi Zhou Dynasty's Zhou You King wanted to please his concubine Bao Si and make her smile, so he lights the emergency fire on the Great Wall calling in help. When the help comes, his concubine smiles, but he loses the trust of the soldiers who were supposed to save him. Later, they do not believe his emergency light. This explains how important accountability is to the government.

Second, discussing the need for the government to work efficiently and implement policies, he argues that government actions should be fast, decisive, and able to seize the opportunities. He gave the example of the Shenzhen special economic zone, which developed much more quickly than others, in order to emphasize the importance of local government action under the policy framework set by the central government.

And lastly, he argues that government needs to have clear goals, and the confidence that it can achieve them (Shen, 2009a). At the time of that speech he was still the local government head, and not yet the CCP secretary. In 2011, at the Wuning CCP's Thirteenth First Conference, he was appointed as the CCP secretary of Wuning. Becoming the top official gave Shen the means to realize his ambitious development plan.

"Green Rising-Up" strategy

On July 22, 2011, Shen declared his blueprint for Wuning in his report: "Gather Power and Efforts for a 'Green Rising-Up, Struggle for a Happy Wuning'." It is the first time that the "Green Rising-Up" strategy appeared in Wuning.[10] The core of the "Green Rising-Up" strategy is that "ecological protection must be the precondition, economic rising is the core, cultural development is the support, social development is the base and political development is the guarantee" (Shen, 2011).

Shen's policy agenda focused on the next five years and five construction projects. After this report was issued, there were many policy and institutional innovations not only in industry but also in government in Wuning. Under the leadership of Shen Yang resources were restructured and significantly mobilized. The spirit of his policies was delivered to the Wuning people through different educational conferences and project engagements.

Restructuring of the local government and resources

There are three key development aspects under the "Green Rising-Up" strategy: new industries are to be developed, ecological tourism is to be promoted, and the best living environment is to be realized to make the county strong and attractive. Implementation ideas concentrated on rural gardening areas, a livable industrial park, landscaping the city, and integrating the rural and the urban environments. The government primarily focused on the city and the industrial park. This section will sketch the actions of the local government under the "Green Rising-Up" strategy.

Under Shen, there was big change in the county's government structure. His power as CCP secretary allowed Shen to require each local official to work for his plans and aims. Shen required that every government unit or department develop ideas for what they must do, distribute responsibility to every official, and keep specific records of their work. The local officials were organized into different groups to take responsibility for big projects. They were called the big projects headquarters and had the responsibility of promoting the implementation of these projects (Wuning Government, 2011a).

In this reorganization the government chief Rao was given a new position as the chief executive of all the projects. There were different offices; instead of the normal government departments, Shen created offices for the promotion of: urban construction projects, industrial projects, ecological tourism, urban transportation, and agriculture. He also set up a coordination office. Each command office set up five working groups focusing on coordination, advertising, promotion, performance evaluation, and maintaining social stability.

These different command groups deployed one third of the local officials across different governmental units or departments, which demonstrates how many personnel resources the local leader mobilized for implementation of his "Green Rising-Up" strategy. These local civil servants were required to keep a diary of their work for their performance evaluation by the local leader. The leader held a promotion conference to encourage passionate young civil servants to be at the front line of project construction, which meant to fight for the projects and solve problems. These actions show how much power the local leader had to implement his aims in the county; indeed, it was like a political movement to generate all resources available to reach the local development aim. Shen, the CCP secretary, is responsible for punishing and promoting local officials. He controlled the incentive system and defined relevant time, tasks, responsibilities, rewards, and punishments.

Shen was also careful not to confront all local officials. He made a statement that he would not change county leaders, as they were powerful officials and important for local stability. Other local officials were to be evaluated in relation to their work on the "Green Rising-Up" projects. If they did a good job they would be promoted, and otherwise they would be removed. In order to have a good team Shen published the work style of local officials, setting behavioral norms, and improving their efficiency of work. He also banned gambling, laziness, and abuse of public funds or seeking private benefits from public power. The regulation was titled "Ten Strictly Prohibited Things Six Not Allowed Things" for local officials to regulate the behavior of local officials (Y. Wang, 2012).

The local leader not only restructured the incentive systems for local officials, but also restructured locally owned assets. These assets were grouped into an investment and development company and included buildings and land. With the founding of this company, the local government obtained loans from local banks.[11] Later, modifications to the infrastructure of the city began; officials planned to remove 2,189 households to make space for a new city (Zhang, 2012). Due to these construction projects, land prices rose quickly, as did housing prices. A local interviewee commented that the housing prices are around 3,000–4,000 RMB per square meter, which is almost half of the annual income of a farmer. With the sale or rent of land, the local government gathered capital to use for development.

A similar process happened to the region's water, as the local government planned to regain water usage rights from private fishermen and labeled it as a government resource for investment. They called it clean water fishing, although compensation or share rights were given to the fishermen (Wuning Fishing Office, 2013). This phenomenon is called land revenue; most of the localities rely on land for government spending, in the form of the rent or sale of land or water rights to developers. The revenue from land obtained by Wuning's government is over 10 billion RMB in one year. This reconstruction of local assets was the foundation for further development.

Innovative policies

Under his leadership, numerous new regulations were promulgated. These regulations came in many forms, from industrial policies to political and social policies, all of which aimed to support the "Green Rising-Up," happy Wuning strategy. This section will focus on the new local policies from industrial, political, and social perspectives.

Wuning's local government created preferential policies for the energy-saving lamp industry, ecological tourism, agriculture, and the mineral, biopharmaceutical, and housing industries. For every industry, one group of local officials was chosen to be responsible. Industrial policies aimed at benefiting the new key industries and evaluation systems were drafted. Altogether 82 officials and 16 groups were involved in Wuning. They were responsible for attracting business and investment in the six industries. They set up offices in other cities to attract investment.

As one of its first measures, the Wuning government closed some old and polluting factories, such as the cement factory. In addition, a waste water discharge system was set up and illegal cage aquaculture was prohibited (Hu, 2013).[12] The energy-saving lamp industry was chosen as the core industry to support in the industrial park; this will be discussed at length in the next section. To support ecological tourism, the government established forest parks, wetland parks, and other cultural parks. Wuning released specific forest regulations to encourage reforestation. Wuning tried to attract environmentally friendly industries and also made specific preferential policies for them.

Wuning also declared local regulations to realize the three governing principals of Secretary Shen. First, to achieve government credibility or accountability, Wuning's government distributed the "Openness of CCP and Government Affairs" regulations to improve the transparency of the government

(Wuning Government, 2008). A special website for the publication of Wuning CCP and government affair documents was set up. On the website of the CCP affairs, there are local leaders' speeches and documents that show government institution building, the decision-making process, and anti-corruption efforts. On the website of the government, there are publications that show local fiscal income, special funds, and land transfers.

Second, to enhance government efficiency, the local government published many regulations that support the incentive system. Local cadres were strictly controlled related to their work for the rapid development of projects. Their performance can be accessed on the website of the projects, as specific project plans with brief progress reports. The government also set up a very efficient land transfer system so that in two years the appearance of the county had completely changed. The inner lakes do not smell anymore and have been turned into scenery with wetland parks. A large amount of new buildings were built to support the real estate industry.

Shen's third governing principle was to set high aims and to have Wuning become the most beautiful county. Secretary Shen ordered three cleaning targets: the city, illegal buildings, and fish farming in the lake. The three cleaning actions are closely related to the city's image (Shen, 2012). Wuning applied for a four A tourism resort to the National Tourism Administration to attract more tourists.

These policies and regulations, such as the new city planning, have brought some negative changes to local people. One big issue related to the land transfer, are the complaints from farmers about the low compensation they received from the government and the high profits made by the local government and developers, especially real estate developers who gained from their land. There were some conflicts around compensation issues, such as how to calculate the area of the old house and garden. The confiscation of farm land for the Wanfu Industrial Park caused a loss of land for farmers. The ecological tourism projects had an adverse influence on the forest farmer's livelihood, because they were required to move out of the place and lost the use rights of the forests.

Secretary Shen's leadership also opened new channels and created new methods to control social conflicts and maintain social stability during the process of rapid development. One significant method is an online blog to communicate with the public (which is mentioned in the following Analysis section) (Chen et al., 2009; Ma, Chung, & Thorson, 2005; Seifert & Chung, 2008). Most of the development conflicts resulted from the negative impacts grand governmental programs had on the life of local people, especially farmers. The government used ecological migration and disaster-induced migration to persuade farmers in deep mountains to move into the city and expected this would be successful. This policy was set up in order to realize a 50% urbanization level, as the level was only 20% in 2007, and it reached 47.38% in 2016 (Xu, 2010). With the deep mountain resettlement project, the Wuning government made a promise that every person would have a place to live. There were thus several low-rent housing and low-price housing areas developed by the government (Shen, 2014). In addition, the local government promised it would help poor farmers to build safe houses in rural areas (Wang, 2012). The local officials tried their best to persuade the people to move in order to finish their tasks.[13] For these big projects that were the will of the local government, a lot of people had to be relocated to make way for the "Green Rising-Up."

During this period of city construction and the processes of resettling and compensation, the government set up a group to keep stability and control. The government website states that the group's task is to keep the big projects running smoothly.

This section has introduced the local policies initiated to promote green development. The analysis shows how powerful the local government is in its territory. The local leader chose to use his power to direct the local cadre system to work for his aims and to restructure local resources to financially support green development. The next section will focus on how the energy-saving lamp industry has been developed in the Wuning industrial park with the support of the local government. The preferential policies that were put in place to support this industry will be explained in detail.

Energy-saving lamp industry

Secretary Shen selected the energy-saving lamp industry as the key industry for the Wuning industrial park. As early as 2008, Wuning addressed this topic in the document "Implementation Opinions about Promoting Energy-saving Industry" (Y. Li et al., 2012). In addition, the Wuning government issued the "Implementation Opinion about Promoting Green Lighting and Electricity in Full Efforts" in 2011 (Wuning County Party Committee & Wuning Government, 2011). These two local regulations are the main source of preferential policies for the energy-saving lamp industry.

The Wuning government set targets for the industrial park. In five years, the energy-saving lamp industry was supposed to reach over 300 companies. The local government came out with aims for each product, for example, 2 billion energy-saving lamps, 1 billion whole energy-saving lamps, and 0.5 billion LEDs per year. The total income from the energy-saving lamp industry was to reach 20 billion RMB and 0.4 billion RMB of tax revenue. The quality and technology of energy-saving lamps was expected to meet the standards of the international market (Wuning County Party Committee & Wuning Government, 2011). The government defined clear targets and aims for each year. It also sent working groups to Guangdong, Hong Kong, Wujian in Taiwan, Zhejiang, and Jiangsu provinces to attract energy-saving entrepreneurs to Wuning.[14] In this sense, the local government functioned like a company distributing its "salesmen" to sell its preferential policies to entrepreneurs.

One key advantage the Wuning industrial park has is the lowest electricity prices among companies in Jiangxi Province (N. Fu & Wang, 2011). Many energy-saving lamp production processes are very energy intensive, so this is a great advantage. The electricity price within the industrial park is 0.6154 RMB/kW for factories, it is much lower than coastal areas; outside the industrial park it is 0.8164 RMB/kW, and for big consumers of over 315 KVA it is only 0.5654 RMB/kW. For water, land, and other services, companies are charged less than the local people (Wuning Industrial Park, 2012). Each government department signed a service contract with companies to promise they will not charge companies, since entrepreneurs are often negatively impacted by fees and charges from the local government in most regions, particularly in poor inland areas (Wuning Government, 2009).

In addition to these preferential policies, the Wuning local government set up institutions to support the upgrading of companies and connect this process to the performance evaluations of some governmental departments and officials. The government also started a quality check center to monitor the companies. It published a magazine and a website on green lighting to advertise in the market. The government also holds a forum for green lighting every year (Wuning County Party Committee & Wuning Government, 2011). The support provided to the energy-saving lamp industry demonstrates the local government's strong intervention into the local economy with its efforts to support local economic growth.

With the help of the local government, the energy-saving lamp industry developed quickly in the industrial park; the local economy still faces fierce competition in the domestic and international market. Support of the local government alone cannot assure an industry will win in the market. Additional factors beyond the industrial policies are behind the region's "Green Rising-Up." The next section will illustrate other aspects of Wuning's "Green Rising-Up" strategy.

Social development in "Green Rising-Up"

The "Green Rising-Up" strategy is not only about industrial development, but also about urban and rural development. CCP Secretary Shen developed this strategy further to include ecological and green industrial parks, and the overall quality of the city and countryside. The appearance of the city is hardly recognizable for the people who have returned after green development. The city became more beautiful, but also more expensive. As negative consequences of the green development the price of housing rose to city levels. Housing prices reached 3,000–5,000 RMB/m^2 in 2012 dramatically up from 500–1,000 RMB/m^2 in 2007. Similarly, the price of living became as expensive as that of the big cities, which is hardly acceptable for a small county.

Keep environmental protection as a bottom line

Wuning's industrial park aims to be an ecological industrial park which can also provide comfortable living conditions for its workers. Regulators created 29 indicators in the areas of economic development, industrial park greenery, pollution control, material reduction, recycling, and evaluation as an ecological industrial park. The government set up a working group for constructing the park in 2009.

Wuning environmental bureau officials claimed that the government refused some attractive projects because their environmental impact did not meet Wuning requirements. The local leader supported the work of the local environmental protection bureau with the goals of preventing polluting industries from settling down at the industrial park and ultimately protecting the water. Simultaneously, the environmental bureau closed many polluting factories in fulfillment of the environmental requirements of the local government. The courage to turn down projects and close polluting industries demonstrates as the strong will of the local government to achieve economic development and ecological protection at the same time.

To the outside world, Wuning is widely portrayed as a green lighting city. The preferential industrial policies have attracted over 130 energy-saving lamp companies to this industrial park as of the beginning of 2013 (Wei & Yang, 2013). Even though there are many positive reports about the environmentally friendly nature of the energy-saving lamp industries, some environmental problems still appeared. One significant issue is the use of mercury during the production of energy-saving lamps.

As Wuning is a water county, the mercury problem is a threat to its clean water. To address this threat, the Wuning government issued a regulation that required the upgrading of the energy-saving lamp industry. One key technology component was to shift from liquid mercury filling technology to solid mercury filling technology in order to reduce the levels of skin exposure to mercury, and mercury release into the air and water during the production process. Additionally, the local government required recycling facilities to further reduce mercury pollution, and the local government listed a time schedule for doing so (Wei & Yang, 2013). To help the companies to install these new facilities, the local government set up a fund and spent two million RMB on it (Kuang, 2011). The local government later encouraged the energy-saving lamps companies to move towards LEDs. Beyond these greening actions in the industrial park, many other greening projects took place in the city.

Green city projects

To improve the image of the city, the old city was pulled down and a totally new city was rebuilt in its place. With the high aim of being the most beautiful county in China, the new city was designed to look picturesque and clean. The Wuning government invited famous architects with advanced ideas for an ecological city to plan a new city for Wuning. Its inner lake, Chaoyang Lake, became a key part of the model for an ecological city with water. The new city was designed according to five principles: nature, human needs, sustainability, character, and regional culture (W. Fu, Zhou, Li, & Li, 2012).

Wuning has published its implementation policies for building a livable city. The first action taken was cleaning the appearance of the city, including small ads, shop signs, restaurants, residences, roads, public facilities, etc. The policies then required that the greenery rate of the city should be over 30% of the city.

The local government made a time schedule and designated officials responsible for this work. Following these changes was an increase in residential property management to make them clearer. Lastly are the maintaining of the public infrastructure and the security of the city (Wuning County Party Committee & Wuning Government, 2013). The policies set out a new geography for the city, embracing the Zhelin Lake in its city plan. The new city was built around the lake and two rivers, and these waters and lakes are connected with each other.

One special point in Wuning's city plan is the focus on the water view and the restrictions on any construction within 100 meters or 38 km along the scenic lake road. For residential buildings, they must be lower than four stories or higher than 10 stories. The government also plans to import some water recreation programs to Wuning.

To protect its water, Wuning aimed to become a water ecological city in line with the 2013 requirements of the Ministry of Water Resources. In its implementation policy, the city listed principles, targets, space distribution, a time schedule, and content for this development goal. It aims to be the first pilot water ecological city. Wuning set three red line standards: the total water usage volume, the efficiency of water usage, and the pollution capacity of the water. Its water protection and restoration, water security, water saving, and pollution reduction programs have been set up at urban and rural areas. The strictest water management system and highest water ecology awareness and culture exist among the local people. In the space distribution plan, the government has outlined a mountain and water system, city water and rivers system, and a Lushan west lake water system. The time schedule was set at one month for gathering of public opinion, more than two years for expert planning and projects, and one month for application and evaluation of those plans. The project will clean the rivers, especially in rural areas, as farmers have a habit of throwing waste into the river. The government gave rural household a garbage bin for free and organized people to collect them regularly which greatly reduced the rural waste issue (Wuning Government, 2017). The implementation policy again set up a promotion group to carry out this program (Wuning County Party Committee & Wuning Government, 2013).

Commercialization of natural resources

Wuning has a large rural area with forests and is dedicated to using them with ecological principles, so that there will be more ecological villages. The "Green Rising-Up" in the rural area includes projects for forestation, forest tourism, the wellness industry, a film-park, and eco-agriculture.

As a heavily forested county, Wuning's responsibility is to protect the forest. Since forest rights are distributed to farmers, farmers have the right to determine how the forests are to be used. Some farmers began to invest in the development of economic trees and products, while other farmers sold their wood quota to companies. On the one hand, the government has strictly controlled the quota of wood that can be cut, so that it can keep deforestation to a minimum. On the other hand, the Wuning government has encouraged farmers to plant trees, especially trees with higher rates of return to increase the income of farmers. In this, there are several big issues for forest rights reform. Many farmers are forced to sell or transfer their forest rights to businessmen by village officials acting in secrecy. Another problem is that the forest rights of farmers are infringed upon by the mineral mining companies. Some farmers complained about the low compensation for their forest rights by developers (Wuning Government, 2013). The process is not as transparent as the government claimed. Some developers even lay claim to the forest for other purposes while hiding their real interest in mining.[15] Local people wrote about this in their opinions online (Wuning Government, 2005).[16]

Forest tourism relied on farmers' forests. The local government developed the local ecological resources into products and aimed to sell them to developers. Several forest parks were included in the government plans which obtained the forest and land from the farmers and sold them as tourism products. The Yin mountain nature ecological conservation park displaced 2,300 people in 250 households and received 14,500 ha of forests for it (Wuning Government, 2011c). All the natural resources that were discovered by the local government were then developed to sell to tourists. The cleaner air, water, and mountain environment are products in the market.

A third big developer is the wellness industry. The air and water quality degraded in many cities, especially in big cities. It is popular for people to use their holidays to spend time at places with good environmental conditions. There is a growing market for senior citizens to live in places with good ecological conditions. Some projects are designed to provide fresh air, fresh water, and a mountain environment. Total investment in the Lushan West Lake International Ecological Health Pension Center was 2.7 billion RMB on 1,500 mu (0.0667 ha) of land (Cai, 2013). The huge compensation fund caused distribution problems among villagers, since village leaders got more compensation than others. The hot springs were sold to some developers for business; the Xianguo Shan hot spring owned by the Pinggang Village became an investment project for 30 to 50 million RMB.

Wuning plans to build a film-park, which was hotly debated on the social network website. From the government project report, this program would confiscate 2.7 km^2; that is only 60% of the land it initially planned to use (Wuning Government, 2011a). The whole project requires 4 km^2 of land (Wuning Government, 2011c). The total project has 7 km^2. There are more than 265 households who have had to move (Wuning Government, 2012).

Wuning also aims to develop eco-agriculture. The government has organized the small fruit farmers into a company, and fruit farmers invest their labor, fruit trees, and their mountain as shares in this company. They share the risks and the benefits as a collective. There are 1.35 km^2 for vegetables, 12 km^2 for pecans and a 4.7 km^2 Camelliaoleifera plantation (Wuning Government, 2011b). The local government has provided special funds for fruit and vegetable farmers to improve their earnings. In the fishing areas, the government has removed all private fishermen without a fishing certification and put strict regulations in place for the fishing industries. As the county chief said, the water belongs to the people and the nation (S. Rao, 2012).

All these projects are part of the "Green Rising-Up" strategy of the happy Wuning vision. Some projects are traditional agricultural industries, but the local government has also tried to import some environmentally friendly projects, such as forest tourism and wellness programs. The aim is to make a business out of Wuning's good ecological conditions, and to show this small county to the outside world. During these processes, some actors have experienced gains but others losses.

Analysis

When the local government focused on the "Green Rising-Up," happy Wuning strategy," big projects followed. Wuning is currently undergoing great change in its county appearance, economy, and society because of this strategy. All the projects were promoted and designed by the local government with little public participation in the decision-making process, while local people have only had a role in their implementation. The people have been expected to cooperate with the local government in order to carry out the government's plans. It was the local CCP secretary who decided what was good for local development, representing his view of what is good for the people of Wuning. It is important to encourage more public participation in order to balance social equality in the process of green development.

Key promoting actors and powers

In the case of Wuning, the capability and vision of a local leader and their transformation power is observed. The local leader made the most of local resources for the "Green Rising-Up" strategy. Even though the local leader always cited the central government's ideas, thoughts, and policies, the reason was to justify the local green development strategy. It is important to realize the innovative role of the local leader in developing the locality.

There are several important points about local leadership innovative ideas. First, they have chosen a development strategy which is suitable to local conditions, particularly it has taken the protection of local ecological environment into consideration. Second, they know the skilled way to mobilize resources to implement the strategy to accomplish specific projects. The way to mobilize local civil servants to strive for a better future, the mobilization of land and capital, all reflect a similar spirit of entrepreneurship. Shen said projects mean capital, growth, fiscal income, and potential power (Shen, 2011). So, for urbanization and industrialization Wuning needs the resources of these projects. But different from an enterprise, the local leader needs to take the social and environmental responsibilities into consideration which is the third point. The public spirit of the strategy is reflected in many aspects; the picturesque view of the new city is accessible for everyone. The citizens can take a walk along the rivers, lakes, and parks. There are many improvements in people's lives along with the "Green Rising-Up" strategy. The continuance of local action became a problem when Shen was promoted to the Jiujiang municipal government in 2016.

"Green Rising-Up" is not a new idea, nor was it invented by Wuning. It is a popular concept in Jiangxi Province and in other agricultural and poor areas. This type of areas uses the term "rising-up" in reference to the idea of narrowing the big gap between the coastal areas and the middle and western areas. Recently, development in the middle and western areas of China is proceeding at a faster rate than that of the coastal areas in terms of their GDP growth rate. This is due to a great transfer of industrial facilities from coastal areas to the middle and western areas, especially of energy-intensive, resource-intensive, and pollution-related industries. Wuning is a good case study to show the insistence of localities when facing the big industrial transfer, the ability to say no to certain polluting industries.

The energy-saving lamp industry is one such industry. Entrepreneurs from Zhejiang or Guangdong provinces moved their production to Wuning because of the preferential policies issued by the local government which has supported the energy-saving lamp industry. The other reason for this transfer is the increasing land prices and other costs in the coastal areas. The low prices of electricity and other resources and cheap labor in Wuning have attracted entrepreneurs from the coast. Another important reason why entrepreneurs chose Wuning is because they have relatively more *guanxi* with people in this county than they do in coastal areas. The *guanxi* between the Zhejiang people and local people is relatively high. People of Zhejiang origin settled in Wuning decades ago; they supply *guanxi* to the Zhejiang entrepreneurs. With this *guanxi* network, the entrepreneurs could trust the Wuning government. *Guanxi* helped entrepreneurs to lower transition costs, as well as reducing the possibility of local rent-seeking from local powers. The local government is happy to attract more of the energy-saving lamp industry to the region. It is an industry that is supported by the fact that the Chinese central and provincial CCP require steps be taken for energy saving and efficiency. The energy-saving lamp industry is expected to have a large market.

Wuning, like other rising-up poor areas in the middle and western regions, faces the dilemma between ecological protection and economic development. Furthermore, since the population's environmental awareness has grown, Wuning must be more sensitive to ecological protection than before. Wuning is rich in natural resources, and it can choose either to mine the resources or to sell them as ecological products.

The Wuning government has elected to become a livable city which sells its natural resources as ecological products. The advantages of the local natural landscape are obvious in the eyes of people who have experienced pollution. The recognition of former prime minister Wen has helped to clearly define this branding of Wuning to the local CCP leadership.

In most undeveloped areas, management of the environment is still in the hands of local people, especially the farmers. They maintain a traditional lifestyle, and their conditions for economic development are not as favorable as those of the coastal areas. All that the people have to invest are land and other resources. Local people are eager for capital investment. The poor areas are more interested in the construction of an ecological civilization, since it could raise the value of their ecology and the primary resources which they have available. The Wuning local government shares this perspective: as Secretary Shen said, Wuning should be a pioneer during the ecological civilization, so as to change its ecological advantage to a development advantage.

As the central CCP puts ecological civilization more and more at the center of the political goals of China, the greening efforts of some counties will be further justified. The "Green Rising-Up" is not only closely related to political values, but also to local cultural values and economic interests. Political power has played a decisive role in Wuning's "Green Rising-Up." What do the politicians of Wuning get from the "Green Rising-Up" and what do the other actors get from it?

Who gets what, how, and when?

The main beneficiaries of the "Green Rising-Up" are the green lighting entrepreneurs who produce energy-saving lamps. They have benefited from many local resources, such as land, water, and the local government's services. They are sensitive to the signals of the market. They need to cooperate with the local government or rely on good local governance to guarantee their property rights. As private property right laws are unclear, the services and promises made in local regulations and laws are very important. If they are favorable, the regulations and laws can significantly reduce production costs and barriers, otherwise, they could greatly increase the costs of business activities.

In Wuning, the local government has issued many preferential policies and Secretary Shen has promised to support entrepreneurs. He has required all local officials to serve entrepreneurs, at the risk of losing their jobs if they do not fulfill this responsibility. Those entrepreneurs who choose to settle down in Wuning did so because of the policies and good services made available to them. The support of the local government cannot guarantee their success in the domestic and global market, since they still sell average and not technologically advanced products. The support of the local government has increased negative competition among localities, which has resulted in the phenomenon of overproduction of similar products. Through preferential policies, the local government can lower the costs for entrepreneurs, but they are not able to guarantee their success in the market.

The work of Wuning's local officials has been praised by the higher-level government, and Wuning is often visited by higher officials. An increasing number of counties go to Wuning to learn about green development and to do their fieldwork. The "Green Rising-Up" led to many local policy innovations and new governance structures which are reflected in the urban and rural projects. The government invested a huge amount of money into the city construction and encouraged a transfer of land rights to entrepreneurs as developers.

Wuning's local officials are very active in the "Green Rising-Up" movement. In the process, local officials courted projects to settle down in Wuning. They included a range of collectively owned resources and assets under the local investment company, and then used it as a bank guarantee to get loans from the local banks (Xu, 2010).[17] Later officials started many different city construction projects under the "Green Rising-Up." The city became more modern, more planned, and more beautiful in its aim to be a livable and ecological city. Local officials have also been involved in the re-designation of land and the relocation of local people. To get land and remove local people, some local officials were forced to persuade their relatives to move first. Some officials who used state resources to chase private profit were uncovered by Shen's bloggers, and those resources were returned to the local government. For example, the water rights in the Lushan west lake were returned to the local government for use in the city projects, such as tourism.

The local government has started to more closely regulate its own resources and rights. The local government has received some praise from its city residents, mostly because of its social welfare programs. The government provides housing and health services to farmers and city residents. As in the broader Chinese political system, the local CCP secretary's values have a strong influence on local peoples' lives. Secretary Shen's values and concerns regarding the credibility of the government, the efficiency of the government, and the long-term strategy of the government have changed the political atmosphere in Wuning. The attitude of the government is open to the people. This is reflected in the petitions on Shen's blog and on the official website of the government, reflected in the very specific and detailed answers to the people's comments. In some respect, Wuning government has gained the trust of the people.

Even though Secretary Shen has earned a reputation among some local people, there are still some problems in Wuning. There were many petitions online which revealed the problems of the land and forest right transfers, corruption, and other issues. In the relationships between government, developers, and local people, the government and the developers are usually on the same side while the interests of local people risk neglect. The difference between the compensation for farmers and the income earned by the local government from the land is huge; the farmers had limited negotiating power to keep their land, forest use rights, or old houses. Because of Wuning's urbanization, the certification of land rights was in the hands of the local government and strictly controlled. During the process of green development, some local people's interests were sacrificed for big development projects. Thus, protecting the interests of weak actors and realizing social justice is a key challenge.

Responding to online petitions or comments on Shen's blog is only one method used by the local government to maintain social stability. Common to all the big development projects is the fact that many people lost their homes and their land rights. Wuning's government attempted to solve those problems through compensation, giving other forms of social welfare to farmers who had lost their land. Nevertheless, the big projects were established without the participation of local people. The beautiful dreams of Wuning are the dreams of local government, but not necessarily those of the people. In the project reports, it is clearly stated that some minorities must be removed and sacrificed for the majority's interests, which are represented by the local government (Wuning Government, 2012).

As local people have little say in the process of "Green Rising-Up," they passively accept those green projects that come with it. Some of their land, their water, and their mountains were sold or rented to outside developers, with the justification that this was for the county's beautiful future. As a backward county, Wuning cannot withstand the devastating efforts of market forces, despite the goodwill of its local government. As people complained, the cost of living is rising and will be soon out of reach for the common people. The local environment is in a process of enclosure and will likely end up in the hands of a few rich people instead of belonging to everyone. Furthermore, since the government promised to serve the entrepreneurs in order to court projects to come to Wuning, local people have little ability to supervise and ensure that the projects are sustainable. The question remains: just how "green" is Wuning's green development?

How green is Wuning's "Green Rising-Up"?

It is difficult to determine whether the strategy of "Green Rising-Up" is green or not. To answer this question, we will explore different views on the matter.

Wuning chose the "Green Rising-Up, Happy Wuning" strategy, and it tried to import environmentally friendly projects, in the process realizing both ecological industrialization, and industrialization ecology. It has closed some very highly polluting factories to reduce pollution; from this perspective, it is ecological and green.

As for Wuning's energy-saving lamp industry, this industry produces green products in response to a growing green demand. It provides green products primarily for use in other places. While their use may be greener than traditional lamps, the production process for the energy-saving lamps is not so green. It is labor, energy, and mercury intensive. Mercury is harmful to the workers and the environment, Wuning's air, water, and land. Although the local government has promised to upgrade the production process to one that uses solid mercury, liquid mercury has been used for more than 10 years.

Forest tourism and recreation programs are tertiary industries, which were originally thought of as natural ecology projects and were not as profitable as secondary industries. These ecological services were discovered by the local government which found ways to market them. It is difficult to measure the influence of this activity currently, and difficult to say whether it is green or not. The guiding principle is good: let nature be nature, let local people manage it as they did a thousand years ago.

Wuning County has made visible efforts to profit from going green. Reflected in those efforts is the dilemma of green development and social justice. Wuning is a case that tells us that there is hope, since the county attempts to pursue green development. Although it is difficult to achieve a real green development path, the efforts being made to invest resources into green industries, like tourism, are evidence of a change in the management of the environment.

Conclusion

This chapter has described the "Green Rising-Up" in Wuning. What happened during the "Green Rising-Up" and what influenced it? What can we learn from this case study?

First, Wuning illustrates that a less developed county can have the courage to stay green and choose a development path that differs from the typical Chinese model of pursuing economic development at any cost. One could also argue that this area, with its good ecological conditions, has advantages in pursuing a green development pathway and can easily link to the ecological civilization advocated by the central CCP.

Second, this case study displayed again the importance of entrepreneurs who successfully run businesses that the local government defines as "green" industries. The entrepreneurs stick to the market logic and react to demand signals, even if these signals are generated by government regulations or laws. The energy-saving lamp industry gave the Wuning local government the idea and the hope of becoming a green lighting city, and in this way to combine economic development with ecological protection.

Third, Wuning demonstrates the key role of local officials, especially the decisive role of the local CCP secretary in green development. The behaviors and actions of Secretary Shen exemplify the power of the CCP secretary to lead local officials and to mobilize local resources to realize his aims and targets. In this manner, it is crucial that the local CCP secretary holds ecological values to make a local green development strategy possible.

In the context of Chinese politics, environmental politics should pay more attention to the local CCP secretaries instead of just focusing on such institutions as local environmental bureaus, since local affairs are under the command of the local CCP secretary (Lieberthal, 1997; A. Wang, 2013). To make Chinese environmental laws and regulations more effective, it is important to make the local CCP secretaries responsible, so that he or she will push for more compliance in the region.

Fourth, the gains and losses during the process of implementation of the "Green Rising-Up" strategy suggest that we should pay more attention to the interest of minority groups. The Wuning case exhibits how quickly a local city can develop without public participation and how quickly people's homes can be removed in the name of this development. If the current practices which rarely include local opinions in the decision-making process continue, the current trend of protesting and petitioning for compensation can be expected to grow. Local people are in a vulnerable position compared to that of the powerful local government. How to best protect the interests of local people and include their knowledge in the "Green Rising-Up" is still an issue that Wuning must resolve.

Wuning 127

Finally, the role of Internet petitions implies positive changes in the local-level governance. The Wuning government's practices around Internet communication with local people exposed how this technology can help to resolve conflicts during a process of rapid development. The messages on the site also revealed that local people care about local development and would like to participate in it. For example, they discovered potential problems in some projects and helped the local government supervise implementation. The abilities of the local government are limited in the supervision of the "Green Rising-Up" process, but the participation of local people online can expand that supervisory power.

Notes

1 Just as the household responsibility is carried out with the farm land, the forest rights reform is about the mountain and forests in the hands of collectives.
2 This is not far away from the famous porcelain township, Jingde Zhen. Recently, more white earth has been discovered leading to mining for extraction in the mountains.
3 In the hard times, there were many beggars from other places in Wuning. Kind villagers always gave some rice to them. Now, there are almost no beggars (personal observation).
4 There are many Zhejiang people in Wuning: the Old Zhe represent hard-workers and have business talent. One example is that they always sell their farm products in the market. Opposite one small village, there was a migrant village for the people from other places, but later they all moved out. The second wave of migrants were from the high mountains, but later, they moved out. For the local people, this is their hometown; for the migrants, it is a transit station (personal observation).
5 The abuse of compensation is a big issue. Wuning also competes for immigrants from the Three Gorges Dam but it has failed thus far.
6 There was a bamboo shoot factory down in Wuning which was run by local people; the products were sold overseas. Later it was closed down and those entrepreneurs went to bigger places to conduct business. They were the first group of people to become rich and set an example for others of how to be an entrepreneur (personal observation).
7 Interview 17.
8 Here foreign also includes investment from other Chinese entrepreneurs.
9 Jinagxi Province was the first to open a Minsheng blog service. On the Jiangxi Wenming Net all local chiefs must open their blog to the public. Some blogs are popular, while others have no articles and no visits. Shen is one of the most popular bloggers on it.
10 "Green Rising-Up" was invented by Wuning and it is also widely advocated in Jiangxi Province, a middle poor province with a focus on green investment. The other strategies did not originate from Wuning, but Wuning is very active in responding to the central- and provincial-level CCP's calls for ecological civilization and "Green Rising-Up."
11 Interview 15.
12 The government said it is for greening the city, but on the other hand, it means some fishers lost their living in this way.
13 Interview 19.
14 These four provinces are also the destination of Wuning's migrant workers.
15 Interview 19.

16 From 2005, the government has opened the people pass to communicate with local people. Wuning government will give specific answers to these questions asked by the people.
17 Interview 15.

References

Cai, C. (2013). Lushan xihai shanshui qianghua yangsheng yanglao zhongxin luohu Wuning [Lushan Xihai's good mountain and water conditions strengthen its attractiveness for ecological health cultivation (with elderly services) projects: Zhongxin located in Wuning]. Retrieved from www.jiujiang.gov.cn/xqcz/201307/t20130712_935436.htm.

Chen, A. J., Pan, S. L., Zhang, J., Huang, W. W., & Zhu, S. (2009). Managing e-government implementation in China: A process perspective. *Information & Management, 46*(4), 203–212.

Emma. (2009). Tiaoguang dashi touzi 30 yi zai Jiangxi Wuning jian lvse zhaoming jidi [The master of dimming lamp technology invested 3 billion in construction of a green lighting base in Wuning, Jiangxi Province]. Retrieved from www.china.com.cn/tech/txt/2009-07/13/content_18123043.htm.

Fu, N., & Wang, Y. (2011). Lvse jueqi zhi lu—Wuningxian jienengdeng chanye zhaoshang, shixian kaifangxing jingji chaochang fazhann de diaoyan [The road to a "Green Rising-Up"—Research on the attraction of the energy-saving industry that led to Wuning's leapfrog development with an open economy]. *Ji'an Jingmaoju*. Retrieved from www.jadoftec.gov.cn/news/JLYD/2011/119/111191621106J4G186FC4DBCII8CE92.html.

Fu, W., Zhou, X., Li, Y., & Li, R. (2012). Qian lun chengshi binshui lvde de shengtai guihua sheji—Yi Jiangxisheng Wuningxian Chaoyanghu jingguan guihua sheji [Discussion on ecological planning and design of waterfront greenland in city—A case study of landscape planning and design of Chaoyang Lake in Wuning County, Jiangxi Provinceweili]. *Zhongwai Jianzhu, 6,* 80–82.

Jiujiang Municipal Government (2018). Jiujiangshi 2018 nian nongcun shuidian anquan shengchan "shuang zhuti" zeren luoshi qingkuang biao [Implementation of the "double leaders'" responsibility system of safe production of the hydro power stations in rural areas in Jiujiang in 2018]. Retrieved from www.jjslj.gov.cn/zwgk/tzgg/201803/W020180328223557934732.pdf.

Hu, J. (2013, May 22). Shengtai jianshe zuli shixian meili Wuning meng—Wuning ruxuan Jiangxi shengtai wenming jianshe shijiaxian [Ecological construction supported Wuning's dream—Wuning is one of the ten best ecological counties in Jianagxi Province]. *Jiujiang Ribao*. Retrieved from www.jjxw.cn/2013/0522/95559.shtml.

Huang, H. (2013, May 20). Huashan yifeng.Bashiche weibo hua Wuning [Bashiche's blog on Wuning]. Retrieved from http://blog.sina.com.cn/s/blog_5e3c33e00101igha.html#bsh-75-263194947.

Industrial Park Research Group. (2012). Wuning jieneng zhaoming chanye jiju fazhan xiaoying fenxi [A cluster analysis of the energy-saving lamp industry in Wuning]. *Wuning Jingji*.

Ke, J. (2013). Bizai banxian haozhengce qingxin qingli wei renmin [Environmental disaster-induced migration is a good policy, serving the people wholeheartedly]. *Wuning Jingji*.

Ke, S., & Yuan, H. (Producer). (2002, July 22). Wuning nongmin xiaoshuidian fahui daxiaoyi [Small hydropower operations owned by farmers have had positive social effects]. Retrieved from http://jiangxi.jxnews.com.cn/system/2002/05/20/000149692.shtml.

Ke, Z., & Chen, X. (2012, July 22). Wuning 1197 ming shuiku yinmin fuzu zijin hexiao [Wuning verified and recalled a compensation quota of 1,197 for dam migrants] *Jiujang Xinwen*. Retrieved from www.jjxw.cn/2012/0713/44459.shtml.

Kuang, J. (2011, January 04). Shanshui Wuning shengtai gongcheng, shengtai baohu, shengtai xiaoyi yitihua [Mountain and water Wuning: An integration of ecological projects, ecological protection, and ecological economics]. *Jiangxi Ribao.* Retrieved from www.er-china.com/PowerLeader/html/2011/01/20110104103109.shtml.

Li, B., & Yang, Y. (2013, March 24). Zhu Chenghua—Wuning jienengdeng chanye di yi ren [Zhu Chenghua—The first entrepreneur in Wuning's energy-saving lamp industry]. *Shijie Zhaomingbao*. Retrieved from http://newspaper.worldlightingweb.com/Qnews.asp?id=7990&QID=2137.

Li, Y., Chen, S., Lei, Q., Yang, F., Zhang, H., & Liu, M. (2012). Wuning zhengce geili yuanqu lvse guangdian chanye kuaisu jiju [Wuning's industrial policies effectively fostered a cluster of green lighting industries]. Retrieved from http://jj.jnds.com.cn/news/minshengshehui/2012-04-24/4870.html.

Lieberthal, K. (1997). China's governing system and its impact on environmental policy implementation. *China Environment Series, 1*(1997), 3–8.

Lin, Y., & Wang, Z. (Producer). (2007, July 03). Shanxiang jubian kan Changshui—Jiangxisheng Wuningxian Changshuicun jiti linquan gaige ceji [Mountain villages' transition—A documentary of forest rights reform in Chuangshui village in Wuning county, Jiangxi Province].*Xinhuanet*. Retrieved from http://news.xinhuanet.com/fortune/2007-07/03/content_6323927.htm.

Ma, L., Chung, J., & Thorson, S. (2005). E-government in China: Bringing economic development through administrative reform. *Government Information Quarterly, 22*(1), 20–37.

Mu, F. (2010, June 17). Wuning linquan gaige zongshu [A summary of forest rights reform in Wuning]. Retrieved from http://blog.sina.com.cn/s/blog_682bef4f0100k988.html.

Rao, J. (2011, February 15). Wuning jienengdeng weihe zheme "liang"? [Why are Wuning's energy-saving lamps so "bright"?] *Jingji Wanbao*. Retrieved from http://blog.sina.com.cn/s/blog_4c16edd50100p9qt.html.

Rao, S. (2012). Rao Sihan zai quanxian sanxiang qingli gongzuo dongyuan dahui shang de jianghua [Rao Sihan's speech on the promotion conference for three clean-up projects]. *Wuningxianwei Wuningxianzhengfu Wangzhan*. Retrieved from www.wuning.gov.cn/?thread-7458-1.html.

Seifert, J. W., & Chung, J. (2008). Using e-government to reinforce government–citizen relationships: Comparing government reform in the United States and China. *Social Science Computer Review*. Retrieved from http://ssc.sagepub.com/content/early/2008/04/07/0894439308316404.full.pdf.

Shen, Y. (2012). Shen Yang zai sanxiang qingli gongzuo dongyuanhui shang de jianghua [Shen Yang's speech on the promotion conference for three clean-up projects]. Retrieved from www.wuning.gov.cn/?thread-7459-1.html.

Shen, Y. (2008). Wuningxian Xianzhang Shen Yang daibiao bei mingming yuanlin xiancheng he chenzhen fayan 2008 [Wuning county chief Shen Yang gave a speech on behalf of the nominated garden counties and townships]. Retrieved from www.chla.com.cn www.chla.com.cn/htm/2008/1029/20875.html.

Shen, Y. (2009a). Yan bi xing xing bi guo zhi bi de, quanli jianshe yijv yiye yiyou shanshui Wuning" [Promises must be kept, action must be resolute, and goals must be reached, making all efforts to build Wuning into a livable, entrepreneurial, and tourism-friendly place]. Retrieved from www.wuning.gov.cn/?thread-598-1.html.

Shen, Y. (2009b, July 14). Zhonggong Wuning Xianwei Shuji [The Secretary of Wuning in Jiangxi Province]. Retrieved from http://msblogs.jxwmw.cn/blog/a/2760/115.

Shen, Y. (2011, July 30). Zai quanxian zhili lvse jueqi, jianshe xingfu Wuning zhuti jiaoyu huodong jian xiangmu jianshe dahuizhan dongyuan dahui shang de jianghua [Shen Yang's speech at a campaigning conference of green rising-up and building a happy Wuning]. Retrieved from www.wuning.gov.cn/Item/7382.aspx.

Shen, Y. (2014). Wuning Xianwei shuji Shen Yang zaixian fangtan wenzi shilv [Interview of the Secretary of Wuning County—Shen Yang]. Retrieved from http://jx.sina.com.cn/jj/focus/2014-05-16/19152277.html.

Wanfu Industrial Park. (2003). Jianyao jieshao wanfu gongyeyuan [A brief introduction to Wanfu Industrial Park]. Retrieved from www.cc.ccoo.cn/webdiy/1062-72311-15506/jga_main.asp?id=72311&cateid=621796.

Wang, A. (2013). The search for sustainable legitimacy: Environmental law and bureaucracy in China. *37 Harvard Environmental Law Review 365*; UCLA School of Law Research Paper No. 13–31. Retrieved from http://papers.ssrn.com/sol3/papers.cfm?abstract_id=2128167.

Wang, Y. (2013). Wuning yige yimin zhi xiang yinglai fazhan xin jiyu [A migrant county embraces new opportunity to develop]. Retrieved from www.jxfpym.gov.cn/Item/15981.aspx.

Wang, Y. (2012). Xiqing shibada, Jiujiangzhan fengcai [Jiujiang Wuning celebrates the Eighteenth National Congress of the CCP]. *Wuning Xinwen*. Retrieved from http://daj.wuning.gov.cn/?thread-1862-1.html.

Wang, Y., & Tong, S. (2013, January 30). Yizuo Quanguo zuimei xiancheng zhengzai jueqi [The rise of one of the most beautiful counties]. *Wuning Xinwen*. Retrieved from www.jjwn.com/news/bencandy.php?fid=48&id-1483.

Wei, Q., & Yang, Y. (2013, March 15). Wuningxian weiyuchoumou yi shiji xingdong yingdui guangdian chanye "gong wenti" [Wuning took precautionary actions to deal with the "mercury pollution problem" caused by the energy-saving lamp industry]. *Shijie Zhaoming Bao*, p. B2. Retrieved from http://newspaper.worldlightingweb.com/Qnews.asp?id=16405&QID=9256.

Wuning Archives Bureau. (2013a). Dashi jizai 1994 [Milestones of Wuning 1994]. Retrieved from http://daj.wuning.gov.cn/?list-1470-2.html.

Wuning Archives Bureau. (2013b). Dashi jizai 1993 [Milestones of Wuning 1993]. Retrieved from http://daj.wuning.gov.cn/?thread-2067-1.html.

Wuning Archives Bureau. (2013c). Dashi jizai 1988–1992 [Milestones of Wuning 1988–1992]. Retrieved from http://daj.wuning.gov.cn/?thread-2066-1.html.

Wuning Archives Bureau. (2013d). Dashi jizai 1996 [Milestones of Wuning 1996]. Retrieved from http://daj.wuning.gov.cn/?thread-2070-1.html.

Wuning Archives Bureau. (2013e). Dashi jizai 2001 [Milestones of Wuning 2001]. Retrieved from http://daj.wuning.gov.cn/?list-1470-2.html.

Wuning Business Bureau. (2009). Xianwei fushuji, daixianzhang Shen Yang shuaiyuan fu jiangsu Zhejiang kaizhan zhaoshang anshang huodong [As Vice County Secretary and acting Chief, Shen Yang was in charge of business attraction activities]. Wuning County Government Disclose of Information. Retrieved from http://218.65.3.188/wlx/bmgkxx/zhaosj/gzdt/zwdt/200911/t20091118_141769.htm.

Wuning County Party Committee & Wuning Government. (2007). Guanyu jiaqiang quanxian chunjie qianhou zhaoshang yinzi gongzuo de tongzhi (wubanzi [2007 6 hao]) [Notice about accelerating businesses and investments attraction during spring festival No. 6 (2007)]. Wuning Industrial Park Website. Retrieved from http://jxwnip.cn/?thread-45-1.html.

Wuning County Party Committee & Wuning Government. (2009). Kaifang de Wuning [Wuning is open]. Retrieved from www.wuning.gov.cn/Category_13/Index.aspx.
Wuning County Party Committee & Wuning Government. (2010). Wuning gaikuang [A brief introduction of Wuning]. Retrieved from www.wuning.gov.cn/?thread-287-1.html.
Wuning County Party Committee & Wuning Government. (2011). Guanyu quanli tuijin lvse guangdian chanye fazhan de shishi yijian [Implementation opinions on promoting the green lighting industry]. Wuningxian Renmin Zhengfu wangzhan. Retrieved from www.wuning.gov.cn/?thread-7465-1.html.
Wuning County Party Committee & Wuning Government. (2012). Wuningxian 2011 nian guomin jingji he shehui fazhan tongji gongbao [Statistical Communiqué of Wuning on the 2011 national economic and social development]. Retrieved from www.wuning.gov.cn/?thread-9513-1.html.
Wuning County Party Committee & Wuning Government. (2013). Wuningxian chuangjian quansheng shui shengtai wenming chengshi shishi fang'an [Wuning's impelmentation plan for establishing a water ecological pilot in Jiangxi Province]. Wuningxian Renmin Zhengfu wangzhan. Retrieved from www.wuning.gov.cn/?thread-13056-1.html.
Wuning County Party Committee & Wuning Government. (2018, May 29). Wuningxian 2016 nian guomin jingji he shehui fazhan tongji gongbao [Statistical Communiqué of Wuning on the 2016 national economic and social development]. Retrieved from www.wuning.gov.cn/Item/79570.aspx.
Wuning Fishing Office. (2013). Shishi qingshui yuye de sikao yu duice [Some thoughts and advice on implementing clean water fishing]. *Wuning Jingji*.
Wuning Government. (2005). Mingsheng tongdao [Green pass for public affairs]. Retrieved from www.wuning.gov.cn/Category_5/Index.aspx.
Wuning Government. (2008). Guanyu dali fazhan jienengdeng chanye de shishi yijian [Opinions about supporting energy-saving lamp industries]. Retrieved from http://wnxswj.2008red.com/wnxswj/article_703_1045_1.shtml.
Wuning Government. (2009). Fuwu chengnuo [Promises and regulations on services]. Retrieved from http://gongyeyuan.wuning.gov.cn/Item/18124.aspx.
Wuning Government. (2010a). Wuningxian ziran ziyuan jianjie [Wuning's natural resources]. Retrieved from www.wuning.gov.cn/?thread-293-1.html.
Wuning Government. (2010b). Wuningxian dili qihou [Wuning's geography and climate]. Retrieved from www.wuning.gov.cn/?thread-292-1.html.
Wuning Government. (2011a). Wuningxian 2011 niandu xiangmu jianshe dahuizhan huodong shishi fang'an [Wuning's implementation plan for big projects, 2011 report]. Retrieved from www.wuning.gov.cn/?thread-5561-1-4.html.
Wuning Government. (2011b). Xianmu dahuizhan jianbao di 9 qi [Brief report on project progress No. 9]. Retrieved from www.wuning.gov.cn/?list-108.html.
Wuning Government. (2011c). Yinshan ziran shengtai baohuqu [Yinshan natural conservation and ecological park]. Retrieved from www.wuning.gov.cn/Item/1031.aspx.
Wuning Government. (2012). Xiangmu dahuizhan jianbao di 10 qi [Brief report on project progress No. 10]. Retrieved from www.wuning.gov.cn/?list-108.html.
Wuning Government. (2013). Wuningxian Zhengfu he wangmin jiaoliu [Communication between the Wuning government and the citizens in Internet]. Retrieved from www.wuning.gov.cn/Category_461/Index_2.aspx.
Wuning Government. (2017). Wuningxian nongcun shenghuo laji tishengnian huodong fangan [Implementation plan of improving rural waste treatment in Wuning County]. Retrieved from www.wuning.gov.cn/Print.aspx?id=85543.

Wuning Industrial Park. (2012). Quanyu yongshui ji yongdian chengben [The costs of water and electricity]. Retrieved from http://gongyeyuan.wuning.gov.cn/Category_1876/Index.aspx.

Xu, Y. (2010). Pojie xinxing chengzhenhua Jianshe de Nanti—Yi Jiangxisheng Wuningxian Weili Ran Ruhe Tuijin Xinxing Chengzhenhua Jianshe [Solving the problems in new mode of urbanization—A case study of Jiangxi Wuning's breakthrough].*Xuexi Yuekan*, 18, 016.

Zhang, X. (2012). Renzhen lvxing zezhi zhili xiangmu jianshe [Strive to perform in implementing projects]. *Wuning Jingji*.

Zhongguowang (Writer) & X. Zhang (Director). (2011). Wuning Xianwei Shuji Dong Jinshou: Linquan zhidu gaige chengjiu "Shanshui Wuning" [Wuning County Secretary Dong Jinshou: forest rights reform contributed to a Wuning with "mountain and water"]. Retrieved from www.china.com.cn/fangtan/2010-10/13/content_21116586.htm.

Zhongshan Daily. (2009, March 24). Wuning fu Zhongshan zhaoshang 10 xiangmu chao 3 Yi [Wuning's businesses and investment attraction in Zhongshan yield 10 projects over 0.3 billion RMB]. *Zhongshan Ribao*. Retrieved from http://info.lamp.hc360.com/2009/03/24064350853.shtml.

6 A comparative analysis of green development

Green development strategies have altered the appearance of these three places, Shanghai, Baoding, and Wuning, and have accompanied their industrialization and urbanization processes. The powers of entrepreneurs, local officials, and *guanxi* together have shaped the pathway of the local green development.

According to political ecology theory, the control or access to the resources that entrepreneurs and local officials have are indicators of their power as actors as seen in Shanghai, Baoding, and Wuning. The entrepreneurs used their social capital to gain access to resources to support their innovative ideas for new green businesses. The local officials trusted these ideas from the entrepreneurs and worked to incorporate them as a local development strategy. During the process, local officials used their *guanxi* to overcome political obstacles, such as the approval of local leaders. When local leaders decide to pursue green development strategies, they can invest large amounts of resources in them.

Green development has common patterns in the Chinese context. The power of local officials, entrepreneurs, and their *guanxi*, is related to Chinese economic, political, and social systems. The entrepreneurs were the first to believe in the future of green business, and often set up their own companies to realize this vision. To achieve the goal, the entrepreneurs had to first build relationships with the local officials through their *guanxi* in order to gain access to certain resources. The local officials, especially the local leaders, have strong political power to control or distribute local resources. It is their *guanxi* which influences trust and cooperation between entrepreneurs and local officials. This is reflected in the transfer of ideas or resources between the two groups.

This chapter analyzes the common driving forces and powerful actors in the three case studies. It then compares their patterns of green development. It highlights the common implications of their green development. Finally, this chapter will offer conclusions about the impacts of local green development. Hopefully, it will shed some light on the relationship between development and ecology at the local governmental level.

Common driving forces

Green development strategy in Shanghai, Baoding, and Wuning was closely related to their "green" businesses. The idea to develop "green" businesses was born in the minds of entrepreneurs. They then communicated their ideas to the local officials whom they trusted in order to gain resources for their businesses. The reform-minded local officials trusted the entrepreneurs with "green" businesses and helped to develop a single company or industry into similar or complete industries.

These local officials cared about developing local interests in a more environmentally friendly and economically successful way. These local officials are usually described as scholar-type officials who are long-term thinkers and are willing to accept new ideas about local development. Wang Daohan advocated transforming Shanghai from a socialist industrial city into a trade and finance center in the "Develop Pudong" strategy. In Baoding, Ma Xuelu strived to develop environmentally friendly and high-tech industries in a relatively poor city; that is why he appreciated Miao Liansheng's idea to develop solar energy and decided to develop renewable energy in Baoding HTZ. Wuning's local leader, Shen Yang, went all out to build up the most beautiful county from a poor, inland, and agricultural place, and emphasized the smart use of the area's ecological advantages in the market.

The entrepreneurs and local officials have lived or worked in these cities for years. This meant they had considerable regional knowledge making it easier for them to judge the potentials of the "green" businesses which would be most suitable for the local context. They also had rich *guanxi* networks in these regions, which they could use to support their development ideas. Their common preferences for supporting the local interests provided a strong basis for their cooperation and resource transfer work.

Based on the common green ideas, entrepreneurs and local officials not only used their economic and political power to mobilize resources, but also their *guanxi* to obtain resources for their "green" ideas. Their ideas and efforts faced competition. Entrepreneurs with green businesses had to compete with other businesses; local officials with green ideas had to win the support of the local leader who could have different local development ideas. The success of a green development strategy depended on the willingness of the local leader to advocate for the local development strategy. With the support of the local leader, the entrepreneurs could enjoy numerous preferential policies and the support of the local government.

Innovative power: entrepreneurs

The green development strategies can be traced back to the entrepreneurs. The entrepreneurs first searched for an alternative development path for the locality. After the period of reform and opening-up, the liberty to pursue economic wealth was nurtured, enabling entrepreneurship and dynamic changes (Guo, 2011; Nee

& Young, 1991; Zapalska & Edwards, 2001). "The entrepreneurs must experiment with new production lines. They must tinker with technologies from established producers abroad and adapt them to the local conditions" (Rodrik, 2008, p. 105). The entrepreneurs are the first actors to have innovative "green" ideas and to take actions to invest resources in order to set up their businesses. Later entire "green" industries follow in their footsteps. These point out the importance of entrepreneurs in exploring new business opportunities, including "green" businesses. There are many examples of this.

In Shanghai, entrepreneurs tried to persuade the government to reform Shanghai into a finance and service center with a good living environment, in contrast to the industrial center planned by the central government. The entrepreneurs came together and discussed the possibility of setting up a financial service center by attracting international businessmen to Lujiazui at the beginning of the 1980s, although the finance and services were still strictly controlled by the governments at that time (G. Wang, 2008). After reading an article about the solar energy industry, Baoding entrepreneur Miao sold all his other businesses to set up a solar company in 1993 (P. Chen, 2010). This company became a world-leading solar PV company, and brought other renewable industries to Baoding. In the hard business environment at Wuning, entrepreneurs searched for different ways to develop the county. Finally, in 2003, an energy-saving lamp factory was able to survive and profit in the market (B. Li & Yang, 2013).

In parallel with these business entrepreneurs, another group of entrepreneurs were also searching for solutions for local development. The local officials who were responsible for local economic development were searching for entrepreneurs and industries that were suitable for the local context. In Shanghai, local officials organized conferences and trips to other places to learn from their experience in economic development. In Baoding, it took many years for Ma Xuelu to find out which industry was suitable and promising for Baoding HTZ. For Wuning, it took decades to find a suitable industry to be supported.

Many studies regard local officials as entrepreneurs, since they aim to promote economic development and are involved in business activities (Cannon, 2000; Lieberthal, 1997, 2007). Local officials were entrepreneurs in these three case studies, but they were different from business entrepreneurs. Entrepreneurs focused only on specific business activities, aiming to be competitive and gaining more market shares. Local officials were busy with industrial policies attempting to attract more entrepreneurs and businesses to their jurisdictions. In this way, local officials were more like policy entrepreneurs, since they are responsible for issues of local public interest, including improving local economic growth and ecological protection.

These groups of cadre-entrepreneurs built industrial clusters in their regions. In Shanghai, the cadre-entrepreneurs made an integrated plan for developing Pudong, including industrial development, city planning, as well as environmental protection. In Baoding, Ma and others worked to develop other renewable industries, such as wind energy companies as well (Shin, 2017). As a result, the Baoding HTZ became a center of not only solar energy companies but also many other renewable energy companies. Under the leadership of Shen Yang, who had working experience in tourism, Wuning developed ecological tourism, ecological agriculture, and so on. These local officials accepted the suggestions of entrepreneurs, and then developed single factories or companies into group factories and industries.

As Rodrik writes, "growth strategies require considerable local knowledge" (Rodrik, 2008, p. 42). Successful growth strategy needs rich local knowledge, and the successful industrial policies need the combination of both innovative entrepreneurs and local officials. These three cases showed the coming together of entrepreneurs and local officials who favored environmentally friendly industries.

The group of environmentally aware local officials developed entrepreneurs' ideas into industrial policies which favored "green" industries. They had the power to decide which entrepreneurs to trust, what to give whom, and which industry to offer preferences to. It is easy for local officials to collude with businessmen to expand short-term economic interests. Some local officials were worried about preserving the local ecology for future generations. They witnessed the environmental pollution and disasters, had sympathy for the environment and with local people. They usually tended to cite Confucian or Buddhist sayings emphasizing the importance of the harmony between humans and nature. Those local officials were more willing to accept the "green" entrepreneurs.

In Pudong, local officials from different government departments came together and established relationships to support the "Develop Pudong" strategy, which they thought was best for Shanghai (Long, 2012). The officials took environmental pollution issues and ecological protection into consideration in the new development areas (Liu & Zhang, 1991; F. Zhao, 1991). They used their political power and *guanxi* to place their ideas on the government's agenda.

In Baoding, Ma Xuelu was the director of Baoding HTZ, worked to bring high-tech industries to Baoding, and rejected polluting industries in the HTZ (interview 3). As a local official, Ma chose to support Miao and his solar company with the resources he could mobilize, even though other local officials did not think renewable industries had a promising future.

In Wuning, the local leader Shen Yang insisted on the value of the local environment to prevent polluting industries from coming to Wuning during the promotion of attracting business investment. He worked in tourism and saw Wuning's ecological conditions as a resource for the industry. The government of Wuning set preferential industrial policies for entrepreneurs in tourism and the energy-saving lamp industry.

In pursuit of green development, these local officials balanced economic development aims and ecological protection issues. They showed their concerns for the local ecological costs and benefits during the process of development. It is important to notice that it was the local officials and leaders as policy entrepreneurs who enlarged the content of green business into green development. From these three case studies, it is clear these innovative green ideas were from entrepreneurs who have substantial awareness about local conditions and who experimented with different activities.

Local officials cooperated with entrepreneurs to develop green ideas into a cluster of green businesses, and local leaders further developed it into a green development strategy. The entrepreneurs and local officials usually made successful progress with their "green" ideas as they had rich local knowledge (Ostrom, Schroeder, & Wynne, 1993). The two innovative groups have some similar values regarding economic development and environmental protection. There are many entrepreneurs doing green businesses in different places in China, there are also local officials in different localities who care about local ecology. The first key issue is how these two groups of innovative people come together, and the second key issue is how their ideas could stand out as an attractive local development strategy in order that green business may gain its priority to be supported by local leadership.

Political power: local leadership

In the Chinese political and economic contexts, the power of the local CCP leader is a decisive factor in terms of which industry receives support and which development strategy is pursued. The local CCP leader's power is also reflected in his control and access to resources and further distribution of the local resources.

Why do some local leaders pursue green growth when the evaluation system of the government's performance criteria is economically oriented? It is true that economic development is crucial for the promotion of local officials, but there are also other responsibilities for local officials, like keeping social stability (So, 2007; Zhu, 2011). There is still space for local leaders to pursue green development. The central government is putting more and more efforts on environmental protection. When there are environmental protests, the promotion prospect of relevant local officials will be negatively influenced. Of course, not every local official wants to be promoted and promotion also depends on other factors, like good connections with upper-level government officials (Opper & Brehm, 2007). In the case of Pudong, Wang Daohan was already 65 years old and a senior CCP member, he would not care about further promotion because the chances of becoming a top leader were thin due to the age restriction. Another reason is that, to catch the attention of the upper-level leaders, it is important for a local leader to differentiate his or her region from other similar local states. For poor localities, like Baoding and Wuning, it is hard to achieve the kind of economic growth achieved by Beijing or coastal counties. That is the reason why both local leaders advocated being an "ecological civilization" pilot.

The green development strategy must compete with other development strategies, in order to win the support of local leaders. In the three case studies, the entrepreneurs and local officials with their "green" ideas and industrial policies advocated their green development ideas for a long time to local governments; green development did not become a key development strategy until it received the support of the local leader. The local entrepreneurs took risks in starting their "green" practices long before local green development strategies were implemented.

Shanghai, as a provincial-level city, had its local policies closely supervised by the central government. Shanghai was thus an important battlefield for different political powers and actors. Shanghai was deleted from the chance to be the first group of Special Economic Zones (Xinhua, 2008); although as early as 1984 the central government agreed to develop Pudong and open Shanghai (H. Li, 2013; J. Li, n.d.). Historically, Shanghai was an international city at the leading edge of global development. By the 1980s, Shanghai was not only behind many international cities, like Hong Kong, but also was far behind newly developing cities, like Shenzhen (Xu, 1995; Yuan, 2012; Q. Zhao, 1994). Many stakeholders from civil society and government departments were concerned about Shanghai's development and discussed how to reform Shanghai (G. Wang, 2008). From archival materials, we can see that the reformers advocated for opening and reform of Shanghai, so that it would resemble other special economic zones and cities. They wanted Shanghai to be a pioneer in experimental development strategies (Ma, 2008; Xu, 1995). Conservative powers insisted on keeping Shanghai as a politically stabilized city with a socialist economy instead of taking risks.

The reform-minded leaders in the 1980s intended to solve many problems in Shanghai, including pollution. They reached a common consensus on strategy: "Develop Pudong." Wang Daohan as the local leader supported the "Develop Pudong" strategy, but the central government did not agree with him initially. Wang Daohan invited many scientists and city planners to help design the "Develop Pudong" strategy to ensure the quality of the planning. The Pudong development strategy needed the support of the central government leaders, especially that of the chief engineer of reform and opening-up: Deng Xiaoping. It was the 1989 student movement which helped Shanghai to obtain Deng's approval of "Develop Pudong" (Yuan, 2012). "Develop Pudong" was a local strategy with green ideas from the beginning, but later became a demonstration program for China's reform and modernization. Its state-led urbanization became a successful showcase for other cities.

The acceptance and support of the local leader, the local CCP secretary, and, in the case of Shanghai, of the top leader, Deng Xiaoping, played an important role in turning entrepreneurs and local officials' ideas for green development into a local development strategy. The Shanghai case showed the insistence of local leaders' support of green development strategy until it got the approval of the central government.

There were local officials who favored "green" businesses early on. Their ability to develop their ideas was limited without the support of the local leader. Local officials can only mobilize those limited resources which are within their power boundaries. Ma could only use political resources in the Baoding HTZ, and not in the entire city. Green industries were not mainstream industries, since they were new and higher-risk compared to other industries. The entrepreneurs and a few "green" local officials were the minority in the local government who supported a development strategy that took green into consideration. Success in obtaining the support of local leaders was a turning point, after which time green businesses developed much faster than before and enjoyed many favorable policies.

In Baoding, Miao and Ma's efforts were not noticed by local leaders for a long time, and their peers even laughed at their ideas (interview 3). Ma tried to introduce renewable energy industries to the Baoding leaders, and was unsuccessful until Mayor Yu took his advice. After Mayor Yu visited Europe and saw the huge potential of renewable energy development there, he justified the development of the renewable energy industries in his "Electric Valley" development strategy. With the cooperation of WWF, he developed the "Solar city" and "Low-carbon city" strategies to promote the concepts of a low-carbon economy and ecological protection. Yu argued for low-carbon and renewable energy development at several conferences and was accordingly named as the low-carbon mayor by the media (Shi, 2008). His power to mobilize resources was much greater than Ma's, because he could mobilize the entirety of Baoding's resources to support the green development strategy. The Baoding HTZ received more land from the local government for the enlargement of the renewable energy industry. Mayor Yu supported private renewable energy companies with local government-owned company resources, such as labor, capital, and technology. Yingli benefited very much from its membership in the Tianwei Group, a strong state-owned company in electricity equipment. The acceptance and advocacy of Mayor Yu, as the local leader, determined Baoding's green development strategy and supported the development of Baoding's renewable energy companies.

Initially, all kinds of industries in Wuning were welcomed at the industrial park as long as they were willing to come to Wuning. As the saying goes, "*jiandao lanli doushi cai*," "all are fish that comes to his net."[1] Since the strong incentives system distributed the task of attracting business to every government department, there were officials who did not care about the quality of industries. Wuning did not have a clear development strategy and lacked city planning before 2011's "Green Rising-Up."

Gradually, the local officials who cared about the local ecology started to realize that some industries were not good for the local air and water quality and some were not successful within the industrial park. Local leader Secretary Shen further highlighted environmentally friendly industries, such as the energy-saving lamp industry and ecological tourism. Secretary Shen valued the environment in Wuning, and it was his responsibility as the local leader to take care of it. Under his leadership, the good ecological conditions were transformed into ecological products in the market, and this attracted entrepreneurs to invest and settle down in Wuning.

Why did the local leaders approve green development in their territory? One common factor is the attitude of the local leader in each of these three cities. Shanghai's Wang, Baoding's Yu, and Wuning's Shen all wrote about the importance of the environment. Their articles revealed that they are familiar with Chinese traditional culture, and they were willing to accept new ideas. The local leaders' ecological awareness was crucial in deciding upon a local green development strategy.

Combination of two powerful groups: guanxi

Guanxi is the glue to draw the business and political power together. The entrepreneurs rely on *guanxi* to overcome many challenges in the Chinese market, as well as to gain certain necessary resources for their businesses. The political actors also rely on *guanxi* to attract competitive entrepreneurs to their regions for development.

In the three cases, entrepreneurs with their "green" businesses need to overcome many challenges in the Chinese market. While market principles have developed, many market institutions to protect entrepreneurs have not developed at a similar pace. Private property rights are insufficiently protected, the rule of law is still weak, and free trade is restricted (Cai, Wu, Zhong, & Ren, 2009; Harvey, 2005). As a result, entrepreneurs actively try to use *guanxi* with local officials to gain political protection. Doing business, especially "green" business, is not easy for Chinese entrepreneurs because of the difficulty in gaining access to resources, which are controlled by local officials. Scholars have concluded that entrepreneurs are strategically allied with the local CCP: "the CCP encourages its members to join the private sector and simultaneously recruits successful entrepreneurs into the party" (J. Chen & Dickson, 2010, p. 66).

The entrepreneurs in Shanghai utilized *guanxi* to put their ideas on to the government agenda. In Baoding, the *guanxi* between Miao Liansheng and Ma Xuelu was the precondition for the cooperation necessary to develop a renewable energy industry. Ma Xuelu had known Miao Liansheng for many years (interview 3), which is why Miao Liansheng asked him for help to develop his solar company and was willing to share his knowledge about solar energy with Ma Xuelu. Solar entrepreneur Miao in Baoding mobilized *guanxi* to put on a "red" hat (i.e., become closely related to the communist party) to turn his private company into a collective holding company to gain national projects, technologies, as well as capital. Farmer entrepreneurs in Wuning relied on *guanxi* to avoid rent-seeking in the inland county. In Wuning, entrepreneurs and local officials are like "brothers" when they describe their *guanxi* (interview 13). Local officials made use of a fellow *"laoxiang"* network to open the door for returning businessmen, encouraging them to return and invest in Wuning. That is why the local government published a document for the spring festival to persuade fellow entrepreneurs to invest back home (WuningCCP & WuningGOV, 2007).

Local officials also need *guanxi* to find capable entrepreneurs to settle down in their regions. Take the local officials in charge of the industrial parks as a case. There are thousands of industrial parks. Local officials compete for entrepreneurs who are searching for suitable places to start their businesses (Coase & Wang, 2012). Local officials need the entrepreneurs' innovative ideas and capital. In Pudong, entrepreneurs created new concept definitions and blueprints for Shanghai as a finance, services, and trade center. In the case of Baoding, Ma Xuelu searched for suitable high-tech industries to develop, and entrepreneur Miao led him to an answer. Wuning's local officials needed the entrepreneurs with energy-saving lamp and tourism industries to invest in his county.

The communication between local officials and entrepreneurs based on *guanxi* nurtured trust and cooperation between them. The *guanxi* base is their common good wish for a better future for their localities. The business and political entrepreneurs communicated about the green development to the locality. In Shanghai, the conference about Shanghai City Development Strategy gathered Wang Daohan Mayor and various experts in 1986 (G. Wang, 2008). A conversation between entrepreneur Miao Liansheng and director Ma Xuelu became a turning point for Baoding's renewable energy development (Zhou, 2010). Shen Yang went to the coastal areas with his team to find successful entrepreneurs, in order to persuade them to contribute to the region's development.

These entrepreneurs with their "green" ideas and businesses provided "green" ideas for the local officials and opened possibilities for a green development strategy. For "green" ideas from entrepreneurs to be taken up in local green development strategies, there are still many challenges. They must gain the attention of leaders at the same time other entrepreneurs are trying to do so. It is a challenge to persuade the local leader to support their "green" businesses, since "green" businesses are still new and associated with high risks. Among these cases, a dense network of *guanxi* is constructed between the entrepreneurs and local officials, particularly regarding their common value regarding environmental protection.

Guanxi played an important role in the combining of power and resources to promote green development. Social capital is not only formed by blood relationships, but also by strongly held common ideas and values. People holding green values came together and became a stronger force for green development. In Baoding, Ma and Miao came together to promote the solar energy company, Yingli, at Baoding; their social capital allowed them to overcome difficulties. In Shanghai, the common ideas to develop Pudong formed a strong social group with experts from different fields and local officials from different governmental departments, and they used their social capital to put their ideas on the governmental agenda. The common aim to develop Wuning drew entrepreneurs and brought local officials together who then further developed their *guanxi*. The green development strategies in each case study provided vivid examples of how *guanxi* works.

First, the entrepreneurs used their *guanxi* to reach the local officials that they trusted to obtain resources for their businesses. In Shanghai, for example, the commonly shared ideas about the importance of developing Pudong brought many experts, scholars, and local officials together. Later these actors used their *guanxi* to reach the local leader—Wang Daohan. In Baoding, Miao reached Ma through his personal *guanxi* to gain the qualification to apply for the national light program which aims to use solar energy to eliminate the situations where poor people are without access to electricity.[2] Although Miao and Ma failed, they trusted each other about the bright future of solar energy. In Wuning, in the name of *guanxi* many entrepreneurs tried different businesses and developed close relationships with local officials to guarantee their property rights and prevent rent-seeking in this inland county.

Second, *guanxi* not only allowed local officials to support entrepreneurs but also advanced green ideas within the government's agenda. There were many obstacles making it difficult for entrepreneurs and local officials to turn their ideas into real actions, including how to persuade the local leader to believe that green businesses are better than other industries to be supported. This was a big challenge as green businesses usually are new which makes it hard for them to gain capital and other resources.

Social capital helped to overcome these problems. Furthermore, their social capital developed during the process of advocating their shared green ideas. In Pudong, Wang used his *guanxi* to push the "Develop Pudong" strategy to the central government's table even after he retired from the position as mayor. In Baoding, when Ma learned about renewable energy, he nurtured *guanxi* with the national and international renewable energy experts and then used it to convince the local leader. The local officials in Wuning relied on their social capital to win entrepreneurs back home.

The power of social capital can be recognized in the ways that entrepreneurs and local officials gained the necessary resources for their green ideas. There were local regulations which guaranteed the services of local government for entrepreneurs and the transfer of local resources to them. The local officials trusted the entrepreneurs and helped them to obtain the local resources for their businesses, including land and capital. In Baoding, Ma gave Miao the access to land and capital to realize the production of solar PV products. He helped Miao to get the national program to support his business with enormous loans. In Wuning, the local officials provided cheap electricity and land to the entrepreneurs for the energy-saving lamp factories and to attract tourism developers. In Pudong, Wang encouraged research on finance and land leasing for "Develop Pudong."

Guanxi played a key role in realizing local development strategies, which is reflected in the way that local officials gained the approval of political leaders. Local officials with green development ideas used their *guanxi* to persuade the local leader to accept their green development strategies. The *guanxi* of local officials allowed the local leader to trust and believe in their ideas. In Shanghai, Wang believed "Develop Pudong" to be a solution for many of the problems of Shanghai, including environmental pollution. Wang had a strong *guanxi* with his student—Jiang Zemin (Zhong, 2005). Wang recommended Jiang as the next mayor of Shanghai, which was the key step for Jiang later to become the leader of the central government. In 1984, Wang proposed the plan to the central government. It was approved in 1985. There was no concrete implementation plan, however. Wang Daohan had waited for five years and was no longer mayor. Finally, Jiang suggested that Shanghai's leaders persuade Deng Xiaoping to agree to "Develop Pudong" after the Tiananmen Square Event. Still, he used his *guanxi* to connect to president Yang Shangkun on the spring festival day, to turn over the documents about "Develop Pudong" to Deng Xiaoping in 1990 (Ifeng, 2010).[3] Deng Xiaoping was afraid that the international investors would not trust the Chinese government's reform; he used Pudong as a strategy to prove his determination for reform (Yuan, 2012).

The *guanxi* did not stop at the realization of local green development strategies. It continued during the implementation of green development strategies. The stronger the *guanxi* network for green development, the more likely the local leader would accept it as a local strategy. *Guanxi* mobilized resources for green development by establishing trust among entrepreneurs and local officials. The actors who share their beliefs in green development can develop their *guanxi* further.

The entrepreneurs used their *guanxi* to connect with the local leader and to allow their ideas to become a key development strategy for the local government. It is common that entrepreneurs have ideas for local green development, but the unique quality of these three case studies was that the entrepreneurs' ideas entered the sights of the local leader. Eventually the local leader developed and implemented these ideas within their local green development strategies.

Chinese-style local green development

The power and social capital of entrepreneurs, local officials, and local leaders mobilized resources to realize green development at the local level in the three cases examined here. They helped the "green" businesses to overcome market barriers and invest huge amounts of local resources into "green" industries and projects. In the Chinese context, local governments are the real owners of the local resources in their territories, although they need to justify the use of these resources and show they are in the interest of local people.

We can observe a common pattern in the implementation of green development strategies in the three cases. The justification for local green development was carried out by the local government's propaganda system. After this justification, the local government set up different working groups, published laws and regulations, and gathered resources to implement green development. Finally, the local government invested local resources, such as land and capital, into green development.

Justification for green development strategies

For local government leaders, their support for green development satisfied the demands of the central government and local people who are affected by pollution. After the coastal areas' rapid development, heavy pollution warned less developed areas that they should search for an alternative development path. All case studies emphasized that green development was in line with environmental protection or ecological civilization. They were pilots in the search for a new development mode.

The justification for "Develop Pudong" was not only Shanghai's strategy, but also a national strategy. Development in Shanghai was different from the other two cases because it was under stricter supervision by the central government. The justification for "Develop Pudong" was strongly influenced by the will of the central government. Shanghai's local government leaders emphasized the demonstrative potential of "Develop Pudong." They argued that "Develop Pudong" could serve as a signal to the world that China would remain open to the world after the Tiananmen Square Event.

At the beginning, the justification for "Develop Pudong" was by reform-minded local leaders, who aimed to solve the problems in Shanghai. The justification for "Develop Pudong" was difficult in the 1980s because of the importance of Shanghai in China's socialist politics and planned economy. The "Develop Pudong" strategy planned to urbanize a large area in a short time. Shanghai's reform and policies were examples for other areas.

"Develop Pudong" was a far-sighted plan which focused on the tertiary industry. Shanghai was polluted by heavy industries during the planned economy era, so "Develop Pudong" was designed with green ideas to avoid similar pollution problems. Most of the tertiary industries were clean industries and the city planning of the Pudong area took environmental protection into consideration.

The justification for "Develop Pudong" was the second wave of reform and opening-up. There was a saying that went "in the 1980s looking up to Shenzhen, in the 1990s looking up to Shanghai." Shanghai opened its tertiary industry sector to the outside world, especially its finance and service sectors. "Develop Pudong" included a free trade zone, a high-tech zone, and a finance center to explore these new markets. The justification for "Develop Pudong" incorporated new ideas and experiences from the international community. Shanghai invited world famous city planners who connected the city to the world community. The comparison of Shanghai to other world cities supported the construction of a new city of modern science and technology along the river.

Baoding Mayor Yu used the same methods to argue that Baoding's Electric Valley strategy was also in line with ecological civilization (W. Chen & Wang, 2009; Yu, 2008). When Baoding's Mayor Yu decided to build China's Electric Valley, he was very active in advocating for the importance of renewable energy and a low-carbon economy. The justification for renewable energy and low-carbon development was very strong and widely reported by the government.

At first, there were different opinions among the Baoding government officials on the renewable energy industries, but this situation changed when the Mayor Yu turned towards the renewable energy industries. Renewable energy was interpreted by Yu Qun as the third industrial revolution in history, and the future energy for people (Yu, 2008). Mayor Yu chose the concept of ecological civilization as the path for Baoding's development (Zhang, 2008). Baoding thus made its name as a low-carbon city because of its strong support of renewable energy.

Baoding was a city with heavy pollution from industries, which polluted the Baiyangdian Lake for years. As a city near Beijing, Baoding was the preferred destination for many polluting industries that were banned from Beijing. The renewable energy industries were Baoding's opportunity to change this situation. Baoding's justification for renewable energy came much earlier and more strongly than from the Chinese central government. After the Renewable Energy Law came out in 2006, Baoding's support for renewable energy fostered low-carbon city development and climate change actions. Baoding sought support from international organizations, such as the WWF, to strengthen its justification for renewable energy development. Although Baoding was a less developed city, it adopted the ecological concepts and ideas of the more developed areas. It was an interesting case which has important implications for other cities in developing countries.

Even in a hinterland county like Wuning, the local leader argued that the natural local ecology is a rich resource. The county Secretary Shen framed the use of the environment as a part of the "Green Rising-Up" strategy, in the CCP spirit of ecological civilization. Shen, as the county CCP secretary, decided that Wuning would be a pilot county in the construction of an ecological civilization (Shen, 2013). The Wuning government held several mobilization meetings to motivate local officials to put all their effort into the "Green Rising-Up" strategy. To advertise the "Green Rising-Up" strategy, slogans were put up around the county, especially near highways. Wuning's propaganda for the "Green Rising-Up" strategy regarded the beautiful local environment as a source of wealth for the local people.

The justification for green development strategies was mainly discussed by local leaders. Plans were made by local governments and green issues were defined by officials and experts. They argued that green development was in the interests of local people and the nation.

Politicized local resources by local governments

After the justification for the local development strategies, the process of controlling and distributing local resources began. In the decentralized political system, the central government has loosely supervised the performance of local governments, including the implementation of state-advocated green development. It was left to local governments to choose what to do with its local resources. The risk in this process was instability or conflicts of interest from local people, which could attract the attention of the central government, and was usually followed by punishing measures of the central government with removal of local officials. Local government officials knew quite well the expectations and preferences of the central government.

Local government has strong regulatory powers, which enable them to make laws and regulations which were relatively effective at the local level. It also had some power to interpret laws and regulations from the central government according to its own interests, when they did not cause serious social instabilities. Furthermore, the courts were under the leadership and control of the local government, so local governments may protect the polluting companies (Van Rooij, 2010). Thus, it is hard for the environmental victim to sue the local governments and industries. For these reasons, local governments had a strong say in their territories.

During the implementation of the green development strategy, the power of local governments was reflected in their ability to distribute local resources. The cooperation between local officials and entrepreneurs was reflected in the resource mobilization for their green development strategies. One important indicator is the commercialization of land by the local government. Through these development strategies, the local government gained access to confiscate land from collectives and to develop the land in the market. It is common for local government to set up development companies as local government-owned companies to gain loans from banks for developing the confiscated land, then sell or rent land use rights in the market. Land transfer is a key point to relocate resources in a market way at the local level in China.

Shanghai Pudong New Area had the greatest access to resources, as the whole Chuansha County was turned into Pudong New Area. It was industrialized and modernized in a very short time. The Develop Pudong Committee formed the Pudong New Area government in 1993, and the old local governments, like Chuansha County government, were dismantled. Shanghai and the national government invested huge amounts of resources to develop the Pudong New Area as "the window of China." The "Develop Pudong" working group started with a few people, but later developed into an entire government body to oversee this new district in Shanghai (Sun, 2010).

Pudong enjoyed many preferential policies from the central government which allowed Pudong to further obtain domestic and international resources. Pudong was able to rent land to the international financial companies and gain capital for development; the central government contributed to this access to capital by ordering the Chinese national banks to relocate in Pudong. The central government allowed Shanghai to keep more revenue in order to build Pudong, and at the same time, it asked the national banks to give loans to Shanghai Pudong. The Pudong government officials used their social capital to find international companies to lease the land. The Pudong government also found developing companies and encouraged them to bring their business to Pudong. Later the developmental companies became four administration districts of Pudong.

Pudong founded four developmental companies to take responsibility to develop four areas, namely Shanghai Waigaoqiao Free Trade Zone Development Company with $10\,km^2$ of land, Jinqiao Export Processing Zone Developmental Company with $27.38\,km^2$ of land, Lujiazui Finance & Trade Zone Developmental Company with $28\,km^2$, and Zhangjiang High-Park Developmental Company with $17\,km^2$ of land.

In Baoding, the local government also controlled and distributed local resources in support of the "Electric Valley" strategy, and low-carbon city development, especially for renewable energy industries. First, Baoding had clear industrial policies which supported renewable energy production. Baoding claimed to be an electric valley, comparable to Silicon Valley in America. Baoding then created an incentive system to encourage innovations in renewable energy technologies (Shin, 2017). The Baoding HTZ provided office buildings for small businesses. Second, Baoding expanded its industrial zone and changed the landscape of the old city. It started to build a solar city and a low-carbon city with specific local laws and regulations. Drawing on the solar city plan, the

Baoding government required public facilities to adopt solar PV systems, like the traffic solar system. In its efforts to become a low-carbon city, Baoding demanded more action in energy reduction and renewable energy generation from companies. Baoding also distributed tasks among different government departments and working groups, especially the low-carbon city working group and renewable energy promotion working group.

The Baoding HTZ expanded its land under the "Electric Valley" strategy, from $16\,km^2$ to $130\,km^2$. Baoding set up working groups to promote low-carbon activities and a solar city. Mayor Yu was the leader of the low-carbon pilot city working group, which also included the other leaders from 27 different governmental departments. The same happened in Wuning. The civil servants were distributed in different groups and tasked with attracting projects.

In Wuning, different working groups appeared to gather resources for the "Green Rising-Up" strategy. The first working group attracted green businesses to Wuning with preferential local policies, such as Jiangxi Chenyang Dengye Youxian Gongsi. The local government promulgated a series of regulations which support the energy-saving lamp industries in the industrial park and ecological tourism projects. The second working group constructed the new city. The local government invited famous city planners to draw up a new city, aiming to build a livable, ecological city and attract tourists and new residents. The Wuning government called civil servants in different government departments together to participate in the new city planning. These civil servants held public positions and were under the control of the local leader.

The third working group managed the mountains, the forests, and land rights. As Wuning was one of the pilot cities for forest rights reform, forest and mountains belong to local peasants according to the central government's reformed forest laws. Interviewed farmers said that forest rights licenses were actually in the hands of local government officials rather than in their hands.[4] The Wuning government had ecological immigrant working offices that asked the farmers to move into the city or concentrated villages (Ong, 2014). Since the new city was developing, it needed more land for its many new projects. There were local government officials specifically responsible for the transfer of land from farmers to developers. The entire Jinkou village was moved to make way for the Zhongxin Lushan Xihai's high-quality tourist resorts (Y. Wang & Tong, 2013). The fourth working group managed the conflicts that arose during the development process. The county leader opened his blog and e-mail to receive the public's questions and complaints.

It is important to bear in mind that the access to and control of local resources depended on the local leader's political position. In the case of Baoding, when Yu left, his programs and regulations were either not well implemented or abandoned after his leave. An interviewee in the Baoding HTZ said that it was possible that Baoding would shift away from renewable energy industries towards other high-tech industries.

In the Chinese local political system, the rotation of local leaders has a negative impact on the consistency of local development strategies (Kostka, 2014).

148 *Comparative analysis of green development*

It is said every mayor introduces his or her own city planning concepts and ideas. In the case of Pudong and Wuning, green development was accompanied through the building of a totally new city.

The power of the local leader to control and distribute local resources is reflected in the process of green development. Another important power is the strong personnel appointment rights of local leaders. Since the local leader has the local personnel power, it is common that local officials are motivated to finish local leader's policies. In the three case studies, each of the local leaders restructured the local government to encourage green development, and the civil servants further worked to obtain resources for green development. The local leader issued laws and regulations to define the preferential policies towards green entrepreneurs and an incentive system for implementing green development. The three cases all set up new government bodies to implement their green development strategies; they all rely on their land to found developmental companies in order to attract businesses.

Environmental justice and distribution pattern of local resources

A local leader's power to control local resources explains how the game of green development worked. The flow of resources does not only obey the rule of the market, but also of the local government's interventions in the market. The government has the right to manage local resources, so it is up to the local government, especially the local leader, to decide whether to sell their local resources. To a certain extent, it is the leader's wishes or beliefs that decide the distribution of local resources. Leaders can ignore certain market rules or behave unreasonably in the market as they are not themselves concerned with making profits. Local leaders are motivated by the national CCP's expressed desire to solve economic development and ecological problems at the same time. If local leaders believe in the green development strategies, they may gamble and invest local resources for this strategy rather than pursue other opportunities.

The rapid development of Pudong is the best example of how local government leaders could change the face of a city in a socialist country. Pudong was planned by the local government and was created as a city in a short period of time. Shanghai invested a huge amount of resources to build the bridges and the Lujiazui finance center. As the central government agreed to make Pudong as a showcase to the world of China's openness, resources for transformation came not only from Shanghai but also from the central government. Develop Pudong persuaded the central government to let Shanghai keep some of its revenues.

Develop Pudong also invested in the environment, according to its own city plan. The amount of greenery in Pudong was much greater than that of the old city. The preferential policies allowed Pudong to lease land to businesses; "Develop Pudong" relied on leasing huge amounts of land to obtain the necessary capital for development. Pudong created the land business model, which set an example for new city development. The government granted a whole county to Pudong as land to attract businesses. Because of the geographic advantage and preferential policies, the price of land rose quickly in Pudong.

In Baoding, the local government enlarged its HTZ under the "Electric Valley" strategy. The Baoding government tried its best to support the renewable energy industries. It favored the renewable energy companies with land gifts and helped the renewable energy companies to get loans from local and national banks. The local government lobbied the central government to define renewable energy industries as national key industries. Baoding was involved in the renewable energy industries itself, as a key shareholder and a pilot city in the national low-carbon city program. The Baoding government invested huge amounts of capital to apply solar PV products in its city, with the goal of promoting applications of solar PV products in other cities.

The Baoding government, under the leadership of Mayor Yu, devoted itself to supporting renewable energy industries. Yu became a low-carbon mayor. After Mayor Yu left office, local green efforts were discounted, as the new leader decided he needed new political achievements to distinguish himself from his predecessor. Renewable energy industries lost favor. The will of local leaders changed the market rules in Baoding, fostering the development of strong renewable energy industries and a pilot low-carbon city, but once the supportive local leader left or retired, their policies and ideas could be weakened or disappear as well.

In Wuning, the local government invested huge amounts of land and capital in the "Green Rising-Up" strategy. The land was given to the entrepreneurs cheaply or even for free to support their energy-saving lamp industries. The government built the industry infrastructure with local revenues to provide good services for the entrepreneurs. To construct the new city, the local government further relied on revenues from land leasing, which sold the use of local land to developers, especially to real estate developers. To develop ecological tourism, the potential of the local environment to attract entrepreneurs was explored by the local government. Wuning's ecological advantages, such as its forest and hot water spring, became selling projects. The lake was cleaned so that a big developer from the outside could manage it alone. These efforts were made to promote green development in Wuning, but there was also abuse of the local environment as natural resources were sold in the market and local communities' rights in the name of green development.

During the process of big projects, the land and water in the hands of farmers in collectives were taken over by the developers. The fever within the real estate industry was one indicator that the local leader tried to sell the local environment to successful people. Wuning's aim to develop ecological tourism, good living, farming, and forest was consistent with its aim to sell the local environment to the outside world. They built many luxury houses and buildings along the water line, with the goal of selling them to successful people from the cities. The Zhongxin Lushan Xihai is a big project. Secretary Shen put value on the environment and posited it as a key resource in Wuning's development strategy.

In this section, we have observed that the pattern of leasing land to obtain capital for green development was similar in the three case studies. The power of local governments to intervene in the market was significant, because its support of "green" businesses, along with huge amounts of local resources, helped the entrepreneurs to gain market shares across the world. Green development appeared to be an alliance of a few key actors in local governments who tried their best to mobilize resources to support their green vision. This pattern suggests that if more and more powerful actors in local governments believe in green development, local governments will have a broader platform from which to advance their economic development goals. Local governments can make a difference in relating environmental protection to economic development, but its ultimate success depends on the perceptions and goals of powerful actors.

Environmental justice of local green development

"All ecological projects are political and economic projects at the same time. The cost and benefits of these green developments are different among different actors" (Bryant & Bailey, 1997, p. 28). Local green development projects are connected to political and economic structures and influence different actors accordingly. Schmink Wood said that "ideas are never innocent but either reinforce or challenge existing social and economic arrangements winning the battle of ideas, over human use of the environment" (as cited in Bryant & Bailey, 1997, p. 41). Entrepreneurs and local officials used green development to realize their policies and goals.

Green development results in a change in the structure of competition for local resources. Green development was dominated by local government leaders and entrepreneurs as they decided how to use local resources. Were they really advocating for green development for every group in society? What were the effects of green development on the local environment and local people? Our political ecology perspective directs us to look at the gains and losses for different actors as a result of the process of green development.

Gains of green development supporters

The local officials in these case studies were praised or promoted because of their efforts for green development. The entrepreneurs gained resources for their businesses and with the support of local governments they were competitive in the green market. Through their efforts to realize their aims, *guanxi* of entrepreneurs and local officials were strengthened.

The entrepreneurs realized their aims to do "green" business. They gained resources to develop their companies, which helped them to produce green products. Miao's Yingli Green became one of the largest solar PV companies in the world. Furthermore, the justification for the green industries overcame the barriers to realizing production at the local government level. Pudong's financial sector, which had been strictly controlled by the central government, gradually became freer. Since the free market and rule of law principles do not work very well, the local government's approval provided necessary protection for the entrepreneurs. Moreover, the local governments promised to provide goods and services to them, attended company activities and even used their governing power to sell the entrepreneurs' products. The entrepreneurs thus became successful and managed to realize their green business visions.

The local officials also benefited during the process of green development. In terms of their political careers, they were promoted either to higher positions or their efforts were recognized by upper-level governments. Local government officials finally found a way to balance the demands of the local economy and local ecology through green development. They, however, were the ones to define green development. In implementation of the "Develop Pudong" strategy, some local officials were promoted by the Chinese national government. For that reason, the "Develop Pudong" model became very popular in other local governments. In Baoding, the "Electric Valley" strategy saved the Baoding High-tech zone and Ma's career. Even after his retirement, Ma remained active in renewable energy associations. Wuning copied significantly from the "Develop Pudong" model. At Wuning, local government officials were praised by the higher-level governments. Wuning's rapid development demonstrated the success of local officials; these local officials gained political achievement, which encouraged other local governments' officials to mimic their experiences.

The *guanxi* among local officials and entrepreneurs was strengthened because of their cooperation to promote green development. Baoding's Ma still has a position in Miao's Yingli company as an advisor on climate change policies. Shanghai's supporters of "Develop Pudong" brought their knowledge and *guanxi* with them to new places and implemented development in other local governments. One key entrepreneur at Wuning said: "Wuning's entrepreneurs and local leader were like brothers in the same boat with the same purpose to develop Wuning" (interview 13). Although the political positions of the local officials may change during their careers and they may not have access to the same resources they once did, their *guanxi* can support further cooperation in the future.

Once a local leader who had been supportive of green development was promoted and moved to other places, the continuity of the local government's green development strategy faced uncertain change. In Shanghai, the local government did not change "Develop Pudong" after the local leader left for a national government post, since "Develop Pudong" had become a national strategy, which is hard to change. In Baoding, after Yu and Ma left, the continuity of green development was in question because the new local leader revaluated the sustainability of the renewable energy industry because of its high energy consumption. In contrast, in Wuning, Secretary Shen left Wuning in 2016, which greatly influenced the further development of the green development strategy and the continuity of the institutions or practice he invented were in question.

Briefly put, the powerful actors who advocated for green development were also the people who gained the most from it.

Effects on local people

In all three cases, the voices of local experts were included in the process of green development. The opinions of the general population, however, were rarely asked for in decisions related to the green development strategies. Local citizens were divided by different gains and losses during the process of green development. While people were forced to move away from their homes because of the green development that required land, others got jobs in the new "green" industries.

Each of the green development strategies mobilized huge amounts of local resources which brought fast development, especially within the industrial parks. During the development process, the price of land rose, and some farmers benefited from it. Compared to the benefits obtained by the local government, they gained relatively little. Significantly, more and more farmers lost their collective land to the development programs. There were land conflicts between local people and the local government; farmers and local residents complained about the price gap between their compensation and the land revenue gained by the local government (interview 19). Local people were at a disadvantage in the conflicts, since local governments made new laws and regulations and were the ones to set up working groups to deal with the land conflicts. Some farmers received compensation and appeared satisfied since their farmland was much more expensive than other farmland in more rural areas. Many farmers moved into the new and modern flats, and some even got more than one flat. As housing prices rose, they benefited from this as well.

Another positive effect of green development was that more job opportunities in green businesses became available. The Baoding HTZ provided thousands of jobs in renewable energy for farmer workers. In the three case studies, local people automatically became workers in the new industries, especially farmers who lived near the industrial parks. There were farmers who immigrated to work in the industrial parks, which brought prosperity to local governments to a certain extent. Will the development continue? One local private entrepreneur argued that "it was fine as the local governments created the urbanization rather than a process of natural urbanization; as long as there were more people coming into the city, it will lead to development gradually" (interview 19). Many farmers gave up their land in rural areas and became workers, renting rooms near the industrial areas. Many local young farmers now had the choice to stay near their hometowns, rather than having to leave to find work in big cities.

The third benefit of green development was that the living conditions of the urban citizens improved. Each of these three cities used modern concepts to build their new cities or city districts, including more greenery, parks, and protection of the local environment. In Wuning, a wetland park was created in the city which connects rivers and lakes in a natural way. Wuning was the first county in Jiangxi Province to build a waste water discharge system, instead of discharging waste directly into rivers and lakes. In Baoding, the industrial park was more modern. The booming real estate business happened alongside the green development strategies, which allowed the developers who promoted a better environment to sell their real estate at higher prices. Local people praised local governments for the improved living conditions in the cities.

There were also costs to green development. Local people living near the new industrial parks still suffered from environmental pollution, even though the parks were made up of "green" industries. In the Shanghai Pudong area, local people complained about the chemical and pharmaceutical industries. In Baoding, local people believed that the solar PV factories negatively influenced their health. Some young couples protested the pollution, arguing that it made it difficult for them to have babies. In Wuning, the local people near the Wanfu industrial park complained of the foul-smelling air, especially during the night. They saw yellow water flowing from the pumps into the local rivers. The workers in the factories revealed that the factories did little for the environment and they did not believe that the local government strictly controlled the factories (interview 18). For local people, the green development was a "face-saving project" for the sake of local government officials.

Besides the health costs, there were some farmers and citizens who lost their homes and lands because of the development strategies. Although there were compensations, there was no room for the local people to fight to save their homes and lands. The will of local officials and entrepreneurs was so strong that they easily took the land and houses for relatively low prices. There were some complaints from the local people about the unfairness of the land and housing compensations; it is said that local government bought the land at low prices and then sold it for a hundred times more in the market (interview 12). Due to the political system, it was hard for the local people to get the right price for their land. In Wuning, the ecological tourism projects confiscated land from the farmers to sell it to the developers. There were some petitions by the farmers, but they failed because local governments prevented them from reaching the upper-level government (interview 18). Shanghai also had problems with land conflicts.

There have been many sad stories related to land conflicts after development strategies went into effect. It was a common pattern that land conflicts went along with development, regardless of whether it was green development or not. Development strategies were based on local resources that were initially in the hands of local people but were then taken by the local government.

In each of the three case studies, the local people enjoyed some benefits brought about the green development strategies, but they also suffered significantly from the green development's side effects. The local people had little weight in how green development was done and they were in a weak position to challenge the changes brought about by the process.

Effects on the local environment

Shanghai Pudong, Baoding, and Wuning connected their local green development to the ecological civilization concept in the CCP ideology. How was the local environment treated by local government officials and entrepreneurs? As local officials and entrepreneurs were the primary decision-makers determining what is good for the local environment, their interpretation of local ecological protection was closely related to their powers and interests. Our political ecology perspective takes into consideration the changes in the local environment during the process of development.

Along with green development, a huge amount of farmland disappeared. It was turned into industrial parks or new cities to demonstrate the achievements of green development to the outside world. Local environmental resources were used to create "a beautiful environment" that would attract entrepreneurs and residents. The industrial parks were established for green industries, even though they sometimes had negative impacts on the local environment.

Many ecological resources were developed into programs to attract business. The development strategies are human-centered and treat the environment as a resource to bring wealth to the local government. In Shanghai, "Develop Pudong" attracted lots of businesses but also damaged the local environment. In Baoding, the pollution related to renewable industries was not measured for the local environment. In Wuning, the mercury pollution related to the production of energy-saving lamps threatened the local environment.

In the conflicts between the local environment and the "green" industries, local government officials and entrepreneurs chose "green" industries, but sometimes the local environment suffered as a result of these "green" industries. Some ecological projects were emphasized as pilot projects to show to the media that local governments did well in environmental protection, even though at the same time the environment was being polluted to serve the industries.

Policy suggestions

There is a wave of cities advocating for green development and copying the experience of pilot cities like Baoding. Hundreds of renewable energy parks appeared after the success in Baoding. Without entrepreneurs and local advocates, many of these efforts failed or turned into real estate development programs (Huang, 2012). As the central government encourages development in line with its ecological civilization vision, some local officials have seized the opportunity to alter the development model. It is difficult to say all the green cities are truly green.

The central government should create more specific ecological criteria for the performance of local government officials. There are still no hard criteria for local officials' efforts in ecological protection; economic growth is the key indicator for promotion (Rauch & Chi, 2010). As such, all green cities have focused on developing green industries still focusing on achieving economic growth. As green industries may not have green impacts on the local environment or people, it would be better that many green industries did not enjoy all of the preferential policies they receive.

In the Chinese political system, the local CCP leader has the power to mobilize resources and restructure the local government bodies, innovatively make new laws and regulations; the local people do not have much influence in decision-making processes. There should be more supervision of the local leader by the public. There should be more participation of local people in green development processes, in order to make their voices heard and protect their interests. Otherwise their interests will continue to be ignored or sacrificed by local governments in the name of green development.

For international actors, green development cooperation and investment should not always focus on the Chinese central government. They should communicate more with local governments, and especially with the local CCP leaders. As there are more and more local officials who plan to visit developed cities to learn about their experiences, the visions of these leaders will greatly influence their policies at home.

For research on China's environmental issues, a focus on local governments in making and implementing laws and regulations is crucial to understanding the huge ecological changes taking place. Local governments interpret many central policies in the economic and environmental interests of its locality. In fact, the local laws and regulations are more effective than the central government's regulations and laws at the local government level (Tanner & Green, 2007).

Notes

1 Interview 15.
2 This policy was inspired by the Chinese government after attending the 1993 "World Solar Summit." It is called "*Guangming Gongcheng*" light project, which was published in 1997, with the aim to send electricity to 8 million people in the form of renewable energy, like solar and wind energy.
3 Deng Xiaoping went to Shanghai to spend the spring festival from 1988 to 1994.
4 Interview 19.

References

Bryant, R. L., & Bailey, S. (1997). *Third world political ecology*. London: Routledge.

Cai, W., Wu, Y., Zhong, Y., & Ren, H. (2009). China building energy consumption: Situation, challenges and corresponding measures. *Energy Policy, 37*(6), 2054–2059.

Cannon, T. (2000). *China's economic growth: The impact on regions, migration and the environment*. London: Macmillan.

Chen, J., & Dickson, B. J. (2010). *Allies of the state: China's private entrepreneurs and democratic change*. USA: Harvard University Press.

Chen, P. (2010, October 27). Guangneng yu mengxiang [Solar energy and dreams]. *Jin Xiu 2010, 10*. Retrieved from http://blog.ifeng.com/article/8298209.html.

Chen, W., & Wang, X. (2009, March 24). Baoding Shizhang Yu Qun Qinghua fabiao yanjiang changdao shengtai wenming [Baoding Mayor Yu Qun delivered a speech at Tsinghua University to support ecological civilization]. Retrieved from www.tsinghua.edu.cn/publish/news/4205/2011/20110225232235734101283/20110225232235734101283_.html.

Coase, R., & Wang, N. (2012). *How China became capitalist*. Hampshire: Palgrave Macmillan.

Guo, R. (2011). *An introduction to the Chinese economy: The driving forces behind modern day China*. Singapore: John Wiley & Sons.

Harvey, D. (2005). *A brief history of neoliberalism*. Oxford: Oxford University Press.

Huang, S. (2012, November 27). Guangxi guangfu zhi du guren biaoyan shangban [The solar city in Guangxi hired people to fake production]. Retrieved from www.21so.com/HTML/zgzqb/2012/11-27-503.html.

Ifeng (Producer). (2010). Du jin jie bo xiongdi zai—Wang Daohan [Through all conflicts and hardships, brotherhood remained—Wang Daohan]. *Wo de Zhongguo Xin*. Retrieved from http://news.ifeng.com/history/phtv/wdzgx/detail_2010_12/02/3314716_3.shtml.

Kostka, G. (2014). Barriers to the implementation of environmental policies at the local level in China. *World Bank Policy Research Working Paper* (7016).

Li, B., & Yang, Y. (2013, March 24). Zhu Chenghua—Wuning jienengdeng chanye di yi ren [Zhu Chenghua—The first entrepreneur in Wuning's energy-saving lamp industry]. *Shijie Zhaomingbao*. Retrieved from http://newspaper.worldlightingweb.com/Qnews.asp?id=7990&QID=2137.

Li, H. (2013, September 10). Deng Xiaoping di qi ci nanxun cuisheng Pudong kaifachao [Deng Xiaoping's 7th southern tour accelerated "Develop Pudong"]. Retrieved from *Shangwu Koukan* http://history.eastday.com/h/20130910/u1a7651243.html.

Li, J. (n.d.). Huigu Pudong Xinqu de guihua he jianshe [A review of the planning and construction of Pudong New Area]. *Shanghai Committee of Chinese Political Consultative Conference*. Retrieved from http://news.eastday.com/epublish/gb/paper167/2/class016700001/hwz322627.htm.

Lieberthal, K. (1997). China's governing system and its impact on environmental policy implementation. *China Environment Series, 1*(1997), 3–8.

Lieberthal, K. (2007). Scorched earth: Will environmental risks in China overwhelm its opportunities? In E. Economy & K. Lieberthal (Eds.), *Harvard Business Review, 85*, 88–96.

Liu, T., & Zhang, M. (1991). Lun Pudong Xinqu huanjing guihua de yuanze he neirong [A discussion of environmental protection principles and content in developing Pudong]. *ShanghaiHuanjing Kexue*, 1, 003.

Long, H. (2012, February 03). Pudong kaifa kaifang qianqi yanjiu he yunniang [The research and preparation for opening and developing Pudong]. *Pudong Shizhi*. Retrieved from http://szb.pudong.gov.cn/pdszb_pdds_dsyj/2012-02-03/Detail_411714.htm.

Ma, Y. (2008). Wo de fuqin Ma Hong [My father: Ma Hong]. *Yanhuang chunqiu*, 3.

Nee, V., & Young, F. W. (1991). Peasant entrepreneurs in China's "second economy": An institutional analysis. *Economic Development and Cultural Change*, 293–310.

Ong, L. (2014). State-led urbanization in China: Skyscrapers, land revenue and "Concentrated Villages." *The China Quarterly*, 217, 162–179.

Opper, S., & Brehm, S. (2007). *Networks versus performance: Political leadership promotion in China*. Department of Economics, Lund University.

Ostrom, E., Schroeder, L., & Wynne, S. (1993). *Institutional incentives and sustainable development: Infrastructure policies in perspective*. Boulder: Westview Press.

Rauch, J. N., & Chi, Y. F. (2010). The plight of Green GDP in China. *Journal of Sustainable Development* 3(1), 102–116. Retrieved from www.consiliencejournal.org/index.php/consilience/article/viewFile/112/28.

Rodrik, D. (2008). *One economics, many recipes: Globalization, institutions, and economic growth*. Princeton: Princeton University Press.

Shen, Y. (2013, June 26). Zai jianshe shengtai wenming zhong zhengdang xianfeng [Strive to become a pilot in ecological civilization]. *Shenyang' minsheng blog*. Retrieved from http://msblogs.jxwmw.cn/blog/c/2760/116120.

Shi, C. (2008, March 13). Yu Qun, dazao Zhongguo Diangu jianshe ditan Baoding [Yu Qun, creating Electric Valley of China, constructing low-carbon Baoding]. Retrieved from www.cenews.com.cn/xwzx/dh/200803/t20080313_222964.html.

Shin, K. (2017). Neither centre nor local: Community-driven experimentalist governance in China. *The China Quarterly*, 231, 607–633.

So, A. Y. (2007). Peasant conflict and the local predatory state in the Chinese countryside. *Journal of Peasant Studies, 34*(3–4), 560–581.

Sun, X. (2010). 800 zhuangshi in anzai [Where are the 800 pioneers?]. *21 Shiji Jingji Baodao*. Retrieved from http://finance.sina.com.cn/roll/20101204/02539054687.shtml.

Tanner, M. S., & Green, E. (2007). Principals and secret agents: Central versus local control over policing and obstacles to "rule of law" in China. *The China Quarterly, 191*, 644–670.

Van Rooij, B. (2010). The People vs. Pollution: Understanding citizen action against pollution in China. *Journal of Contemporary China, 19*(63), 55–77.

Wang, G. (2008). Huiyi Pudong kaifa [A review of "Develop Pudong"]. Retrieved from www.tsinghua.org.cn/alumni/infoSingleArticle.do?articleId=10016213&columnId=10016199.

Wang, Y., & Tong, S. (2013, January 30). Yizuo Quanguo zuimei xiancheng zhengzai jueqi [The rise of one of the most beautiful counties]. *Wuning Xinwen*. Retrieved from www.jjwn.com/news/bencandy.php?fid=48&id=1483

WuningCCP & WuningGOV. (2007). Guanyu jiaqiang quanxian chunjie qianhou zhaoshang yinzi gongzuo de tongzhi (wubanzi [2007 6 hao]) [Notice about acclerating businesses and investments attraction during spring festival No. 6 (2007)]. Wuning Industrial Park. Retrieved from http://jxwnip.cn/?thread-45-1.html.

Xinhua (2008). Jiemi lishi: gaige kaifang shiban jingji tequ de juece neiqing [Uncover the secret: The story of decision-making of special economic zones during the reform and opening-up]. Retrieved from http://news.hexun.com/2008-07-09/107551672.html.

Xu, W. (1995). Kaifa kaifang Pudong de juece shimo [The decision-making model for "develop and open Pudong"]. *Zhongguo Ruankexue, 7*.

Yu, Q. (2008). Baoding: "Ditan" linian zutui shengtai wenming [Baoding: The low-carbon concept supported its ecological civilization]. *Chengshi Zhuzai*, 5(City Dialogue), 22–23.

Yuan, E. (2012). Xiaoping sudu: 60 tian diaoding—"Pudong kaifa kaifang" zhezhang "Zhongguo wangpai" shi zenme da chulai de? [Deng Xiaoping: Deciding to "open and develop Pudong" in 60 days—How did he play out this card?]. *Nanfang Zhoumo*. Retrieved from www.infzm.com/content/75057.

Zapalska, A. M., & Edwards, W. (2001). Chinese entrepreneurship in a cultural and economic perspective. *Journal of Small Business Management, 39*(3), 286–292.

Zhang, C. (2008, April 07). Baoding shizhang Yu Qun: Zou juyou Baoding tese de shengtai wenming fazhan zhi lu [Baoding Mayor Yu Qun: the road to ecological civilization with Baoding's characteristics]. *Baoding Ribao*. Retrieved from www.heb.chinanews.com/todaybd/news/xyjj/2008-04-07/28551.html.

Zhao, F. (1991). Lun kaifang Pudong huanjing baohu ying jianchi de yuanze [Discussion of the principles of environmental protection in "Develop Pudong"]. *Shanghai Huanjing Kexue, 10*(1), 43–44.

Zhao, Q. (1994). Dier zhang de tiandi zhi duhou Pudong de dili dimao ji renwen jingguan [The second chapter: The geographic, landscape, and cultural history of Pudong] (Zhao, Q., Trans.). In Q. Zhao (Ed.), *Xin shiji xin Pudong* (pp. 19–50). Shanghai: Fudan Daxue Chubanshe.

Zhong, P. (2005, July 08). Shezhe: Rui Xingwen [Shi Zhe: Rui Xingwen]. *Cai Jing*.

Zhou, F. (2010). Yizhang huangpai cuisheng "Zhongguo diangu" [A yellow card was responsible for "China electric valley"]. *Zhongguo Jingji he Xinxihua*. http://finance.sina.com.cn/roll/20100927/10108710049.shtml.

Zhu, R. (2011). *Zhu Rongji Jianghua Shilu (Di Yi Juan) [Zhu Rongji Memoire, "Shanghai Speech 2"]*. Beijing: Renmin Chubanshe.

7 A political ecology of local green development

More and more local governments, especially those in cities, rich and poor, are advocating for green development in the form of ecological, low-carbon, or circular development (Chinese Society for Urban Studies [CSUS], 2013). The role played by local governments in economic transformation has caught the attention of many scholars, some of which doubt the motivations of local governments in environmental protection (Economy, 2010; Lieberthal, 1997; J. Y. Lin & Liu, 2000; Montinola, Qian, & Weingast, 1995; Oi, 1995; Shapiro, 2012; Walder, 1995; C. Zhang, 2006).

This book has tried to understand the powers and factors which have led to local green development, which helps us to understand local green development and its relationship with China's environmental transformation. It specifically asks why some local governments advocate for green development, and what influences they have on the local environment and society. This study has aimed to do the following: first, to use political ecology theory to explore the interaction of political, business, and social powers during the decision-making process of local governments towards green development; second, to compare in detail three significantly different cities, namely the provincial-level city Shanghai, the municipal-level city Baoding, and the county-level city Wuning, to identify the key common factors that fueled their green development; third, to emphasize the leadership of local governments in experimenting with new ideas and policies in green development, moving ahead of the national government and providing valuable experience and knowledge to other local governments domestically and abroad, regardless of their political stature and socioeconomic conditions.

Several main findings are summarized here. The entrepreneurs, local officials, and their personal connections, *guanxi*, are the main explanatory factors behind local green development in the cases examined. The entrepreneurs represent business power, local officials are the agents of political power, and *guanxi* acts as a social power which creates connections between the actors. The entrepreneurs and local officials utilized their power and *guanxi* to mobilize resources in order to advocate for green development. During the process, innovative entrepreneurs promoted green development ideas or experimented with green businesses at the localities. Their goals can broadly be described as gaining access to

160 *Political ecology of green development*

resources currently controlled by political powers and they actively searched for the support of local officials. When local officials accepted and pursued entrepreneurs' green development ideas, the entrepreneurs and local officials worked together to persuade the local leaders to turn their proposals into key local policies. In this process, personal networks and personal relationships, or *guanxi*, play an important role in connecting and building trust between entrepreneurs, local officials, and local leaders.

The second group of empirical findings in this research is the different gains and losses of actors during the process of green development. It is a common pattern that local officials and entrepreneurs receive more of the benefits while the interests of the weak actors, like farmers and the environment, are underrepresented or neglected during the process of local green development. These findings suggest the importance of paying attention to the environmental and social justice dimensions of local green development. In this way, this study makes a contribution to political ecology's analysis of imbalanced power and benefits, and social and environmental justice issues. Political ecology emphasizes the political interests and actions of various actors and their impact on society and the environment (Bryant & Bailey, 1997, p. 2; McCay, 2002; Peet & Watts, 2004). This theoretical approach is well suited to analysis of green development. The Chinese political system is characterized by strong government and industry with a weak society. Political ecology implies that the behavior of powerful actors, in this case, the government and industry, have enormous impacts on the environment. Indeed, the government and industry are the dominant powers in deciding and investing in environmental projects.

The first section of the conclusion focuses on this study's relationship with the broader political economy and environmental politics literature. The second section describes this study's contribution to academic debates over the role of entrepreneurs, local officials, and *guanxi* in China's local green development. The third section is about rethinking the environmental and social justice issues surrounding China's local green development. Finally, the last section discusses this study's implications about green development and potential future research topics.

Struggling local power

The empirical findings of this study demonstrate that Chinese local governments do take action toward green development on their own initiative rather than only when given orders by the central government. The puzzle posed by the literature is that many scholars conclude that local governments have strong incentives to pursue economic development at the cost of environmental protection (Economy, 2007; Fewsmith, 2001; Jahiel, 1998; J. Li, 2009; Liu & Diamond, 2008). In all three case studies, the local governments were not only concerned with economic growth, but also with environmental protection. As evidence of this, this study shows that the concern has translated into policy. All three regions have achieved economic growth with a focus on green industries.

Political ecology of green development 161

This study agrees with many scholars of China's environment that local governments are crucial in environmental governance; most of this scholarship focuses on criticizing the destructive actions of local governments, while paying little attention to the positive practices of local governments in environmental protection (Economy, 2010; Lieberthal, 1997). Local governments are negatively portrayed in environmental studies for several reasons: first, it is assumed that positive environmental changes come largely from the Chinese central government or civil society and not from local governments and industries (Knup, 1997; Tang & Zhan, 2008; Yang, 2005); second, a large group of environmental scholars focus primarily on the failure of weak actors to realize environmental protection because of local leaders' protection of local industries and the poor implementation of environmental laws and regulations. They overlook the fact that positive environmental changes at the local level would not be possible without the support of powerful local actors, such as the departments for economic and industrial policies (Jahiel, 1998; Ma & Ortolano, 2000). They tend to argue that local government and industry care only about economic growth and have no incentive to take responsibility for environmental protection. The central government, NGOs, and EPBs all have limited power to induce environmental policy change on the part of Chinese local governments (Schwartz, 2004; Van Rooij, 2006).

Numerous studies in political economy point out that local government is the driver for China's rapid economic development (Oi, 1995; White, 1998). They argue that decentralization allows the central government to create strong incentives for local governments and industries to pursue economic growth in collaboration. In relation to the environment, they say little, or conclude that local officials pursue economic interests without consideration of the environmental and social costs (J. Chen & Dickson, 2010; Guthrie, 2012; Li, Meng, Wang, & Zhou, 2008; Naughton, 2007; Oi, 1995; Walder, 1995). Based on such political economy studies, it is reasonable to question whether local governments could also be a driver for China's environmental transition because it lacks incentives to do so. In exploring this question, this study employed political ecology theory, which adds a strong environmental element; political ecology goes beyond the role of government in economic development and expands the impacts of government policies to the environment and society.

This book seeks to improve our understanding of local environmental politics. Some studies on this topic exist, but none attempt to explain in depth how green development policies came into being or who the actors behind them are. This is to say, the existing studies lack a basic understanding of green development in the Chinese context (Beyer, 2006; Crooks, Nygard, Zhang, & Lui, 2001; Economy, 2005; Ho, 2001; Knup, 1997; Kostka & Hobbs, 2012; Kostka & Mol, 2013; Ma & Ortolano, 2000). This study addresses the gap in previous studies by looking much more closely at three variables: the role of the local officials in charge of devising local regulations, particularly industrial policies, the influence of businessmen on how local resources are distributed, and the *guanxi* between local officials and businessmen as it contributes to gathering resources for their

162 *Political ecology of green development*

common goals. The latter is particularly significant, as the positive impact of businessmen on the local environment is underestimated in the aforementioned studies. Most of the literature focuses on their role in economic activities, while little attention is given to their role in local environment management (Baumol, 1968; Deyo, 1987; Fan, 2002; Gartner, 1988; Hamilton & Harper, 1994; Hébert & Link, 1989; Kiong & Kee, 1998; J. Y. Lin & Liu, 2000; Luo, 1997; Montinola et al., 1995; Oi, 1992, 1995; Zhu, 1999).

This study portrayed a more complicated picture of local powers in local development. There are local officials, who have lived or worked in a region for a long time and they have rich local knowledge, they do wish a better future for the local region. They would like to gain economic development as well as protection of the local environment, or at least reduce the negative impact of industries. In selecting industries to support this, these local officials do consider the environmental impact of different industries. More attention regarding local environmental politics should be given to powerful local actors instead of focusing on local-central relationships or the weak role of civil society, or the role of local environmental protection bureaus.

Entrepreneurs, local officials, and *guanxi*'s power to control and access resources

As explained in the previous section, many studies focus on the practices of low-carbon or ecological cities, introducing indicators and ranking cities' green development; there is a lack of studies explaining the politics and dynamics behind these green policies and actions (Song et al., 2010; Xin & Zhang, 2008; 1999). This book is an in-depth review of entrepreneurs, local officials, and *guanxi*'s power to control and access resources, mainly in the form of land and capital.

Applying political ecology theory, the key role of businessmen in environmental issues can be explained by their ability to take control over local land and other environmental resources (Bryant & Bailey, 1997). In this way, this book is aligned with many studies about China's economic development, which point out the importance of entrepreneurs, local officials, and their reciprocal relationships (Gartner, 1988; Huang, 2008; Oi, 1992; Knup, 1997; Naughton, 2007; Walder, 1995; Wank, 1996; Xin & Pearce, 1996; Yang, 2005). This study goes beyond these actors' influence on economic development to emphasize their influence on the local environment and society. This multi-faceted influence will be described in more detail in the second section of the conclusion.

Private entrepreneurs' innovative ideas to organize resources for green development

An entrepreneur is "someone who specializes in taking responsibility for and making judgment and decisions that affect the location, the form, the use of goods, resources, or institutions" (Hébert & Link, 1989, p. 39). After reform and opening-up, private entrepreneurs set up thousands of firms that contributed to the nation's rapid economic development; they are "the new rich" who have gathered huge amounts of wealth (Fewsmith, 2001; Goodman, 2008; Liao & Sohmen, 2001). In the field of green businesses, Chinese entrepreneurs also set up companies and some have been entered onto *Forbes'* list of Chinese billionaires.

One of the key findings of this study is the innovative role which private entrepreneurs play in identifying market opportunities for green products and creating firms to profit from them. In this study they are represented by Chen Kunlong and other experts in Shanghai, Miao Liansheng and his company Yingli in Baoding, and Zhu Chenghua at Wuning (K. Chen, 1980; interview 3; B. Li & Yang 2013).

The scholarship on private entrepreneurs typically analyzes private entrepreneurs' role in economic development as well as political and social change in the nation, e.g., broader political participation (J. Chen & Dickson, 2010; Dickson, 2003; Malik, 1997; McMillan & Woodruff, 2003; Nevitt, 1996; Tsai, 2005, 2007). This study complements this literature by highlighting the role of entrepreneurs in environmental protection. It demonstrates that private entrepreneurs play an important role in encouraging local economic development towards sustainability.

The entrepreneurs were the first actors to introduce green businesses at the local level. In Shanghai, for instance, entrepreneurs wrote articles about finance and trade in the early 1980s and were frontrunners of the subsequent development of these industries (Long, 2012). More broadly, entrepreneurs are also the actors who experiment with different businesses and ideas. Miao Liansheng, for example, opened several different businesses in Baoding until he settled on solar energy (Zhou, 2010). Sometimes, entrepreneurs fail; even such cases can be an example from which new entrepreneurs can draw experiences and lessons. Zhu Chenghua's energy-saving lamp business did not prove successful in the end (B. Li & Yang, 2013). He inspired other entrepreneurs to start their own, more successful energy-saving lamp factories.

Chinese private entrepreneurs are very active in green businesses, especially the renewable energy industry (Han, Mol, & Lu, 2010; S. Zhang & He, 2013). In each of the three case studies in this research, the entrepreneurs were actively involved in the local government's environmental projects; they provided products and financial support for local experimental environmental projects; and they pushed local officials towards a more ambitious low-carbon or ecological development pathway.

Many risks and difficulties lie ahead of private entrepreneurs doing business because the country lacks the rule of law, free markets, and free trade. It is still a problem for private entrepreneurs to legitimate and protect their private property (Bai, Lu, & Tao, 2006; Clarke, 2003; Tsang, 1994, 1996). All these problems were overcome by the private entrepreneurs, the key lies in *guanxi*. *Guanxi* are social relationships with relatives and friends.

First, we must consider: why are political relationships necessary in local green development? They are necessary because many resources, like land and credit, are in the hands of local governments (Cannon, 2000; J. Chen & Dickson,

2010; Guthrie, 2012; Naughton, 2007). It is common for private entrepreneurs to use their *guanxi* to connect with local officials to gain capital and land for their companies. Some entrepreneurs even participate in politics and become members of the CCP to nurture *guanxi* with local officials (J. Chen & Dickson, 2010; H. Li, Meng, & Zhang, 2006; Zhu, 1999).

Local officials' political power to mobilize resources

As Kenneth Lieberthal concludes, local leaders control environmental regulation and access to local resources (Lieberthal, 1997). Local officials are the key to understanding environmental issues.

This book presents local government officials who advocated for green development and did so without receiving mandatory orders from the central government. This study is based on a large body of studies about local officials which emphasize the strong incentives of these officials to develop their local economies (Tsui & Wang, 2004; Wong, 1991; C. Zhang, 2006). Most of these studies argue that local officials act as entrepreneurs by finding the industries suitable to local conditions (Landry, 2008; J. Y. Lin & Liu, 2000; Montinola et al., 1995; Nee, 1992; Oi, 1992; Walder, 1995; Wong, 1991; T. Zhang & Zou, 1998). One aspect these studies overlook is the impact of the local officials' efforts on the local environment. In a similar vein, this study also found that some local officials care not only about personal career promotion and their economic achievement, but also about local public interests, including environmental protection. The local officials in these three cases are very familiar with local context, and they are actively searching for entrepreneurs in environmentally friendly industries to work together for local development.

The empirical finding of this study demonstrated that local officials proposed new ideas, created new policy, and established organizations to develop their localities (Lieberthal, 1997; Nee, 1992; Walder, 1995). A good example of this is land developers in industrial parks (Lichtenberg & Ding, 2009). The local officials in charge of industrial parks in Pudong, Baoding, and Wuning were granted land and staff. They set up new governments tasked with attracting businesses and investments. Some local officials even seized this opportunity to establish their own companies and gave up their jobs in the governments, in what is known as the "*xiahai*" phenomenon (R. Guo, 2011).

Local officials in charge of industrial parks have control and access to land and capital resources. Local government is authorized to transfer the collective land, mainly agricultural land, into urban construction land (Naughton, 2007). The national bank branches in the localities are also under the purview of the local government, which means that local officials can get loans more easily than private entrepreneurs (Lu & Sun, 2013; Shirk, 1993). Local officials are entitled with their political power to control and distribute local resources; they can play an important role in directing the development of the local economy.

This study has found two common approaches used by local officials. The first is using land and capital to build infrastructure in industrial parks to attract businesses (Cartier, 2001; Lichtenberg & Ding, 2009; Zhu, 1999). This is primarily carried out by the development company operating in the industrial park under the leadership of the local government. The second approach includes industrial policies; in this case local governments decide which industries are suitable for the locality and draw up industrial policies aimed at attracting businesses in those industries (Stiglitz, Lin, & Monga, 2013; Wade, 1990).

The development companies formed by local governments are simultaneously a company and a government administration or political institute with a strong economic task (Walder, 1995; C. Wang, 2014; Weingast, 1995). They have taken the place of the old government administrations, and they are responsible for developing the territory under their rule. Later these development companies will become government bodies. Since these companies primarily targeted businesses and capital attraction, it is debatable whether they will satisfy their social responsibilities. This book discussed the Lujiazui development company, which governs the Lujiazui area and developed finance industries. Subsequently, this company further began developing real estate and other businesses.

An important finding of this study is how local governments relied on land revenue. Land has been a big source of local government revenue through transfer fees for the right to use land, land taxes, and credit using land as security (Dong, 2009; Qiu, Teng, & Wang, 2009; Shao, 2010). Shanghai's Pudong district was one of the first places where a development company used land use rights to gain capital for development (Wan & Yuan, 2001; J. Zhang, 1991). Later this model of land development and urbanization spread to other local governments. Both Baoding and Wuning have used this strategy to develop their industrial zones and urban areas. This study concludes that this development model has a huge impact on China's environment and local people, especially farmers.

The second measure for local officials to shape the development of their regions is through industrial policy. Correspondingly, this study emphasized how local officials chose what industries and businesses to support. In doing so, it questioned whether, as many scholars argue, local officials pick the winners of the economic transformation and specifically support them in their industrial policies (Naughton, 2007; Rodrik, 2008; Steinfeld, 2000). In the cases chosen in this study, it seems that the green companies were not initially the obvious go-to industries. It is only through favorable industrial policies, the support of local government, and the development of the green market that they were ultimately successful. The local officials leading the development of industrial parks picked industries that they predicted would have a promising future in the market. For instance, Miao Liansheng's solar energy company was very new and not yet successful when Ma Xuelu chose to support it. As Ma Xuelu learned more about solar energy and other renewables, he came to believe that renewable energy should be the focus of Baoding's HTZ. It was the same in Pudong: even though there was no finance and trade in the market economy at the beginning of the 1980s, the local officials and entrepreneurs believed in the promising future of these industries.

166 *Political ecology of green development*

Local officials who do choose green industries to support are motivated by the potential economic and environmental benefits of green industries. Renewable energy industries have a huge market and are considered environmentally friendly. There is a paradox posed by the literature and the empirical findings of this study about why local officials pursue green development, given that economic development is the key indicator for their political performance and career promotion (Landry, 2008; H. Li & Zhou, 2005; Wong, 1991). Several conclusions have been drawn here to resolve this paradox. First, when local officials pursue green development, they also create local economic development. Local officials not only compete with other local officials in GDP growth, but also in the creation of new policies regarding solving economic as well as social problems (Xu, 2011). It is possible that they may be more outstanding than others because of the "green" element in their policy formation. Second, the assumption that local officials will pursue economic development at all costs is too rational and does not take into account the cultural environment and other values of local officials. Albeit the fact that local officials act as entrepreneurs, they are not private entrepreneurs who care only about profit-making; the local officials have other responsibilities as well, such as environmental protection. Lastly, some local officials, such as those who will not be promoted because of their age, might not be working towards a promotion at all and thus have more freedom to work towards policies which do not explicitly benefit economic development. In sum, there are multiple reasons that economically minded local officials pursue green development.

Guanxi—*the connections between entrepreneurs and local officials*

Guanxi are interpersonal relationship or connections, which involve reciprocal obligation (Davies, Leung, Luk, & Wong, 1995; Tsang, 1998; Xin & Pearce, 1996; Yeung & Tung, 1996). The word is composed of two Chinese characters. One is "*guan*," which means closed, and the other is "*xi*" which means tied together. As mentioned before, entrepreneurs face many challenges when doing business, such as the lack of rule of law and insecure property rights. Under these circumstances, it is *guanxi* that helps them to overcome these challenges and "substitutes for formal institutional support," particularly for private entrepreneurs (Davies et al., 1995; Farh, Tsui, Xin, & Cheng, 1998; Lee & Dawes, 2005; Luo & Chen, 1997; Xin & Pearce, 1996; Yeung & Tung, 1996). This study focuses on the *guanxi* between entrepreneurs and local officials. *Guanxi* has consequences, such as bribery, corruption, and other negative social impacts, as it is "personal gains at social costs" (Fan, 2002; L. Li, 2011; Smart, 1993). That was not a research aim of this book.

As is evident in this study, *guanxi* is necessary to help private entrepreneurs and local officials realize local green development (Ahlstrom & Bruton, 2001; Batjargal & Liu, 2004; Wank, 1996; Xin & Pearce, 1996). Entrepreneurs use their *guanxi* to connect with local officials who can help them to obtain resources or protection (Ahlstrom & Bruton, 2001; Batjargal & Liu, 2004; Wank, 1996).

Local officials in turn use their *guanxi* to find out the right entrepreneurs and connect with key local leaders in order to realize their vision for green development.

The empirical evidence gathered in this study represents a rebuttal to scholarship which deemphasizes the role of *guanxi* in China's development (Guthrie, 1998; Yang, 2002). This study stresses the role of *guanxi* in supporting innovative ideas and polices to overcome various challenges, and particularly in realizing local green development.

Guanxi's significance is very clear in all three case studies. A good example of the power of *guanxi* is Miao Liansheng whose company was not qualified to apply for the national solar program as it was privately owned (interview 3). He thus used his *guanxi* to obtain support and resources from his friend—Ma Xuelu, who was the director of the Baoding HTZ. Later, when Ma had no more capital to help Miao, he encouraged the state-owned company management to help Miao (interview 3). The transferable nature of *guanxi* allows the actors to build bridges among parties with common connections (Dunning & Kim, 2007; Luo, 2007; Standifird & Marshall, 2000).

In addition to fostering connections, *guanxi* plays a crucial role in sharing information and transferring knowledge between entrepreneurs and local officials (Buckley, Clegg, & Tan, 2006; Ramasamy, Goh, & Yeung, 2006; Shin, Ishman, & Sanders, 2007). Many studies place emphasis on the negative impacts of *guanxi* between entrepreneurs and local officials, most prominently corruption, and its positive effects have not been fully examined in literature (Dunfee & Warren, 2001; Fan, 2002; L. Li, 2011; Luo, 2008; Su & Littlefield, 2001). This study found that *guanxi* is reciprocal and forms trust between local officials and private entrepreneurs, which is why entrepreneurs can then gain resources from local officials (Lee & Dawes, 2005; Park & Luo, 2001). This is not to say that the previous studies are wrong; rather this study calls for a more comprehensive understanding of *guanxi*, including its positive effects.

Guanxi fosters a deep mutual trust between private entrepreneurs and local officials, especially in the case of new businesses (So & Walker, 2013; Xin & Pearce, 1996). It is usually entrepreneurs who share their innovative ideas about green businesses with local officials whom they trust. Entrepreneurs need to explain their new ideas in detail to persuade local officials to support them. In this way, local officials obtain business information from entrepreneurs.

It is interesting to observe that local officials are also entrepreneurs. In all cases local officials did not interfere in entrepreneurs' businesses except when the entrepreneurs were confronted with problems. This again shows the trust between the two parties. After learning about the entrepreneurs' ideas, local officials are often involved in the development of the local industrial parks. In this, they put significant effort into attracting more entrepreneurs with similar businesses to settle down in their vicinity. The ideas behind green development provide common interests and benefits for entrepreneurs and local officials alike.

Because of the fierce competition among different localities, it is important to point out that local officials also seek to build *guanxi* with entrepreneurs in order

168 *Political ecology of green development*

to attract more businesses and entrepreneurs to settle down in their region (Saxenian, 2003). This is particularly obvious in the case of Wuning. The local officials utilized their *guanxi* to persuade entrepreneurs in coastal areas to move their businesses to the county. While the findings of this study support this idea, they also suggest that there is not enough attention paid in the literature to how local officials use their *guanxi* to connect with entrepreneurs.

Local officials also use their *guanxi* to form coalitions to advocate for their green development strategies over other development strategies. For instance, the common aim of promoting the development of trade and finance in "Develop Pudong" appealed to many local officials. They formed a coalition to advocate for "Develop Pudong" and mobilized their collective *guanxi* to reach out to the local leader in order to realize this idea. When the local leaders Wang Daohan and Zhu Rongji agreed to "Develop Pudong," they also used their *guanxi* to connect with Deng Xiaoping in order to gain the central government's approval.

The *guanxi* between "green" entrepreneurs and local officials further developed during the process of green development. These actors came together because of a common interest in green development at the local level, and their commonly held green values served as a basis for *guanxi*. Similarly, a love for one's home, a wish for a better future, and a concern for future generations were all important reasons for the formation of *guanxi* in the case studies.

Guanxi is necessary both for local officials and entrepreneurs to realize their aims. *Guanxi* can help entrepreneurs to gain the resources in the hands of local officials and help local officials to gain industrial information from entrepreneurs. *Guanxi* provides trust and cooperation between entrepreneurs and local officials. It is *guanxi* that brought together the entrepreneurs and local officials for green development in the three cases.

Political ecology and local green development

Political ecology has a profound meaning for environmental studies, especially with its concern for weak actors in environmental issues. One focus of political ecology is to rethink the costs and benefits of environmental pollution or protection. They criticize environmental projects which are not socially equitable and participatory (Forsyth, 2008; Swyngedouw & Heynen, 2003). This study contributes to the field of political ecology with empirical findings about the impacts of local green development. It examines two categories of impact: the impact on the environment and the impact on society, both of which result in gains and losses for different actors during the process of green development. China's local green development is decided by powerful political actors. It has had enormous impacts on the local environment and society. As Robbins (2012, pp. 19–20) argues "[…] environmental change and ecological conditions are the product of political processes."

The most powerful actors are local officials who make policies and projects, which cause both positive and negative environmental and social change. At the same time, local businessmen provide ideas and capital to develop the local environment. This study specifically looked at land use as an indicator of environment development, and how local officials and entrepreneurs have changed land use patterns and realized urbanization through green development. In China's urbanization literature, many scholars argue that green development is led by the local government, which absorbs resources such as land from rural areas (Berg & Björner, 2014; Ding, 2003, 2007; Hsing, 2010; Hui & Bao, 2013; G. C. Lin & Yi, 2011; Lu & Sun, 2013). Some scholars demonstrate that China's urbanization has shifted from government-led to market-oriented; from the empirical findings of this study we can conclude that local governments still dominate the urbanization process (LeGates & Stout, 2011; Zhu, 1999).

In analyzing local government land policy as it supports green development, this study focuses on social and environmental justice issues like other political ecology studies (Peet & Watts, 2004; Vásquez-León & Liverman, 2004; Warren, Batterbury, & Osbahr, 2001). This study has examined the gains and losses during the process of green development; this is in contrast with the majority of political ecology studies, which focus on the causes of environmental degradation in rural areas and pay limited attention to social justice and environmental impacts in the process of urbanization (Bryant, 1992; Walker, 2003). In the three case studies, green development necessitated access to environmental resources, like land. This is a major issue for China where there has been wide-scale change of land ownership at the local level. From 1996 to 2004, roughly 7.6 million hectares of arable (agricultural) land was lost. A primary reason is urbanization, which has driven transfers in land ownership from farmers in collectives to municipal governments (Cartier, 2001; Ji & Qi, 2006; Tan, Li, Xie, & Lu, 2005). In the name of green development, local officials and entrepreneurs successfully gained land rights from collectives, mostly farmers. Given these findings, this study urges us to rethink green development by clarifying who has or does not have the power to decide how green development is managed (Adams, 2009). What is more, this study asks who benefits from green development and who loses. In this way, it is aligned with the broader political ecology literatures (Heynen, Kaika, & Swyngedouw, 2006; Robbins, 2012).

Political ecology—politicized environment

Political ecology stems from the study of land degradation issues in developing countries, and later expanded to a study of land-based resources and environmental resources like forests (Blaikie & Brookfield, 2015; Bryant, 1992; Rocheleau, 2008). A large body of the political ecology literature on land use or environmental resources focuses on small land or environmental resource users and connects their experiences to the broader political and economic power context. There is a lack of attention paid to large land use change patterns, such as those present in the process of China's urbanization (C. Adams, Murrieta, Neves, & Harris, 2008; Bryant, 1992; Vásquez-León & Liverman, 2004; Warren, Batterbury, & Osbahr, 2001). This study examined political land users—namely the local leaders. Thus, this study contributes to the land studies with a political

170 *Political ecology of green development*

ecology perspective on China's urbanization. This study elaborated how rural land was turned into urban land during the process of green development through political power. The land use pattern changes were also accompanied by social change at the localities, which will be explained in the following.

Since this study uses cities as case studies, it is rooted in urban political ecology. This study stresses the negative impacts of local government-led urbanization on society and environment. Thus, in line with urban political ecology, it emphasizes that the process of urbanization neglects social and environment issues (Heynen et al., 2006). Many scholars dispute the social and environmental problems related to China's urbanization (J. Chen, 2007; Lichtenberg & Ding, 2009; T. Zhang, 2000). This study warns that there is a tendency to use green development as a new justification to continue government-led urbanization.

Urban political ecology is a dynamic field of study. There are various topics, including urban reforestation, floods, infrastructure, pollution, environmental rights, and justice issues (Heynen, Perkins, & Roy, 2006; Keil, 2005; Monstadt, 2009; Njeru, 2006; Pelling, 1999; Swyngedouw & Heynen, 2003). Despite this dynamism, there are no studies about China's urbanization from a political ecology perspective. This study argues that the way in which social and environmental problems are addressed is decided by the political power structure, in which local officials and entrepreneurs are the decision-makers while weak actors, like farmers and the environment, have few channels to participate in decision-making processes.

A key finding of this study is that, during the process of green development, a large area was urbanized and a planned city was formed. Both the economic and political systems influence the form of this new urbanized area. During the process of urbanization, the natural environment is transformed into an urban environment (Swyngedouw & Heynen, 2003). In the three cases studied, we can see how cities expanded rapidly by taking over neighboring villages and even a whole county, in the case of Pudong. Pudong's urbanization model, rapid urbanization in an agriculture area, happened in other regions as well. From the regional and national perspective, it raises concerns that urbanization is leading to the loss of arable land, which may trigger food security issues and further environmental degradation (Brown, 1995; Cartier, 2001; J. Chen, 2007; Skinner, Kuhn, & Joseph, 2001; Tan et al., 2005; A. G.-O. Yeh & Li, 1999).

During the process of green development, it is the local officials and entrepreneurs who define what is green, control access to environmental resources, and decide where to settle industries. Their concept of environment is limited in the way that local officials and entrepreneurs still care more about economic growth than about environmental protection, thus they are not able to represent the environment and the local people's interests. This is evidenced in the way that local leaders in each case study always emphasized the development of "green" industrial zones over creating policies for environmental protection. Moreover, some of the "green" industries emit pollutants to the local environment, most prominently the solar PV and battery industries at Baoding (Ifeng,

2010). A key challenge for China's local green development is to realize more public participation in the decision-making process.

There is also the phenomenon of the "commoditization of nature" during the process of green development, especially in the case of Wuning (Liverman, 2004). Good environmental conditions are developed into ecological tourism projects or high-quality real estate programs (A. D. Wang, 2013; Shen, 2013). It is in question whether the local villagers can hold onto their forest rights, continue their traditional livelihood, and enjoy the benefits of these ecological projects.

In the process of green development, the environment is politicized. The strong political actors define what green development is and how to manage the environment, while the weak political actors face the risks of losing their rights to manage the environment. Thus, it is important to engage key stakeholders into green development decision-making processes in order to protect the interests of the weak.

Rethinking green development—winners and losers

Political ecology calls for more detailed and in-depth studies about green development (Tim, 2003, p. 20). Political ecology questions the effectiveness of sustainable or green development, since the structure of global capitalism in which it is embedded does not change (Bryant & Bailey, 1997). As W. Adams argues, "green development is not about the way the environment is managed, but about who has the power to decide how it is managed" (Adams, 2009, p. 408). In the current Chinese political system, the powerful political and economic actors dominate local affairs, so it is hard for the weaker actors to protect their rights during the process of green development. It is true that sustainable and green development has brought positive environmental changes; it is also important for us to understand how green development has had a negative impact on the environment and weaker actors' rights.

Political ecology aims to find out the winners and losers, or costs and benefits, in relation to environmental issues (Bryant & Bailey, 1997; Robbins, 2012; Rocheleau, 2008). There is a strong tendency in political ecology studies to argue for the weaker political actors, particularly peasants, and criticize the strong political and economic forces that are behind environmental degradation (Bryant & Bailey, 1997).

As green development is both a political campaign and activity, the costs and benefits of the use of environmental resources are distributed unequally among actors. Usually it is the weak political actors who bear the cost (Bryant, 1992; Swyngedouw & Heynen, 2003). There is a large body of literature in political ecology about peasants and the enclosure of resources in environmental management (Bassett, 1988; Grossman, 1998; Peet & Watts, 2004; Vásquez-León & Liverman, 2004; E. T. Yeh, 2000). There are also many studies about Chinese peasants; these do not pay enough attention to how the environmental projects advocated by strong political and economic factors influence the peasants (Cai, 2003; X. Guo, 2001; Pils, 2005; Ya-hua, 2004).

172 *Political ecology of green development*

In the three case studies, the costs and benefits are distributed unequally among farmers, local officials, and entrepreneurs. Farmers were the marginalized group who lost during the process of green development; they sacrificed their land for the green development strategies, usually still live near the industrial zones, and are exposed to environmental damages. Green development strategies have enabled the local officials and entrepreneurs to control access to local resources that formerly had been in the hands of local people, especially farmers' land. It is important to point out that industrial parks are the most common mode of transforming rural land into urban land (Cartier, 2001).

The entrepreneurs benefited from gaining access to local resources and many were successful in the market. Their gain may be the losses of other actors. The solar PV and energy-saving lamps have improved the environment in the areas where the consumers live. Meanwhile the environment of the people producing them is degraded. As green development progresses, it is likely that more land will go into the hands of local governments and business people. Consequently, there will be more landless farmers and a disappearance of arable farm land.

Political ecology is a useful theory to analyze green development and explain how green development affects the local environment and people. During the process of green development, local politics determines who can derive benefits and who will experience losses. As green products become more and more popular, it is important to keep a watchful eye on the costs and benefits to different actors in the process of green development.

Implications of local green development

The way that China chooses to develop influences the world. Local green development is closely related to the Chinese political, economic, and social contexts, and its popularity will have broader implications for China's environmental protection, development, and that of the world as well.

This study demonstrates that innovative green development policies and actions come from local governments (Schreurs, 2008). Baoding launched its low-carbon city in 2007, the first one in China (Baodingribao, 2007). Local governments like Baoding and others make regulations and start new organizations to support their green development. Yet, despite this leadership in green development, the role of local government is still not fully researched in the field of environmental protection and climate change. It is entirely possible that the local experiments with new policies may later be applied more broadly by the national government (Heilmann, 2008). A very interesting finding is that green development is not only possible in rich areas, but also in poor areas like Baoding and Wuning. The process of green development turns a poor area's underdeveloped status from a disadvantage to an advantage, as the unpolluted environment attracts new businesses and ecological tourism. This has broader meaning for the developing world: green development is possible in poor areas.

This study addresses a gap in research on China's environmental politics about the power of local political actors. Most of China's environmental studies focus on the role of environmental laws or environmental officials (Dasgupta, Laplante, Mamingi, & Wang, 2001; Jahiel, 1998; A. Wang, 2006). As this study concludes, the real power is in the hands of the government bodies in charge of economic affairs or local leaders, instead of weak political departments like the EPB. The reason for bad implementation of environmental laws and regulations lies in the political power structure as well. The authority of environmental departments is lower than those in charge of development in the Chinese political system (Lieberthal, 1997).

It is the will of strong political actors and their policies that greatly influence the Chinese environment. This study demonstrates that local leaders' power has a strong effect on the local ecology. This study does not explore how to consistently motivate powerful actors to pursue more sustainable development, or how to check and supervise the strong power of local leaders. In what is a solid first step, the CCP's ecological civilization ideology enables local government leaders to legitimate green development. There is still a lack of performance measures and concrete incentives for local leaders to pursue green development. Whether a state will pursue green development or not is determined by the local leader's willingness to find alternative ways to develop industries.

The decentralization enables local leaders to mobilize resources to achieve their aims (Guthrie, 2012; Naughton, 2007; C. Zhang, 2006). Local leaders control the national banks at the local level, since they have the power to appoint local bank officials (Hsueh, 2011; Naughton, 2007; Shirk, 1993). Because of the local leader's personnel power within the local government, many local officials have been involved in implementing the local leader's development strategy. In the case of Pudong, for instance, the New Pudong Government replaced the old government body in Chuansha County with the mission to carry out the "Develop Pudong" strategy. In all the three case studies, the local leaders set up new working groups, development companies, and industrial zones. Some of the local officials were endowed with huge amounts of land to start government-owned companies. These companies would sell or rent the land; they primarily developed rural land into industrial land. Local civil servants served as salesmen at the same time; they were encouraged to go out and use *guanxi* to serve the local development strategy. Some civil servants were even forced to persuade their relatives to move away from their land in order to leave space for development, under the threat of losing their jobs in the government. The power of the local political system to implement such tasks is quite high at the local government level, since the local leader has the power to punish or reward the local officials.

Future research topics

Regarding future research topics about China's local green development, this section will address it through the lens of political ecology theory, and the role of local officials, entrepreneurs, and their connections, as well as comparative case studies.

Political ecology scholars in geography emphasize the scale of the issue related to environmental studies (Liverman, 2004; Neumann, 2009; Swyngedouw & Heynen, 2003). The scale of this study is very limited as it only focuses on the scale of local politics; similar research on a national or international scale and the impacts on the local green development would be interesting future topics. For example, what is the impact of international demand for green products on the local people where the products are produced? The international and local linkage is observable through analyzing the performance of international companies for green products.

There is also a need for more research on green development from an individual perspective, which would address questions such as what kinds of entrepreneurs are engaged in "green" businesses. What traits or values are common in the local officials or leaders who believe in the promises of green development? Another topic for study is what occurs when the local leader moves to another place: will he carry his ideas and policies with him to his new position? How will the next local leader treat the green development strategy? Will green businesses carry on? These are important questions since a local leader's support is very important for entrepreneurs' businesses.

This study has mentioned that land is a key indicator and resource for green development. There is little known and much to be studied about land transfer and possible conflicts between local governments and farmers in green development. Since the development of renewable energy also requires vast amounts of land, particularly considering the big renewable energy projects which are preferred, farmers and ranchers' lands are often confiscated for renewable energy projects. Will these green development projects also bring land loss to farmers and ranchers, as urbanization has done in the rural regions around cities? What is the public acceptance of renewable projects? Are there also imbalanced costs and benefits among the local people and government? These are all interesting starting points for future research topics. Land conflict is one of the major social issues that local people protest ; these protests against local governments challenge the legitimacy of the political power (X. Guo, 2001; Hui & Bao, 2013; Pils, 2005). It is important to carry out more research about the land compensation or conflicts around green development projects.

Another possibility for extending this research is to include more cities as case studies. There are hundreds of cities which claim they have gone green; studies of some of these other cities would determine whether the same development dynamics found in the three case studies examined here follow a similar pattern in other areas of China. Alternatively, it would be interesting to explore whether a similar pattern exists in cities outside of China.

Since China is still a developing country, its urbanization is planned by the government. Issues of environmental protection related to the urbanization process are also worth researching. Comparisons of the practices for environmental protection among cities in developed countries and developing countries are necessary to determine the best environmental protection practices.

This chapter reviewed the key findings of this book, which revealed how entrepreneurs, local officials, and their *guanxi* came together to pursue local green development. Local green development was initiated by entrepreneurs and local officials, and led by local leaders. During the process, *guanxi* played a key role in connecting and building trust among entrepreneurs and local officials. This book also showed how local green development has been dominated by powerful local actors' efforts. One of the major findings of this study is the complexity of green development. It has brought various benefits, such as the rapid development of green industries which have contributed to China's green development as well as the world's; it has also improved urban environments with the construction of green, low-carbon, and ecological cities. Yet, green development has also caused suffering for weak actors, like the people who have lost their land and homes in the name of green development. The local environment also faces abuse for the rapid development of "green" industries by local governments and industries. The costs of green development have been unevenly borne, and the benefits unevenly distributed.

Advocacy for local green development should be encouraged, but the process and its impacts should also be questioned if only powerful actors define and decide what green development is, particularly if they do so without comprehensive consideration of social and environmental justice. How to engage the public to participate in the green development decision-making process remains a key challenge. As more and more cities advocate for local green development, it is also important to rethink the social and environmental justice issues linked to the process of local green development.

References

Adams, C., Murrieta, R. S., Neves, W. A., & Harris, M. (2008). *Amazon peasant societies in a changing environment: Political ecology, invisibility and modernity in the rainforest*. Sao Paulo: Springer.

Adams, W. (2009). *Green development: Environment and sustainability in a developing world (3rd edition)*. London: Routledge.

Ahlstrom, D., & Bruton, G. D. (2001). Learning from successful local private firms in China: Establishing legitimacy. *The Academy of Management Executive, 15*(4), 72–83.

Bai, C. E., Lu, J., & Tao, Z. (2006). Property rights protection and access to bank loans. *Economics of Transition, 14*(4), 611–628.

Baodingribao. (2007, March 26). Rang "yangguang" zhaoliang Baoding rang "yangguang" wennuan Baoding nuli jianshe jieneng huanbaoxing chengshi—zai quanshi jianshe taiyangneng zhi cheng dongyuan dahui shang [Let "sunshine" light up Baoding, let "sunshine" warm up Baoding, strive to become an energy saving and environmentally friendly city—The promotion conference on constructing a "solar city"]. *Baoding Ribao*. Retrieved from http://zhuanti.bdinfo.net/bdrb/bdrb_info/news_info.asp?news_id=2351.

Bassett, T. J. (1988). The political ecology of peasant-herder conflicts in the northern Ivory Coast. *Annals of the Association of American Geographers, 78*(3), 453–472.

Batjargal, B., & Liu, M. (2004). Entrepreneurs' access to private equity in China: The role of social capital. *Organization Science, 15*(2), 159–172.

Baumol, W. J. (1968). Entrepreneurship in economic theory. *The American Economic Review, 58*(2), 64–71.

Berg, P. O., & Björner, E. (2014). *Branding Chinese mega-cities: Policies, practices and positioning.* Glos: Edward Elgar Publishing.

Beyer, S. (2006). Environmental law and policy in the People's Republic of China. *Chinese Journal of International Law, 5*(1), 185–211.

Blaikie, P., & Brookfield, H. (Eds.). (2015). *Land degradation and society.* London: Routledge.

Brown, G. P. (1995). Arable land loss in rural China: Policy and implementation in Jiangsu Province. *Asian Survey, 35*(10), 922–940.

Bryant, R. L. (1992). Political ecology: An emerging research agenda in Third-World studies. *Political Geography, 11*(1), 12–36.

Bryant, R. L., & Bailey, S. (1997). *Third world political ecology.* London: Routledge.

Buckley, P. J., Clegg, J., & Tan, H. (2006). Cultural awareness in knowledge transfer to China—The role of guanxi and mianzi. *Journal of World Business, 41*(3), 275–288.

Cai, Y. (2003). Collective ownership or cadres' ownership? The non-agricultural use of farmland in China. *The China Quarterly, 175,* 662–680.

Cannon, T. (2000). *China's economic growth: The impact on regions, migration and the environment.* London: Macmillan.

Cartier, C. (2001). "Zone fever," the arable land debate, and real estate speculation: China's evolving land use regime and its geographical contradictions. *Journal of Contemporary China, 10*(28), 445–469.

Chen, J. (2007). Rapid urbanization in China: A real challenge to soil protection and food security. *Catena, 69*(1), 1–15.

Chen, J., & Dickson, B. J. (2010). *Allies of the state: China's private entrepreneurs and democratic change.* USA: Harvard University Press.

Chen, K. (1980). Xiang Pudong guangkuo diqu fazhan [Developing in Pudong in a broad space]. *Shehui Kexue, 5,* 010.

Chinese Society for Urban Studies [CSUS] (2013, June 25). Characteristics and development trend of Chinese eco-city. Retrieved from www.ens.dk/sites/ens.dk/files/politik/vedvarende-energisamarbejde-kina/bibliotek/Seminar/characteristics_and_development_trend_of_chinese_eco-city.pdf.

Clarke, D. C. (2003). Economic development and the rights hypothesis: The China problem. *The American Journal of Comparative Law 51,* 89.

Crooks, R., Nygard, J., Zhang, Q., & Lui, F. (2001). China air, land, and water: environmental priorities for a new millennium. The World Bank, Washington DC. Retrieved from http://documents.worldbank.org/curated/en/2001/08/1631741/china-air-land-water-environmental-priorities-new-millennium.

Dasgupta, S., Laplante, B., Mamingi, N., & Wang, H. (2001). Inspections, pollution prices, and environmental performance: evidence from China. *Ecological Economics, 36*(3), 487–498.

Davies, H., Leung, T. K., Luk, S. T., & Wong, Y.-h. (1995). The benefits of "Guanxi": The value of relationships in developing the Chinese market. *Industrial Marketing Management, 24*(3), 207–214.

Deyo, F. C. (1987). *The political economy of the new Asian industrialism.* New York: Cornell University Press.

Dickson, B. J. (2003). *Red capitalists in China: The party, private entrepreneurs, and prospects for political change.* Cambridge: Cambridge University Press.

Ding, C. (2003). Land policy reform in China: Assessment and prospects. *Land Use Policy, 20*(2), 109–120.

Ding, C. (2007). Policy and praxis of land acquisition in China. *Land Use Policy, 24*(1), 1–13.

Dong, Z. (2009). Difang zhengfu "tudi caizheng" de xianzhuang, chengyin he zhili [Local governments and land-related finance: The status quo, cause and effects analysis, and treatment]. *Lilun Daokan* (12), 13–15.

Dunfee, T. W., & Warren, D. E. (2001). Is guanxi ethical? A normative analysis of doing business in China. *Journal of Business Ethics, 32*(3), 191–204.

Dunning, J. H., & Kim, C. (2007). The cultural roots of guanxi: An exploratory study. *The World Economy, 30*(2), 329–341.

Economy, E. (2005, May 07). China's environmental movement. Testimony before the Congressional Executive Commission on China Roundtable on Environmental NGOs in China: Encouraging Action and Addressing Public Grievances, 7. Retrieved from www.cfr.org/publication/7770/.

Economy, E. (2007). The great leap backward? The costs of China's environmental crisis. *Foreign Affairs, 86*, 38–59.

Economy, E. (2010). *The river runs black: The environmental challenge to China's future*. New York: Cornell University Press.

Fan, Y. (2002). Questioning guanxi: Definition, classification and implications. *International Business Review, 11*(5), 543–561.

Farh, J.-L., Tsui, A. S., Xin, K., & Cheng, B.-S. (1998). The influence of relational demography and *guanxi*: The Chinese case. *Organization Science, 9*(4), 471–488.

Fewsmith, J. (2001). *Elite politics in contemporary China*. Oxon: East Gate Book.

Forsyth, T. (2008). Political ecology and the epistemology of social justice. *Geoforum, 39*(2), 756–764.

Gartner, W. B. (1988). Who is an entrepreneur? Is the wrong question. *American Journal of Small Business, 12*(4), 11–32.

Goodman, D. S. (2008). *The new rich in China: Future rulers, present lives*. Oxon: Routledge.

Grossman, L. S. (1998). *The political ecology of bananas: Contract farming, peasants, and agrarian change in the eastern Caribbean*. USA: University of North Carolina Press.

Guo, R. (2011). *An introduction to the Chinese economy: The driving forces behind modern day China*. Singapore: John Wiley & Sons.

Guo, X. (2001). Land expropriation and rural conflicts in China. *The China Quarterly, 166*, 422–439.

Guthrie, D. (1998). The declining significance of guanxi in China's economic transition. *China Quarterly*, 254–282.

Guthrie, D. (2012). *China and globalization: The social, economic and political transformation of Chinese society*. New York: Routledge.

Hamilton, R. T., & Harper, D. A. (1994). The entrepreneur in theory and practice. *Journal of Economic Studies, 21*(6), 3–18.

Han, J., Mol, A. P., & Lu, Y. (2010). Solar water heaters in China: a new day dawning. *Energy Policy, 38*(1), 383–391.

Hébert, R. F., & Link, A. N. (1989). In search of the meaning of entrepreneurship. *Small Business Economics, 1*(1), 39–49.

Heilmann, S. (2008). From local experiments to national policy: The origins of China's distinctive policy process. *The China Journal*, 1–30.

Heynen, N., Kaika, M., & Swyngedouw, E. (2006). Urban political ecology. In N. Heynen, M. Kaika, & E. Swyngedouw (Eds.), *The nature of cities: Urban political ecology and the politics of urban metabolism* (pp. 1–20). London: Routledge.

Heynen, N., Perkins, H. A., & Roy, P. (2006). The political ecology of uneven urban green space the impact of political economy on race and ethnicity in producing environmental inequality in Milwaukee. *Urban Affairs Review, 42*(1), 3–25.

Ho, P. (2001). Greening without conflict? Environmentalism, NGOs and civil society in China. *Development and Change, 32*(5), 893–921.

Hsing, Y. T. (2010). *The great urban transformation: politics of land and property in China.* Oxford: Oxford University Press.

Hsueh, R. (2011). *China's regulatory state: A new strategy for globalization.* New York: Cornell University Press.

Huang, Y. (2008). *Capitalism with Chinese characteristics: Entrepreneurship and the state (Vol. 1).* Cambridge: Cambridge University Press.

Hui, E. C., & Bao, H. (2013). The logic behind conflicts in land acquisitions in contemporary China: A framework based upon game theory. *Land Use Policy, 30*(1), 373–380.

Ifeng. (2010). Liujiu guiye lvzhao tousu, yingli xinnengyuan xiangmu shexian weigui [Complaints against six and nine silicon company]. Retrieved from http://finance.ifeng.com/news/20101012/2697700.shtml.

Jahiel, A. R. (1998). The organization of environmental protection in China. *The China Quarterly, 156*, 757–787.

Ji, M., & Qi, Z. (2006). Nongyebu Fubuzhang: 2020 nian Zhongguo gengdi quekou 1 yi mu yishang [The Vice Minister of Agriculture: By 2020, China have a shortage of 0.1 billion mu arable land]. *Xinhuangnet.* Retrieved from http://news.xinhuanet.com/house/2006-03/07/content_4267506.htm.

Keil, R. (2005). Progress report—urban political ecology. *Urban Geography, 26*(7), 640–651.

Kiong, T. C., & Kee, Y. P. (1998). Guanxi bases, xinyong and Chinese business networks. *British Journal of Sociology*, 75–96.

Knup, E. (1997). Environmental NGOs in China: An overview. *China Environment Series, 1*(3), 9–15.

Kostka, G., & Hobbs, W. (2012). Local energy efficiency policy implementation in China: Bridging the gap between national priorities and local interests. *The China Quarterly, 211*, 765–785.

Kostka, G., & Mol, A. P. (2013). Implementation and participation in China's local environmental politics: Challenges and innovations. *Journal of Environmental Policy & Planning, 15*(1), 3–16.

Landry, P. F. (2008). *Decentralized authoritarianism in China.* New York: Cambridge University Press.

Lee, D. Y., & Dawes, P. L. (2005). Guanxi, trust, and long-term orientation in Chinese business markets. *Journal of International Marketing, 13*(2), 28–56.

LeGates, R. T., & Stout, F. (Eds.). (2011). *The city reader.* Oxon: Routledge.

Li, B., & Yang, Y. (2013, March 24). Zhu Chenghua—Wuning jienengdeng chanye di yi ren [Zhu Chenghua—The first entrepreneur in Wuning's energy-saving lamp industry]. *Shijie Zhaomingbao.* Retrieved from http://newspaper.worldlightingweb.com/Qnews.asp?id=7990&QID=2137.

Li, H., Meng, L., Wang, Q., & Zhou, L.-A. (2008). Political connections, financing and firm performance: Evidence from Chinese private firms. *Journal of Development Economics, 87*(2), 283–299.

Li, H., Meng, L., & Zhang, J. (2006). Why do entrepreneurs enter politics? Evidence from China. *Economic Inquiry, 44*(3), 559–578.

Li, H., & Zhou, L.-A. (2005). Political turnover and economic performance: The incentive role of personnel control in China. *Journal of Public Economics, 89*(9), 1743–1762.

Li, J. (2009). Scaling up concentrating solar thermal technology in China. *Renewable and Sustainable Energy Reviews, 13*(8), 2051–2060.

Li, L. (2011). Performing bribery in China: Guanxi-practice, corruption with a human face. *Journal of Contemporary China, 20*(68), 1–20.

Liao, D., & Sohmen, P. (2001). The development of modern entrepreneurship in China. *Stanford Journal of East Asian Affairs, 1*(1), 27–33.

Lichtenberg, E., & Ding, C. (2009). Local officials as land developers: Urban spatial expansion in China. *Journal of Urban Economics, 66*(1), 57–64.

Lieberthal, K. (1997). China's governing system and its impact on environmental policy implementation. *China Environment Series, 1*(1997), 3–8.

Lin, G. C., & Yi, F. (2011). Urbanization of capital or capitalization on urban land? Land development and local public finance in urbanizing China. *Urban Geography, 32*(1), 50–79.

Lin, J. Y., & Liu, Z. (2000). Fiscal decentralization and economic growth in China. *Economic Development and Cultural Change, 49*(1), 1–21.

Liu, J., & Diamond, J. (2008). Revolutionizing China's environmental protection. *Science, 319*(5859), 37.

Liverman, D. (2004). Who governs, at what scale and at what price? Geography, environmental governance, and the commodification of nature. *Annals of the Association of American Geographers, 94*(4), 734–738.

Long, H. (2012, February 03). Pudong kaifa kaifang qianqi yanjiu he yunniang [The research and preparation for opening and developing Pudong]. *Pudong Shizhi*. Retrieved from http://szb.pudong.gov.cn/pdszb_pdds_dsyj/2012-02-03/Detail_411714.htm.

Lu, Y., & Sun, T. (2013, January 1, 2014). Local government financing platforms in China: A fortune or misfortune? *International Monetary Fund Working Paper 13*(243), 1–30. Retrieved from www.imf.org/external/pubs/ft/wp/2013/wp13243.pdf.

Luo, Y. (1997). Guanxi: principles, philosophies, and implications. *Human Systems Management, 16*(1), 43–51.

Luo, Y. (2007). *Guanxi and business*. Singapore: World Scientific.

Luo, Y. (2008). The changing Chinese culture and business behavior: The perspective of intertwinement between guanxi and corruption. *International Business Review, 17*(2), 188–193.

Luo, Y., & Chen, M. (1997). Does guanxi influence firm performance? *Asia Pacific Journal of Management, 14*(1), 1–16.

Ma, X., & Ortolano, L. (2000). *Environmental regulation in China: Institutions, enforcement, and compliance*. Maryland: Rowman & Littlefield Publishers.

Malik, R. (1997). *Chinese entrepreneurs in the economic development of China*. Westport: Greenwood Publishing Group.

McCay, B. J. (2002). Emergence of institutions for the commons: Contexts, situations, and events. In National Research Council (Ed.), *The drama of the commons* (pp. 361–401). Washington DC: National Academies Press.

McMillan, J., & Woodruff, C. (2003). The central role of entrepreneurs in transition economies. In G. Fields & G. Pfeffermann (Eds.), *Pathways out of poverty: Private firms and economic mobility in developing countries* (pp. 105–121). Boston: Kluwer Academic Publishers.

Monstadt, J. (2009). Conceptualizing the political ecology of urban infrastructures: Insights from technology and urban studies. *Environment and Planning. A, 41*(8), 1924.

Montinola, G., Qian, Y., & Weingast, B. R. (1995). Federalism, Chinese style: The political basis for economic success in China. *World Politics, 48*(01), 50–81.

Naughton, B. (2007). *The Chinese economy: Transitions and growth (Vol. 1).* Cambridge: MIT Press Books.

Nee, V. (1992). Organizational dynamics of market transition: Hybrid forms, property rights, and mixed economy in China. *Administrative Science Quarterly, 37*(1).

Neumann, R. (2009). Political ecology: Theorizing scale. *Progress in Human Geography, 33*(3), 398–406.

Nevitt, C. E. (1996). Private business associations in China: Evidence of civil society or local state power? *The China Journal* (36), 25–43.

Njeru, J. (2006). The urban political ecology of plastic bag waste problem in Nairobi, Kenya. *Geoforum, 37*(6), 1046–1058.

Oi, J. C. (1992). Fiscal reform and the economic foundations of local state corporatism in China. *World Politics, 45*(1), 99–126.

Oi, J. C. (1995). The role of the local state in China's transitional economy. *The China Quarterly, 144*(1), 1132–1149.

Park, S. H., & Luo, Y. (2001). Guanxi and organizational dynamics: Organizational networking in Chinese firms. *Strategic Management Journal, 22*(5), 455–477.

Peet, R., & Watts, M. (2004). Liberation ecologies: Environment, development and social movements. In R. Peet & M. Watts (Eds.), *Liberation ecologies: Environment, development and social movements* (pp. 1–45). London: Routledge.

Pelling, M. (1999). The political ecology of flood hazard in urban Guyana. *Geoforum, 30*(3), 249–261.

Pils, E. (2005). Land disputes, rights assertion, and social unrest in China: A case from Sichuan. *Columbia Journal of Asian Law, 19*, 235.

Qiu, G., Teng, L., & Wang, C. (2009). Woguo difang zhengfu "tudi caizheng" wenti yanjiu [Research on local governments' land fiscal problems]. *Kaifang Daobao 3*(144), 47–52.

Ramasamy, B., Goh, K., & Yeung, M. C. (2006). Is guanxi (relationship) a bridge to knowledge transfer? *Journal of Business Research, 59*(1), 130–139.

Robbins, P. (2012). *Political ecology: A critical introduction (Vol. 16).* West Sussex: John Wiley & Sons.

Rocheleau, D. E. (2008). Political ecology in the key of policy: From chains of explanation to webs of relation. *Geoforum, 39*(2), 716–727.

Rodrik, D. (2008). *One economics, many recipes: Globalization, institutions, and economic growth.* Princeton: Princeton University Press.

Saxenian, A. (2003). Government and Guanxi: The Chinese software industry in transition. *London Business School Centre for New and Emerging Markets Working Paper, 19*.

Schreurs, M. A. (2008). From the bottom up local and subnational climate change politics. *Journal of Environment & Development, 17*(4), 343–355.

Schwartz, J. (2004). Environmental NGOs in China: Roles and limits. *Pacific Affairs*, 28–49.

Shao, Y. (2010). Guanyu "tudi caizheng" yu caishui tizhi gaige wenti zongshu [A summary of "land finance" and problems with fiscal and tax institutional reform]. *Jingji Yanjiu Cankao, 24*, 36–45.

Shapiro, J. (2012). *China's environmental challenges*. Cambridge: Polity.
Shen, Y. (2013, June 26). Zai jianshe shengtai wenming zhong zhengdang xianfeng [Strive to become a pilot in ecological civilization]. *Shenyang' minsheng blog*. Retrieved from http://msblogs.jxwmw.cn/blog/c/2760/116120.
Shin, S. K., Ishman, M., & Sanders, G. L. (2007). An empirical investigation of sociocultural factors of information sharing in China. *Information & Management, 44*(2), 165–174.
Shirk, S. L. (1993). *The political logic of economic reform in China*. California: University of California Press.
Skinner, M. W., Kuhn, R. G., & Joseph, A. E. (2001). Agricultural land protection in China: A case study of local governance in Zhejiang Province. *Land Use Policy, 18*(4), 329–340.
Smart, A. (1993). Gifts, bribes, and guanxi: A reconsideration of Bourdieu's social capital. *Cultural Anthropology, 8*(3), 388–408.
So, Y. L., & Walker, A. (2013). *Explaining guanxi: The Chinese business network*. Oxon: Routledge.
Song, Y., Qi, R., You, W., Wang, X., Zhu, R. (1999). Shengtai chegnshi de zhibiao tixi yu pingjia fangfa [A study on indices system and assessment criterion of eco-city]. *Chengshi Huanjing yu Chengshi Shengtai 12*(5), 16–19.
Standifird, S. S., & Marshall, R. S. (2000). The transaction cost advantage of guanxi-based business practices. *Journal of World Business, 35*(1), 21–42.
Steinfeld, E. S. (2000). *Forging reform in China: The fate of state-owned industry*. Cambridge: Cambridge University Press.
Stiglitz, J. E., Lin, J. Y., & Monga, C. (2013). The rejuvenation of industrial policy. *World Bank Policy Research Working Paper* (6628). Retrieved from https://openknowledge.worldbank.org/bitstream/handle/10986/16845/WPS6628.pdf?sequence=1.
Su, C., & Littlefield, J. E. (2001). Entering guanxi: a business ethical dilemma in mainland China? *Journal of Business Ethics, 33*(3), 199–210.
Swyngedouw, E., & Heynen, N. C. (2003). Urban political ecology, justice and the politics of scale. *Antipode, 35*(5), 898–918.
Tan, M., Li, X., Xie, H., & Lu, C. (2005). Urban land expansion and arable land loss in China—A case study of Beijing–Tianjin–Hebei region. *Land Use Policy, 22*(3), 187–196.
Tang, S.-Y., & Zhan, X. (2008). Civic environmental NGOs, civil society, and democratization in China. *Journal of Development Studies, 44*(3), 425–448.
Tim, F. (2003). *Critical political ecology: The politics of environmental science*. London: Routledge.
Tsai, K. S. (2005). Capitalists without a class political diversity among private entrepreneurs in China. *Comparative Political Studies, 38*(9), 1130–1158.
Tsai, K. S. (2007). *Capitalism without democracy: The private sector in contemporary China*. New York: Cornell University Press.
Tsang, E. W. (1994). Threats and opportunities faced by private businesses in China. *Journal of Business Venturing, 9*(6), 451–468.
Tsang, E. W. (1996). In search of legitimacy: The private entrepreneur in China. *Entrepreneurship Theory and Practice, 21*(1), 21–30.
Tsang, E. W. (1998). Can guanxi be a source of sustained competitive advantage for doing business in China? *The Academy of Management Executive, 12*(2), 64–73.
Tsui, K.-y., & Wang, Y. (2004). Between separate stoves and a single menu: Fiscal decentralization in China. *The China Quarterly, 177*, 71–90.

Van Rooij, B. (2006). Implementation of Chinese environmental law: Regular enforcement and political campaigns. *Development and Change, 37*(1), 57–74.

Vásquez-León, M., & Liverman, D. (2004). The political ecology of land-use change: Affluent ranchers and destitute farmers in the Mexican municipio of Alamos. *Human Organization, 63*(1), 21–33.

Wade, R. (1990). *Governing the market: Economic theory and the role of government in East Asian industrialization*. New Jersey: Princeton University Press.

Walder, A. G. (1995). Local governments as industrial firms: An organizational analysis of China's transitional economy. *American Journal of Sociology, 101*(2), 263–301.

Walker, P. A. (2003). Reconsidering "regional" political ecologies: Toward a political ecology of the rural American West. *Progress in Human Geography, 27*(1), 7–24.

Wan, Z., & Yuan, E. (2001). *Toushi Pudong sisuo Pudong [A lens through which to look through and think about Pudong]*. Shanghai: Shanghai Renmin Chubanshe.

Wang, A. (2006). Role of law in environmental protection in China: Recent developments. *Berkeley Law Scholarship Repository, 8*, 195–223.

Wang, A. D. (2013). Chengzai guoji jinrong zhongxin shiming de Lujiazui [The mission to be an international financial center: Lujiazui]. Retrieved from www.pdtimes.com.cn/html/2013-04/11/content_6_1.htm.

Wang, C. (2014). Transition from a revolutionary party to a governing party. In K. G. Lieberthal, C. Li, & Y. Keping (Eds.), *China's political development: Chinese and American perspectives* (pp. 73–102). Washington DC: Brookings Institution Press.

Wank, D. L. (1996). The institutional process of market clientelism: Guanxi and private business in a South China city. *China Quarterly—London*, 820–838.

Warren, A., Batterbury, S., & Osbahr, H. (2001). Soil erosion in the West African Sahel: A review and an application of a "local political ecology" approach in South West Niger. *Global Environmental Change, 11*(1), 79–95.

Weingast, B. R. (1995). The economic role of political institutions: Market-preserving federalism and economic development. *Journal of Law, Economics, & Organization*, 1–31.

White, L. T. (1998). *Unstately Power: Volume 1, Local Causes of China's Economic Reforms*. New York: ME Sharpe.

Wong, C. P. W. (1991). Central–local relations in an era of fiscal decline: The paradox of fiscal decentralization in post-Mao China. *The China Quarterly, 128*, 691–715.

Xin, K. K., & Pearce, J. L. (1996). Guanxi: Connections as substitutes for formal institutional support. *Academy of Management Journal, 39*(6), 1641–1658.

Xin, Z., & Zhang, Y. (2008). Low carbon economy and low carbon city. *Urban Study, 4*, 98–102.

Xu, C. (2011). The fundamental institutions of China's reforms and development. *Journal of Economic Literature*, 1076–1151.

Ya-hua, L. (2004). Approaches to the solutions of the insurance of the land-lost peasants [J]. *Journal of Wuhan University of Hydraulic and Electrical Engineering (Social Sciences Edition), 3*, 012.

Yang, G. (2005). Environmental NGOs and institutional dynamics in China. *The China Quarterly, 181*(1), 46–66.

Yang, M. M.-h. (2002). The resilience of guanxi and its new deployments: A critique of some new guanxi scholarship. *The China Quarterly, 170*, 459–476.

Yeh, A. G.-O., & Li, X. (1999). Economic development and agricultural land loss in the Pearl River Delta. *China. Habitat International, 23*(3), 373–390.

Yeh, E. T. (2000). Forest claims, conflicts and commodification: The political ecology of Tibetan mushroom-harvesting villages in Yunnan Province, China. *The China Quarterly, 161*, 264–278.

Yeung, I. Y., & Tung, R. L. (1996). Achieving business success in Confucian societies: The importance of guanxi (connections). *Organizational Dynamics, 25*(2), 54–65.

Zhang, C. (2006, July 03). Sheng di qi ci huanbao dahui zhaokai Yu Qun daibiao Baoding qianding zerenshu [Yun Qun represented Baoding in signing a responsibility contract at the 7th Environmental Protection Conference of Hebei Province]. *Baoding Ribao.* Retrieved from www.heb.chinanews.com/todaybd/news/bdxw/2006-09-01/2764.html.

Zhang, J. (1991). Pudong Xinqu tudi pizu jiaga wenti tantao [An exploratory discussion of land leasing prices in Pudong New Area]. *Tansuo yu Zhengming, 1*, 37–39.

Zhang, S., & He, Y. (2013). Analysis on the development and policy of solar PV power in China. *Renewable and Sustainable Energy Reviews, 21*, 393–401.

Zhang, T. (2000). Land market forces and government's role in sprawl: The case of China. *Cities, 17*(2), 123–135.

Zhang, T., & Zou, H. F. (1998). Fiscal decentralization, public spending, and economic growth in China. *Journal of Public Economics, 67*(2), 221–240.

Zhou, F. (2010). Yizhang huangpai cuisheng "Zhongguo diangu" [A yellow card was responsible for "China electric valley"]. *Zhongguo Jingji he Xinxihua.* Retrieved from http://finance.sina.com.cn/roll/20100927/10108710049.shtml.

Zhu, J. (1999). Local growth coalition: The context and implications of China's gradualist urban land reforms. *International Journal of Urban and Regional Research, 23*(3), 534–548.

Appendix
Interview and fieldwork information

Baoding interviews

Baoding	Interviewees	Date and place	Questions
1	General Secretary of China's Low-carbon Economy Promotion Association	April 18, 2012 Office of the China Low-carbon Economy Promotion Association, Beijing	1 What do you think about the popularity of low-carbon cities in China and why? Which cities have done the best? 2 What's your opinion of Baoding's and Shanghai's low-carbon city development? 3 Why do local governments strive for green development and influence in China's green growth transition?
2	Project Coordinator of the WWF Low-carbon City Initiative—Baoding	April 19, 2012 WWF Office in Beijing, China	1 Why did WWF choose Baoding as a low-carbon pilot city in China? 2 How did WWF cooperate with the Baoding municipal government to carry out the project? Which government departments or organization were involved? 3 What has been done in this project? 4 What is WWF's role and impact on Baoding's low-carbon city? 5 In your opinion, what is the role of the renewable energy industry in Baoding?

Appendix

Baoding	Interviewees	Date and place	Questions
3	The former Director of the Baoding High-tech Zone	April 23, 2012 The Torch Project Park	1 When and how did you learn about the renewable energy industry? 2 Why, when, and how did you support the development of renewable energy at Baoding high-tech park? 3 When, how, and why did the Baoding municipal government choose the electric valley of China as a local development strategy? Who was involved in that decision? 4 How does the Baoding government support renewable energy industries? And did Baoding's municipal government make a difference for the renewable energy industry? 5 What is the role of WWF and the national government during this process? 6 What is your relationship with entrepreneurs in the Baoding High-tech Park? 7 How is environmental protection understood in Baoding High-tech Park? What are the environmental impacts of the renewable energy industry? Can you speak to the public complaints about the Liu Jiu factory? 8 Which government department is responsible for low-carbon city construction?

Baoding	Interviewees	Date and place	Questions
4	Baoding High-tech Committee, Economic Department	April 24, 2012 Office of Baoding High-tech Committee Economic Department	1 When did the Baoding High-tech Zone decide to build up a renewable energy industry base, and why? 2 Which challenges did the renewable energy industries face? How do they work now? 3 What is the role of Baoding's High-tech Park in the relations between renewable energy enterprises and the Baoding municipal government? 4 Which leader has decided to develop renewable energy industries? What are the new High-tech leader's opinions toward renewable energy industry? 5 How does Baoding High-tech implement its industrial policies and cooperation with enterprises?
5	Private Manager of an energy-saving and environmental protection company, Runli	April 25, 2012 Office of Runli	1 What's your opinion of the electric valley in Baoding? 2 How did Baoding government policies, such as the electric valley of China, influence companies in Baoding? 3 What do you think about the environmental protection efforts in Baoding? 4 Which government department is responsible for low-carbon city construction?

Appendix 187

Baoding	Interviewees	Date and place	Questions
6	Taxi driver	April 25, 2012	1 Do you know about the Electric Valley of China and the low-carbon city initiative in Baoding? Do you know what kinds of projects there are in Baoding? 2 What kinds of changes have the low-carbon projects brought to Baoding, and how? 3 How much do you know about the renewable energy industries at Baoding? 4 Why did Baoding's municipal government support the renewable energy industry?
7	Hotel staff	April 26, 2012	1 How did you learn about the electric valley of China and the low-carbon city initiative in Baoding? 2 How much do you know about renewable energy industries in Baoding? 3 Do the low-carbon city and solar city projects bring changes to citizens' daily life?
8	The Development and Reform Commission of the Baoding government	April 26, 2012	1 What progress has been made in Baoding's low-carbon city planning? Note: I was unable to interview these officials, as the person in charge was not there. I tried and failed twice because there were protesters in front of the government office and policemen were there to keep order. The protests were caused by land conflicts between farmers and the Baoding government.

Appendix

Baoding	Interviewees	Date and place	Questions
9	Low-carbon development institute group interview with North China Electric University	April 26, 2012 An informal discussion at North China Electric University	1 Who has advocated low-carbon city development in Baoding? 2 How do you think about the environmental and social impacts of renewable energy industries in Baoding? 3 How was the low-carbon institute involved in low-carbon city projects? 4 How do you judge the electric valley policy at Baoding?
10	Working staff of Wind energy company in Baoding	April 26, 2012 On phone	1 How did the electric valley strategy influence the wind company in Baoding? 2 How is your company's environmental impact? And how about solar PV industries? 3 How is the state of development of wind energy company in Baoding?
11	Working staff at Baoding Tianwei Corporation	Mail correspondence	1 What is the relationship between Tianwei and Yingli? 2 How does the Baoding government support your company? What is the influence of Baoding's industrial policy on your company? 3 What do you think about Baoding's electric valley strategy and low-carbon city initiative? 4 Do you know of the public's complaints about the environmental impacts of solar PV production?

Appendix 189

Wuning interviews

Wuning	Interviewees	Date and place	Questions
12	Civil society volunteer and private manager	November 14, 2013 In a restaurant near Wuning Lake	1 When did Wuning start to pay attention to the green rising-up? 2 In your opinion, what is the current state of the energy-saving lamp industry? 3 Who has advocated for a green rising-up and the energy-saving lamp industry, and why? 4 What do you think about the green rising-up in Wuning, and specific efforts such as the new city planning? 5 What kinds of changes have occurred after the implementation of this strategy?
13	Chairman of the Lighting Industry Association of Wuning	November 14, 2013 General manager's office of Mipai	1 When and why did you decide to move your company to the Wuning industrial park? 2 What is the green rising-up's influence on the energy-saving lamp industry? 3 How does the local government support the energy-saving lamp industry? 4 How is your relationships with local government officials?
14	Environmental NGO leader	November 18, 2013 Luoping Village	1 When did you become aware of the green rising-up in Wuning? 2 What are the impacts of the green rising-up in Wuning? 3 Why did you organize an environmental demonstration and how does it work? 4 What is your relationship with the local government?

Wuning	Interviewees	Date and place	Questions
15	Director of the Wuning Department Industrial Policy	November 18, 2013 Office of Wuning Industrial Policy Department	1 When did Wuning start to develop the energy-saving lamp industry and who made it a key industry to support? Why? 2 How do industrial policies, such as the selection of certain projects, support the green rising-up? 3 How do you imagine the future of the energy-saving lamp industry in Wuning? What challenges does the energy-saving industry face? How do industrial policies support the development of energy-saving lamp and tourism industries?
16	Secretary of the Wuning Environmental Bureau	November 26, 2013 Office of the Wuning Environmental Bureau	1 What the relationship between the green rising-up strategy and the environmental protection work in Wuning? 2 What are the environmental impacts of the energy-saving lamp industry? 3 How do you deal with the mercury problem? 4 How does green rising-up influence environmental protection in Wuning? 5 What is your department's role in the green rising-up?
17	Traffic policeman who introduced the first energy-saving entrepreneur in Wuning Wanfu industrial park	November 26, 2013 Car	1 How and why did Wuning get the first energy saving lamp factory in Wuning? 2 What is your relationship with the entrepreneur who set up the first energy-saving lamp factory at Wuning? 3 Why did the entrepreneur later fail? What was his influence on Wuning's energy saving-lamp industrial policy? 4 How do you think about the green rising-upat Wuning?

Appendix 191

Wuning	Interviewees	Date and place	Questions
18	Rural migrants in Wuning industrial park	Personal observation during the fieldwork	1 Do you know about the green rising-up development in Wuning? 2 What is the influence of green rising-up on your life? 3 How do you perceive the relationships between the local government and entrepreneurs? 4 What kinds of changes occurred after the green rising-up strategy?
19	People living in Wuning including relocated farmers and citizens	Personal communication during the fieldwork	1 What do you think of the green rising development in Wuning? 2 Did the relocation impact your life? How was the compensation? 3 What changes has the green rising-upstrategy brought to your life? 4 What's your role in the green rising development?
20	Civil servants	Personal communication during the fieldwork	1 When, why, and how did the local government decided to strive for a green rising-up? 2 What is the relationship between local government, the industrial park, and the entrepreneurs? 3 What kinds of responsibilities do you have during the process of green rising-up? 4 How does the local government attract projects? And how does the implementation work?

Wuning	Interviewees	Date and place	Questions
21	Journalist	November 28, 2013, QQ, Internet media	1 How much do you know about the decision-making process of the green rising-up strategy? 2 Why and how did the local government leader choose the green rising-up strategy? 3 What is the relationship between the local government and the entrepreneurs? 4 What are the impacts of the green rising-up strategy on locals and the environment?

Shanghai interview

1	University professor who has written her dissertation on "Develop Pudong"	Skype	1 Who has advocated the Develop Pudong strategy in Shanghai, and why? 2 What is the decision-making process for developing Pudong? 3 How does the Develop Pudong strategy impact local people and the environment? 4 What is your opinion of "Develop Pudong"?

Index

abuse 68, 113, 127n5, 149, 175
access 5, 10, 31, 76, 92, 111, 133, 137, 140–2, 146, 147, 151, 159, 162, 164, 169, 170, 172
accountability 111, 112, 114
Adams, W.M. 13, 171
agricultural and forest civilization 82
anti-dam protest, Nu River Dam 3
application 12, 78, 85, 88–90, 93, 94, 119, 149
Asian Development Bank 26
assets 6, 36, 63, 82, 113, 114, 124
authoritarian 4, 25, 29, 35, 36
authoritarian, hierarchical party-state 4
authority 4, 8, 25, 29, 35–7, 173
autonomy 5, 8, 25, 30, 56
average income 64, 65

Baidu chat room 95
Bai Keming 85, 98n8
Bailey, S. 34
Baiyangdian Lake 76–8, 84, 92, 93, 98n7, 144
bankruptcy 92
Baoding 13–15, 26, 38, 76–100, 133–42, 144–7, 149, 151–4, 159, 163–5, 167, 170, 172; development and 96–7; development path, local leaders' search 79–84; Electric Valley of China 85–7; entrepreneurs innovative ideas, solar energy 80–1; environmental and economic problems, city struggle 76–9; green city projects 89–91; green development strategy 85–7; *guanxi* and actors, green development 91–7; HTZ 94, 95; industry, pulling resources 84–9; local leader recognition 84–5; local officials, green development 81–2; local officials and entrepreneurs, cooperation with trust 82–4; low-carbon strategy, decisive factors 92–3; national Hi-tech Zone (HTZ) creator 78–9; renewable energy industries development 87–9
Baoding Huiyang Aviation Propeller Factory 83
Beijing 10, 26, 34, 54, 57, 76–8, 85, 93, 96, 98n1, 137, 144
Belief 67, 85, 143, 148
Biyun international residence 68
blueprint 52, 81, 111, 112, 140
"A Brief Blueprint of Pudong New Area Construction" 52
Bryant, R.L. 34
Buddhist 77, 136
Building Integrated Photovoltaics (BIPV) technology 90
business opportunities 34, 135
business power 159

cadmium pollution 50
cadre-entrepreneurs 6, 7, 135
Cai Dingxin 108
cancer villages 59
capital 5, 6, 8–12, 14, 15, 26, 51, 52–7, 62, 63, 67, 76, 79–83, 86–8, 91, 93, 107–9, 114, 121, 123, 133, 139–43, 146, 148, 149, 162, 164, 165, 167, 168
carbon emission intensity 90, 91
carbon-positive city 96
CCP secretary/secretary 54, 55, 85, 98n8, 110, 112, 113, 117, 121, 124, 126, 138, 145
Center for Legal Assistance to Pollution Victims (CLAPV) 33
Central Economic Working Conference 24
central government 1–5, 9, 11, 12, 24, 25, 27–31, 33–8, 49–53, 56–8, 60–3, 66–9, 76, 78, 79, 81, 87, 88, 91, 93, 94, 96,

194 *Index*

central government *continued*
99n18, 112, 121, 135, 137, 138, 142–50, 154, 155, 160, 161, 164, 168
central government, role of 4–5
central-local government relationship 30
Central Planning Commission for Industrial Production 49
central planning system 6
Century Park 60
challenges 5, 10, 11, 62, 66, 140, 141, 166, 167
Chaoyang Lake 118
chemical and pharmaceutical industries 153
Chen Kunlong 50, 67, 68, 163
Chen Yun 56
China National Human Development Report 2013 15
China South Industries Group Corporation (CSIGC) 87
Chinese Communist Party (CCP) 4, 9, 30, 36–8, 58, 173
Chinese national banks 146
Chinese National Development Bank 80
"Chinese style federalism" 8
Chinese-style local green development 143–50; environmental justice and distribution pattern, local resources 148–50; green development strategies, justification 143–5; politicized local resources, local governments 145–8
Chuansha 62, 146, 173
city planners 138, 144, 147
civil servants 37, 55, 113, 121, 147, 148, 173
civil society 2, 3, 36, 50, 138, 161, 162
clear aims 111
coalition 82, 83, 85, 92, 95–7, 168
collaboration 26, 161
collective 6, 36, 53, 62, 63, 65, 69, 94, 106, 120, 140, 146, 149, 152, 164, 168, 169
collectively owned land 62, 63
commercialization 14, 119–21, 146; of land 146
commoditization of nature 171
common ideas and values 141
common pattern 133, 143, 153, 160
communes 6
communication 127, 141
comparative case design 13
compensation 34, 37, 61, 63–5, 94, 97, 114–16, 120, 124, 126, 152, 153, 174
competition between local governments 29

complaints 31, 78, 92, 95, 111, 115, 147, 153
concentrated villagers 147
confiscation 14, 64, 65, 97, 115
conflict 31–3, 35, 37, 61, 76, 95, 97, 115, 127, 145, 147, 152–4, 174
Confucian 111, 136
Consequences 14, 117, 166
conservative powers 49, 56, 138
Construction and Promotion Committee 86
consumers 24, 26, 27, 117, 172
continuity 151
controlling and distributing local resources 145
cooperation 4, 11, 24–6, 76, 82, 90, 133, 134, 139–41, 146, 151, 155, 168; agreements 26
costs and benefits 136, 168, 171, 172, 174
county 1, 7, 13, 15, 26, 29–32, 34, 36, 54, 62, 105–13, 115–19, 121, 122, 125, 126, 134, 135, 140, 141, 145–8, 152, 159, 168, 170, 173

dam immigrants 107
dang guan ganbu 29
danwei 80, 89
Datang Coal Power Station 86
Dawang Township 31
death of fish 77
decentralization decentralized/ decentralized political system 145
decision-making 37, 175
Deng Xiaoping 52, 54, 56–8, 61, 67, 138, 142, 168
determination 142
"Developing in Pudong in a Broad Space" 50
development companies 63–5, 67, 146, 165, 173
"Development is not necessarily good" 13
development path 24, 69, 79, 80, 126, 134, 143, 163
development strategy 5, 9, 10, 12, 13, 27, 51, 56, 68, 76, 84, 85, 87, 89, 91, 97, 105, 109, 121, 126, 133, 134, 137–9, 141, 143, 145, 149, 151, 173, 174
"Develop Pudong, Build a Big Modern Shanghai" 53
Develop Pudong Committee 146
"Develop Pudong" strategy 13, 15, 50–70, 134, 136, 138, 141–4, 146, 148, 151, 154, 168, 173; accelerated urbanization 62–5; analysis 65–8; government-led

urbanization 61–2; green development 68; new ecological area 59–61; powers and actors 66–7
Develop Pudong United Advising Group 55
Dickson, Bruce J. 6–11, 140, 161, 163, 164
Ding Qiang 83
disappearance 172
disaster induced migration 115
distribution/distribution of local resources 148
domestic green market 28
Donghai Township 32
driving forces 133, 134–43; innovative power, entrepreneurs 134–7; political power, local leadership 137–9; powerful groups combination, *guanxi* 140–3
duanzi juesun 95
ducks 50
Dunhuang solar PV project 88
dynamic private entrepreneurs 7

eco-agriculture 119, 120
ecological awareness 139
ecological civilization 1, 2, 85, 123, 126, 127n10, 137, 143–5, 153, 154, 173
ecological compensation fee system 61
ecological crisis 66, 68, 76, 77, 83, 84, 91
ecological criteria 154
ecological migration 115
ecological products 122, 139
ecological tourism 112–15, 136, 139, 147, 149, 153, 171, 172
ecological villages 119
Economic Daily 80, 85, 98n10
economic development 8, 14, 30
economic growth 1, 2, 9, 11, 30
economic reform policies 8
economic trees 119
efficiency 7, 26, 86, 91, 111, 113, 115, 119, 122, 124
Electric Valley of China (EVC) 84, 85–7, 144, 146, 147, 149, 151
empirical evidence 2, 167
enclosure of resources 171
energy conservation 86, 89, 91
Energy Production and Consumption Revolution Strategy 25
energy-saving and emission-reduction targets 95
energy saving lamps/ energy-saving lamp companies 110, 118
energy sector 7

enforcement 4
enlargement 139
entrepreneurs, entrepreneurship 5–8, 14, 49, 92, 93, 107, 121, 133, 134; in economic development 7; sociocultural power of 10
environmental aid 38
environmental and economic problems, city struggle 76–9; city near capital 76–7; ecological crises, Baiyangdian Lake 77–8
environmental and social justice 14, 160
environmental awareness 1, 31, 37, 66, 81, 122
environmental challenges 5
environmental impacts 3, 9, 14, 25, 31, 33, 35, 62, 169; assessment 34, 95
environmental justice 94, 148, 150–4, 160, 169, 175; green development supporters gains 150–1; local environment, effects 153–4; local people, effects 152–3
environmental Kuznets curve 14
environmental laws and regulations 4, 7, 60, 126, 161, 173
environmentally friendly industries 5, 108, 114, 136, 139, 164
environmentally sustainable development 1
environmental mass events 31, 32
Environmental Non-Governmental Organizations (ENGOs) 3, 33–5
environmental performance 25
environmental petitions 31, 33; data *32*
environmental policies 4, 24
environmental pollution 31
environmental protection 4
Environmental Protection Bureaus (EPBs) 4, 11, 31, 50
Environmental Protection Law 2014 33
Environmental Protection Law 2015 3, 35
environmental protection tax 61
environmental protests 3, 25, 31, 137
environmental reform 37
environmental regulation 164
environmental transformation 159
environmental victims 34
European countries 54
evaluation 4, 25, 52, 54, 98, 113, 114, 117, 119, 137
experience 3, 8, 12, 51, 52, 54, 58, 68, 80, 81, 108, 121, 122, 135, 136, 144, 151, 154, 155, 159, 163, 169, 172
expert entrepreneurs 50
explanatory factors 159

exporter 96
export-oriented 24, 26

farmer-entrepreneurs 6
farmers 62, 172
Farmland 12, 95, 97, 108, 152, 154
federalism 30
Fei Xiaotong 62
Fenghuo Xi Zhuhou 111, 112
Fengyang household responsibility system 12
Finance 7, 27, 58, 61, 146
financial companies 146
findings 5, 159, 160, 163, 166, 168, 169, 175
first base for renewable energy and energy equipment 83
fiscal and administrative reforms 5
fishermen 78, 98, 114, 121
Forbes 163
Forces 6, 32, 38, 125, 133, 134, 171
Foreign Economic and Management Magazine 52
forest farmer 106, 108, 115
forest parks 114, 120
forest reform/forest rights reform 106, 120, 127n1, 147
Four Asian Dragons 66
fragmentation 29, 35
fragmented local authoritarianism *29*, 35-7
future research topics 160, 173, 174

gains and losses 94, 126, 150, 152, 160, 168, 169
GDP growth 25, 29
German Energy Agency 26
global green influences: informal and indirect influence, global green consumers 26-7; international organizations and local governments, cooperation 25-6
global solar photovoltaic (PV) market 27
Golden Sun project 28
gongzai dangdai, lizai qianqiu 61
government leaders, advocacy 53-8; central leaders, approvals of 56-8; "Develop Pudong" 58-65; local leadership, collective efforts 53-6
government-led urbanization 61
Great Leap Forward 59
"green" businesses 6, 134, 135, 138, 140, 141, 143, 150, 174
green city 89, 118
green city projects: low-carbon city 90-1; solar city 89-90

green consumerism 26
green development, eco circular low-carbon green transition 1, 24, 159
green development strategies 1, 4, 8, 10, 12-15, 133, 134, 137, 141-3, 145, 146, 148, 152, 153, 168, 172
"green" entrepreneurs 7, 136, 168
green investment 27, 127n10
green leap forward 105-28
"green rising-up" strategy 112-26; actors and powers, promoting 121-3; analysis 121-6; beneficiaries of 123; energy-saving lamp industry 116-17; environmental protection and 117-18; green city projects 118-19; innovative policies 114-16; local government and resources, restructuring 112-14; natural resources commercialization 119-21; social development in 117-21
green supply chain management 27
Guangdong Province 32-3, 108, 110, 116, 122
guanxi 6, 10-12, 52, 66, 81, 83, 92, 95, 122, 133, 134, 136, 140-3, 150, 151, 159-61, 163, 164, 166-8, 175
Gu Chuanxun 57
Guodian Corporation Group 83
Guodian United Power 83, 88
Guthrie, D. 10

Hamburg 54
Hanxin 111
Hanxin Limu 111
health costs 153
Hebei Province 31, 32
high-tech industries 27, 61, 65, 76, 78, 79, 81, 84, 134, 136, 140, 147
hi-tech zone (HTZ) 78-88, 91, 92, 94, 95, 134-6, 138, 139, 146, 147, 149, 152, 165, 167
Hong Kong 52, 54, 61, 66, 87, 116, 138
household responsibility system reform 6
Huang, Y. 6
Huangpu River 50, 53, 59, 62, 65
Huangpu river pollution treatment plan 50, 68
Huang Qifan 67
Hukou 65, 111
Hu Lijiao 55, 57
Hu Yaobang 51, 56

ICLEI 26
imbalanced power 160
immigrant county 107

Index   197

implementation 3, 4, 7, 56, 66–8, 86, 89, 90, 99n18, 105, 113, 118, 119, 121, 126, 127, 142, 143, 145, 151, 161, 173
incentives 2, 4, 14, 30, 34, 87, 139, 160, 161, 164, 173
incentives and punishment institutions 87
incentive system 4, 86, 111, 113, 115, 146, 148
industrial clusters 135
industrialization 15, 88, 92, 106, 107, 121, 125, 133
industrial parks 9, 11, 14, 15, 94, 95, 97, 99n24, 117, 140, 152–4, 164, 165, 167, 172
industrial policies 6, 8, 9, 11, 36, 61, 81, 89, 91–4, 109, 114, 117, 118, 135–7, 146, 161, 165
infrastructure 11, 49, 55, 60, 63, 69, 109, 110, 114, 119, 149, 164, 170
innovative policies 12, 84, 94, 114
innovative power 134
interaction 159
international cities 60, 66, 138
international designers 68
international organizations 25, 26, 52, 145
internet 31
internet petitions 127
interventions 92, 148
the iron rice bowl *(tie fanwan)* 6
itai-itai disease 50

jiandao lanli doushi cai 139
Jiangsu 56, 111, 116
Jiangxi 7, 105, 107, 108, 110, 116, 122, 127n9, 127n10, 147, 152
Jiang Zemin 53, 55, 57, 142
Jinjiang EVC hotel 90
Jinkou village 147
Jinqiao/ Jinqiao Export Processing Zone Developmental Company 146
Jiujiang 106, 108, 122
Jiusan Society 52
job opportunities 65, 94, 152
"jumping into the sea" *(xiahai)* 7, 80
justification 69, 125, 143–5, 150, 170

Land Administration Law 64
land conflicts 152, 153, 174
land development 63, 165
land leasing 142, 149
landless farmers 65, 172
land loss 95, 174
land nationalization 69
land ownership 169

land revenue 114, 152, 165
land transfers 86, 95, 115
land use rights 63, 146, 165
lantian 77
laoxiang 140
laws and regulations 4, 7, 60, 65, 126, 143, 145, 146, 148, 152, 155, 161, 173
LDK 95
leadership 7, 30, 34, 37, 49, 51, 53–5, 57, 67, 69, 78, 96, 106, 109, 112, 114, 115, 121, 122, 136, 137, 139, 145, 149, 159, 165, 172
liberation of farmers 6
liberty 134
Li Dingfu 108
Lieberthal, Kenneth 164
Lin'an 110
Lin Tongyan 52, 55, 59
Li Peng 57, 58, 98n3
livable city 58, 118, 122
living conditions 49, 59, 117, 152, 153
local actors 25
local CCP 9, 86, 98n8, 110, 121, 122, 124, 126, 137, 138, 140, 154, 155
Local citizens 152
local context 5, 36, 79, 92, 134, 135, 164
local demonstration projects **2**
local development strategies 14
local environmental politics/local environmental governance 2, 4, 5, 7, 29, 161, 162
local governments and people conflict 31–5; local green politics, changing 33–5; local petitions and protests 31–3
localization 96
local knowledge 8, 9, 37, 66, 69, 136, 137, 162
local leaders/ local leadership 53, 67, 69, 121, 137
local officials 4, 5, 8–12, 14, 15, 27, 31, 34–8, 47, 52, 56, 67, 69, 76, 78, 80, 82, 86, 91, 97, 99n25, 99n30, 107, 108, 113, 114, 116, 123, 124, 126, 133–46, 148, 150, 151, 153–5, 159–70, 172, 173, 175
local revenue 8
local state corporatism 30
local villagers 63, 171
low-carbon city 13, 76, 88–97, 144–7, 149, 172
low-carbon pioneering 76–100
low-price housing 115
low-rent housing 115
Lujiazui 60–2, 135, 146, 148, 165

Lujiazui Finance & Trade Zone Developmental Company 146
Lunyu 111
Lushan West Lake International Ecological Health Pension Center 120

Ma, X. 135
market barriers 143
market principles 140
mass demonstrations 33, 35, 36
Ma Xuelu 77, 78, 81, 134–6, 140, 141, 165, 167
Medium and Long-term Plans for Renewable Energy 87
mercury 59, 106, 118, 125, 154
Miao Liansheng 79, 80, 140, 141, 163, 167
mining companies 120
Ministry of Environmental Protection (MEP) 24, 27, 32, 33, 35–6, 91, 106
Ministry of Housing and Urban-Rural Development (MHURD) 111
Ministry of Science and Technology (MoST) 78, 79, 81, 88, 92
Ministry of Water Resources 119
minority groups 126, 138
Minsheng Blog 111
miracle 6, 66, 69
mountain 106, 109, 115, 119, 120, 127n1
Multinational Corporations (MNCs) 26, 27, 68

National Development and Reform Commission (NDRC) 1, 2, 25, 27, 82, 88, 96, 98n14
national ecological pilot 106
national government's influence 27–30; decentralization 29–30; local governments, encourage 27–9
national high-tech industry pilot program 82
nationalization 49, 59, 69
national key industries 149
national low-carbon pilot program 88
"nationally owned but privately managed" *(guoyou konggu minying jizhi)* 82, 83
National Tourism Administration 115
Naughton, B. 36
netizens 35, 93, 111
New Century, New Pudong 60
New Century Residence 90
new development mode 143
new policies 166, 172
New York stock market 87
Ni Tianzeng 51, 55, 70n5

nomenklatura system 37
norms of reciprocity 10
North China Electric Power University (NCEPU) 77
Northern China Plain 76, 98n1, 98n7

obstacles 133, 142
Oi, J.C. 30
one station service 110, 111
online blog 115
Overseas Chinese 52
owners 4, 5, 7, 11, 12, 143

Party Committee 86, 91, 105–7, 110, 116, 117, 119
patterns 14, 133, 169
peasant entrepreneur 109
Pengze nuclear power station 34
People's Congress 33, 65
personal connections 10, 159
personal relationships 160
personnel rights/personnel power 30, 35, 148, 173
petition and complaint system, *xinfang* 34
"Pilot Hygiene City/County" 1
pilot water ecological city 119
Pinggang Village 120
planned economic era 49
planned industrial center 49, 59
policy and institutional innovations 112
policy suggestions 154–5
political achievement 67, 96, 151
political campaigns 4
political careers 34, 37, 151
political control 3
political ecology 5–12, 14, 159–75; Chinese entrepreneurs and "green" businesses 6–8; entrepreneurs, local officials, and *guanxi*'s power 162–8; green development, rethinking 171–2; guanxi, entrepreneurs and local officials connections 166–8; innovative ideas to organize resources, private entrepreneurs 162–4; and local green development 168–73; local green development implications 172–3; local green experiments and experiences 12; local leaders and greener future 8–10; local power, struggling 160–2; political power to mobilize resources, local officials 164–6; politicized environment 169–71; powerful actors, interactions 10–12; social capital and 10–12; theory 133
political economy 5–6, 92, 94, 160, 161

political hierarchy 76
political movement 86, 113
political power 123, 137
political protection 140
political ties 7
pollutants discharge fee system 61
polluting factories 77, 78, 114, 118, 125
positive effects 167
poverty 76
power 5–11, 14, 24, 27, 30, 33–8, 56, 57, 61, 68, 69, 77, 82–4, 86, 88, 92–4, 96, 97, 106, 111, 113, 116, 121, 123, 124, 126, 127, 133, 134, 136–43, 145, 148, 149, 151, 154, 159–62, 164, 167, 169–74; boundaries 138
powerful actors 133
power investment 28
Poyang Lake 111
preferential policies 5, 61, 62, 67, 78, 81, 83, 110, 114, 116, 117, 122, 123, 134, 146, 148, 149, 154
price butcher *jiage tufu* 96
private entrepreneurship 6
private firm 80
private property 11, 123, 163
profits 7, 65, 68, 115, 148
projects 1–3, 11, 14, 24–8, 31–5, 55, 60, 64, 84, 86–91, 94, 96, 97, 107, 109, 112–16, 118–21, 123–5, 127, 140, 143, 147, 149, 150, 153, 154, 160, 163, 168, 171, 174
promotion 25, 37, 67, 87, 89, 91, 113, 119, 136, 137, 147, 154, 164, 166; conference 89, 91, 113; group 119
propaganda 143, 145
property rights 36
protest 3, 15, 25, 31, 33, 35, 137, 174
Provincial Economic and Technology Financial Guarantee Company 82
public enterprises 6
public litigation 3
public participation 4, 14, 25, 35, 69, 94, 121, 126, 171
public property 6, 9
Pudong 13, 15, 50–70, 134–8, 140–4, 146, 148, 149, 151, 153, 154, 164, 165, 168, 170, 173
Pudong Gas Company 60
Putnam, Robert D. 10

Qidong 33
Qu Geping 54

real estate/real estate industries/real estate developers 7, 8, 95, 115, 149, 153, 165

reciprocal obligation 166
reciprocal relationships 162
red capitalists 11
red hat entrepreneur 81
reforestation 60, 114, 170
reformers and anti-reformers 56
regionally decentralized authoritarian system (RDA) 35
regulations 4, 7, 38, 55, 60, 61, 65, 86, 87, 93, 110, 114–16, 121, 123, 126, 142, 143, 145–8, 152, 155, 161, 172, 173
regulatory power 111
relocation 14, 37, 64, 65, 94, 99n27, 124; compensation 65
renewable energy 7, 12, 14, 15, 25, 27, 28, 60, 81–99, 134, 136, 139–42, 144–7, 149, 151, 152, 154, 155, 163, 165, 174
Renewable Energy Industry Under Crisis 85
Renewable Energy Law 85, 144
renewable industries 81, 86, 96, 97, 135, 136, 154
rent-seeking 122, 140, 141
reorganization 113
research design 12–15; local green development, questioning 13–15
reservoir resettlement 107
resettlement projects 107
resource mobilization 146
resources 3, 5, 6, 8, 10, 13, 14, 25–7, 30, 33, 36, 49, 53, 54, 56, 58, 61, 68, 69, 76–9, 81, 82, 84–7, 89, 91–7, 99n17, 105–8, 111–13, 116, 119–24, 126, 133–43, 145–54, 159–64, 166–73
responsibility 5, 6, 8, 12, 25, 34, 36, 38, 54, 84, 87, 98n11, 98n15, 111, 113, 119, 123, 127n1, 139, 146, 161, 162
restrictions 119
restructuring, local government 112–14
revenues 97, 148, 149
Rivers 50–3, 67, 68, 98n1, 106, 119, 122, 152, 153
Robbins, P. 168
Rodrik, D. 9, 136
Rostow, W.W. 6
rotation/rotation of local leaders 4, 147
Rui Xingwen 54, 55
rule of law 4, 11, 140, 150, 157, 163, 166

sacrifice 63, 124, 125, 155, 172
scholar-type officials 134
Schreurs, M.A. 12
Schumpeter 6

Index

services 6, 7, 27, 65, 88, 110, 117, 123–5, 135, 140, 142, 149, 151
shan ding quan, shu ding gen, ren ding xin 106
Shanghai 10, 13, 15, 26, 38, 49–70, 133–6, 138, 140–4, 146, 148, 151, 153–5, 159, 163, 2000 51; government leaders, advocacy of 53–8; local entrepreneurs and 50–1; local leader's efforts 51–3; Pudong strategy, *guanxi* 52–3
Shanghai City Development Strategy 51, 141
Shanghai Local Chronicles of Environmental Protection 59
Shanghai National Land Remediation Office 50
Shanghai Plan Management Bureau 50
Shanghai Planning Commission 49
Shanghai Pudong 15
Shanghai Waigaoqiao Free Trade Zone Development Company 146
sharing information and transferring knowledge 167
shengdi biancheng shudi 79
Shen Yang 110–12, 134, 136, 141
Shenzhen economic policies 12
Shenzhen/Shenzhen special economic zone 49, 112
Shijiazhuang 76
Shi Lishan 83, 98n14
Shirk, S.L. 11
Sichuan Aba 82
Sichuan Province 31
significance 167
Silicon Valley 146
sister cities 26
Six and Nine silicon material factory 95
small hydropower stations 7, 106, 109
social capital 5, 6, 10–12, 51–3, 57, 80, 81, 91, 93, 133, 141–3, 146
social instability/social stability 34–7, 113, 115, 124, 137, 145
social networks 10, 67, 83, 120
social power 159
social responsibilities 165
solar city 85, 86, 89, 91, 95, 97, 146, 147
solar energy 8, 25, 79–82, 85, 86, 88–90, 92, 94–6, 99n18, 134, 135, 140, 141, 163, 165
Solar Program 82
solar PV 28, 80, 83, 84, 88, 95–7, 99n21, 135, 142, 147, 149, 150, 153, 170, 172
Song Yuqin 108
stability 8, 35–7, 62, 113, 115, 116, 124, 137

state-owned enterprises (SOEs) 83
state-owned land 62, 63
State Planning Commission 49, 54
steel production 59
Sunan 61
Sun-tech 92, 95, 99n21
Supervision 11, 95, 99n18, 127, 143, 155
Suzhou River 50, 52, 59

tertiary industry 62, 144
third industrial revolution 144
Tiananmen Square event 53, 56–8, 66, 142, 144
Tianjin 10, 26, 31, 34, 76, 78, 99n19
Tianwei Group 83, 87, 139
Tianwei Yingli 83
Tianya 95
Tongji University 51, 109
Torch Program 92
township and village enterprises (TVEs) 6, 8, 65, 78, 107, 108
Trade and Industry Management Bureau 82
traditional culture 139
traditional petition system 31
transfer fees 165
transformation 24, 62, 89, 121, 148, 159, 165
transparency 114
treating and polluting 77
Trina Solar 27
trust 6, 51, 57, 80–2, 112, 122, 124, 133, 136, 141–3, 160, 167, 168, 175
trustworthiness 10
Tsinghua University 50, 70, 85

understanding 5, 76, 155, 161, 164, 167
unfairness 153
United Nations 15, 26
United Nations Environment Programme (UNEP) 26, 28
urbanization 14, 15, 61–3, 65, 69, 106, 107, 115, 121, 124, 133, 138, 152, 165, 169, 170, 174
Urban political ecology 170
Urban Shifang 33
urban villages 63

Van Rooij, B. 4, 31, 34, 145, 161

Waigaoqiao 60, 61, 146
Walder, A.G. 30
Wanfu industrial park 109, 153
Wang Daohan 51–5, 57, 66, 68, 134, 137, 138, 141, 142, 168

Wang Ganghuai 50, 52, 68
waste water 59, 78, 114, 152
water recreation 119
water resources 106–7
water view 119
Watts, Jonathan 5
weak actors 14, 124, 160, 161, 168, 170, 175
weak social groups 111
wealth 60, 64, 67, 80, 106, 134, 145, 154, 163
wellness industry 119, 120
Wen Jiabao 106
Wenming Net 111, 127n9
Wenzhou 108, 109
Western Development 80, 82
wetland parks 114, 115
wind energy 7, 26, 28, 85, 88, 92
window of China 15
wind turbine 7, 27, 83
winners/winners and losers 171
Wood, Schmink 150
wood quota 119
World Bank 24, 26, 52
World Wide Fund for Nature (WWF) 15, 24, 26, 90, 96, 99n20, 139, 145
Wuning 7, 13, 15, 26, 38, 105–28, 133–7, 139–42, 145, 147–9, 151–4, 159, 163–5, 168, 171, 172; CCP secretary's reform ambition for 110–12; energy-saving lamp industry 125; entrepreneurs and local officials 107–12; entrepreneur's pull effect 109–10; environmentally friendly industries 108–9; "green rising-up" strategy 112–26; immigrant county 107; mountain and water resources 106–7; poor inland county 105–6

xiaguan yiji 29
Xianguo Shan hot spring 120
Xi Jinping 24
xinfang 34
Xingcheng Electric Device Company 109
Xinjiang Goldwind 7
Xu, C. 35
Xu Huoxing 109

yan bi xin, xing bi guo, zhi bi de 111
Yang Chaofei 32
Yang Shangkun 57, 142
Yangtze River Basin 58
Yao Yilin 57
yellow card 79
Yingli Green Energy (Yingli) 7, 27
Yin mountain nature ecological conservation park 120
Yuan Enzhen 57
Yu Jin Chun 50
Yu Qun 78, 84, 91, 98n8, 99n16, 144

Zhangjiang 61, 62, 146
Zhao Ziyang 57
Zhejiang/Zhangjiang High-Park Developmental Company 146
Zhelin Lake 107, 119
Zhelin Power Station 107
Zhonghang Huiteng Wind Energy Company 83
Zhongshan 111
Zhongxin Lushan Xihai 149
Zhou Enlai 50
Zhou Xianwang 31
Zhu Chenghua 109, 163
Zhu Rongji 55, 57, 67, 168